THE ENCYCLOPEDIA OF
ANIMAL
BIOLOGY

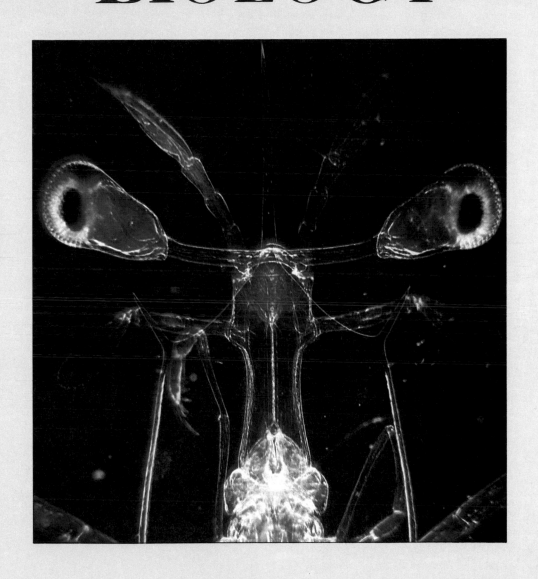

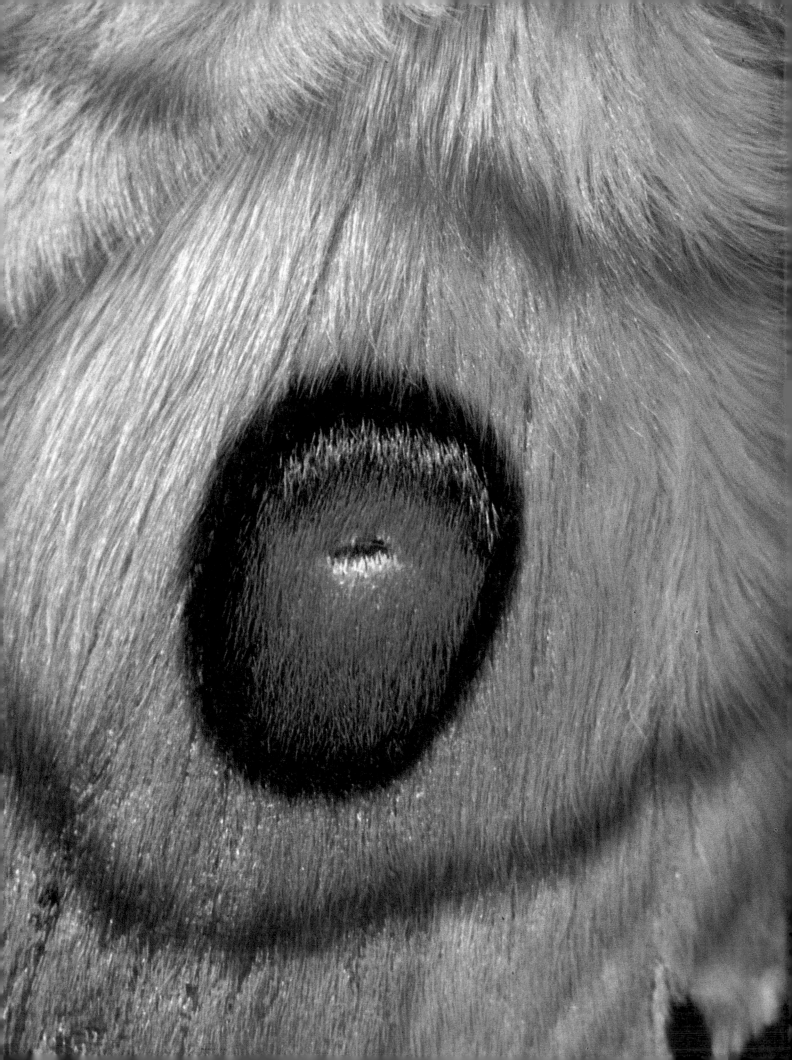

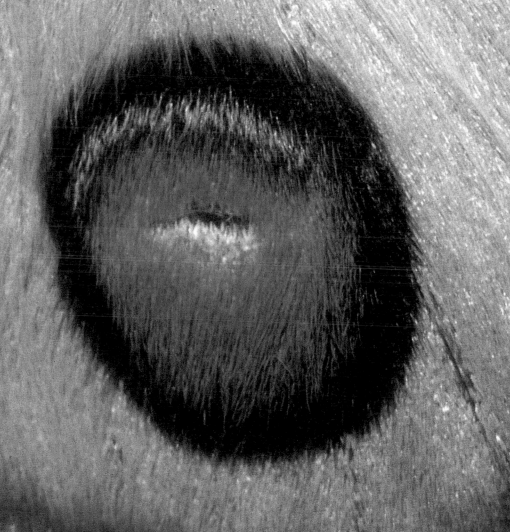

THE ENCYCLOPEDIA OF
ANIMAL
BIOLOGY

Edited by Professor R. McNeill Alexander

Facts On File
New York

Project Editor: Graham Bateman
Editor: Neil Curtis
Art Editor: Chris Munday
Art Assistant: Wayne Ford
Picture Research: Alison Renney
Production: Clive Sparling
Design: Chris Munday
Index: Barbara James

 AN EQUINOX BOOK

First published in the United States of America by
Facts On File, Inc.
460 Park Avenue South, New York,
New York 10016.

Planned and produced by:
Equinox (Oxford) Ltd
Musterlin House,
Jordan Hill, Oxford,
England OX2 8DP

Copyright © Equinox (Oxford) Ltd, 1987

Reprinted 1989

Library of Congress Cataloging-in-Publication Data

The Encyclopedia of animal biology.

  Bibliography: p.
  Includes index.
  1. Zoology. 2. Physiology. I. Alexander, R. McNeill.
QL45.2.E53 1987   591   87–8960
ISBN 0–8160–1817–0

Origination by Fotographics, Hong Kong;
Scantrans, Singapore; Alpha Reprographics Ltd,
Harefield, Middx, England.

Filmset by BAS Printers Limited,
Over Wallop, Stockbridge, Hampshire, England.

Printed in Spain by Heraclio Fournier S.A. Vitoria.

8/16

Advisory Editors

Professor Pierre Dejours
Centre National de la Recherche
Scientifique
Associé a l'Université Louis Pasteur
Strasbourg
France

Professor Malcolm S. Gordon
Department of Biology
University of California, Los Angeles
USA

Professor Kjell Johansen
Department of Zoophysiology
University of Aarhus
Aarhus
Denmark

Artwork and Diagrams

Simon Driver

Richard Lewington

Oxford Illustrators Limited

Contributors

RMcNA	R. McNeill Alexander The University of Leeds Leeds	DCS	David C. Sandeman The University of New South Wales Kensington, NSW Australia
JC	Jack Cohen University of Birmingham Birmingham England	GS	G. Shelton University of East Anglia Norwich England
MSG	Malcolm S. Gordon University of California Los Angeles USA	AJT	Allan J. Tobin University of California Los Angeles USA
CBJ	C. Barker Jorgensen University of Copenhagen Copenhagen Denmark		
MFL	Michael F. Land The University of Sussex Brighton England		

Left: White tern (Gygis alba monte) *in flight with fish in beak (Andrew Henley); half-title: head of larva of the mantis shrimp* Squila maritis *(Oxford Scientific Films); title page: eye spots on wing of moth* Antheraea eucalypti *(Premaphotos Wildlife).*

PREFACE

How do animals breathe, feed, move and perform all the bodily functions characteristic of animal life? And, what are the building blocks of life? This book answers these questions and many more. In other words, it is about how animals work. Most other disciplines of biology stress the differences between the many kinds of animals, but physiological biology often reveals astonishing similarities. It shows how the same basic principles govern life in animals as different as an amoeba and an elephant, or a jellyfish and an ant. Many similarities apply widely or even universally in the animal kingdom: they are features acquired early in the evolution of animals, that have been retained ever since. They are most apparent in the structure and inner workings of cells, which are basically alike in all animals. Other similarities are restricted to animals that engage in similar ways of life. For example, clams and sea squirts use similar structures and processes to filter tiny particles of food from seawater, although other features of their bodies are very different. Fish and octopus have remarkably similar eyes. Such similarities occur because evolution has often found similar solutions to recurring problems.

This book is divided into a number of sections. The first (The Animal Kingdom) introduces the main groups of animals, presenting the essentials of their appearance, structure and ways of life. The remaining sections occupy most of the book. They consist of a series of entries, each giving a coherent account of one of the principal bodily functions, showing how it is performed throughout the animal kingdom.

The first of the main entries describes the proteins and other molecules that make life possible. It shows how they work together in the cells, which are the basic building blocks of animal structure. It shows how heredity depends on the famous mechanism of the double helix and illustrates many of the minute structures that have been found within cells by electron microscopy.

Subsequent entries describe the main organ systems of animals and explain how they work. An entry on feeding explains the basic principles of nourishment, from techniques of food capture to the chemical processes of digestion. It describes how animals deal with a wide variety of food, from the microscopic algae that clams filter from sea water to the huge prey tackled by some snakes and deep-sea fishes. It shows how parasites exploit their hosts and how cattle and corals exploit microorganisms living within their bodies.

The next entries deal with respiration and blood circulation and with the control of the temperature and chemical composition of the body. They show how animals get oxygen, control their water and salt content and avoid freezing or overheating in such diverse environments as polar seas, tropical swamps and deserts.

Subsequent entries are concerned with the senses of animals, their movements and their brains and nervous systems. The echolocation systems of bats and whales and the electric sense

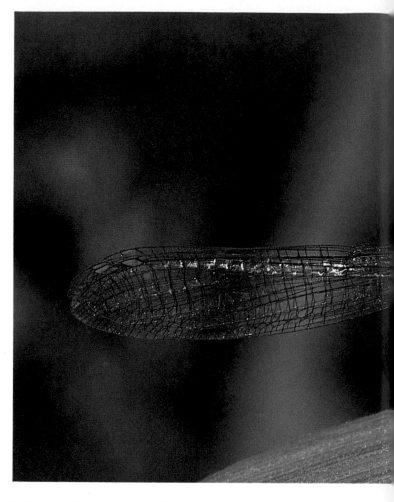

Mating damselflies (*Coenagrion puella*) (Bruce Coleman Ltd).

of some fishes are explained, as well as the more widespread senses of touch, taste, vision and hearing. The crawling of *Amoeba*, the swimming of fish, the flight of birds and insects, the running of mammals and many other techniques of locomotion are all discussed. An entry on nervous systems shows how the relatively simple brains of insects and mollusks are providing clues about the mechanisms of our own, much more complex, brains.

The last main entry is about reproduction and growth. It explains the principal kinds of sexual and asexual reproduction. It shows how simple eggs develop into complex animals and it illustrates the amazing variety of life cycles.

Finally the book ends with a glossary giving definitions and

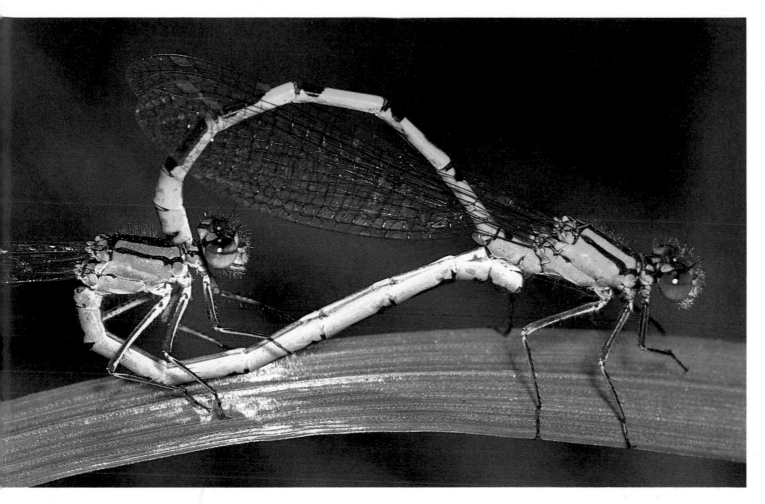

short explanations of important technical terms, and a book list for those who wish to take the subject further.

Each entry consists of a number of interlinking elements. The entry proper is preceded by a discursive section introduction and each entry starts with an introductory panel, which summarizes the contents. It is followed by flowing main text which discusses the main subject concerned. Supplementary and more detailed information is frequently given in charts and tables, boxed feature essays or double page special feature essays.

Illustrations play a major role in this book. Diagrams have been specially commissioned to further expand upon themes within the text, while the numerous color photos constantly remind the reader of the animals whose biology is being discussed.

This book has been written by eight authors, scattered widely around the world. They have been chosen for two reasons. First, they are acknowledged experts, leaders in their various fields. They have made substantial contributions to zoology, by their own discoveries. Secondly, they are people who had shown in their books or other writings that they had the breadth of vision needed for a work of this kind. They have been able to set their discoveries and other recent advances in the broader context of a major field of zoology. In partnership with them we have the editorial team of Equinox (Oxford) Limited, coordinating the project and using their experience and expertise to recruit the best available artists and to find the finest, most telling photographs to illustrate the book. Together we have produced a book which is authoritative and up-to-date, and which we believe the reader will enjoy as well as find informative.

R. McNeill Alexander
DEPARTMENT OF PURE AND APPLIED ZOOLOGY
THE UNIVERSITY OF LEEDS

Stages of frog leaping (Simon Driver).

CONTENTS

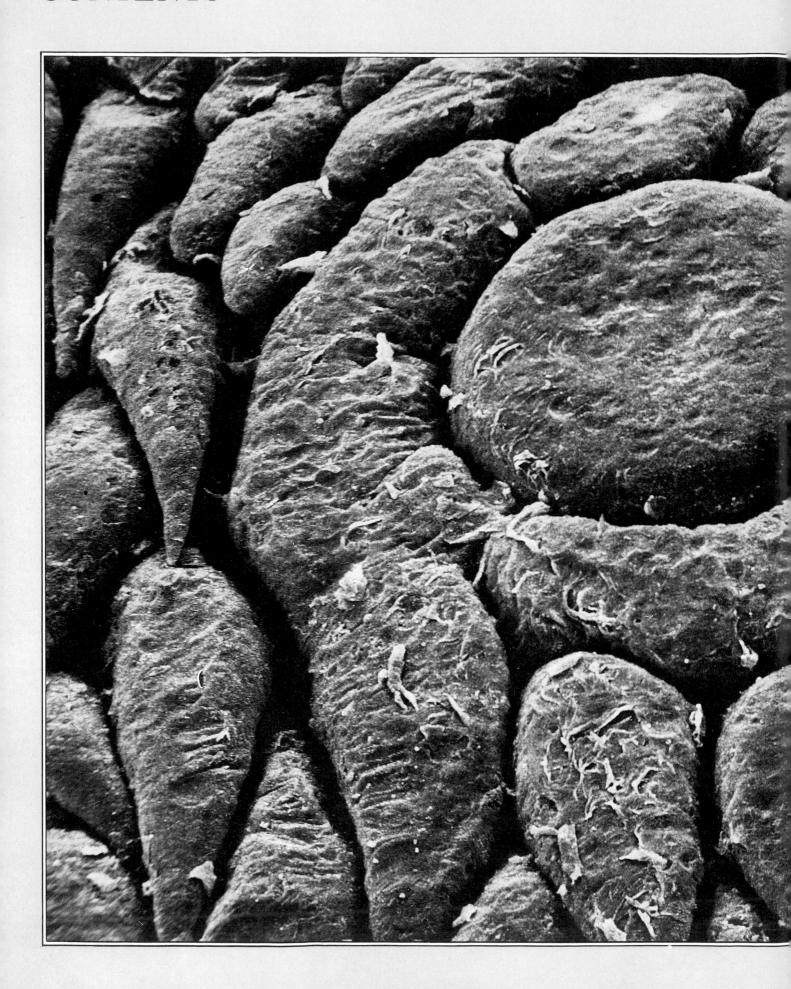

THE ANIMAL KINGDOM   2

MOLECULES AND CELLS   20

FEEDING AND DIGESTION   34

Food for all   48

GAS EXCHANGE AND CIRCULATION   50

Living in Water but Breathing Air   64

THE INTERNAL ENVIRONMENT   66

SENSES   84

MOVEMENT OF ANIMALS   98

Record Breakers   112

COORDINATION AND CONTROL   114

REPRODUCTION AND DEVELOPMENT   128

BIBLIOGRAPHY   144
PICTURE ACKNOWLEDGEMENTS   144
GLOSSARY   IX
INDEX   XIV

Papillae on surface of dog's tongue, with taste buds in trenches between papillae; scanning electron micrograph (Science Photo Library).

THE ANIMAL KINGDOM

Animal names. . . Classification of animals. . . Evolution of animals. . . Plurals of animal terms. . . Protozoans—amoeba, flagellates, ciliates. . . Animals with two layers—sponges, jellyfish, sea anemones, corals. . . Simple worms and wheel animalcules. . . Symmetry in animals. . . Segmented animals—earthworms, crustaceans, insects, spiders. . . Mollusks—snails, clams, octopus. . . Echinoderms—starfish, sea urchins, sea lilies. . . Animals with backbones. . . Sea squirts and lancelets. . . Fish—sharks, hagfish, bony fish. . . Amphibians. . . Reptiles. . . Birds. . . Mammals— monotremes, marsupials, placental mammals. . .

ANIMALS exhibit staggering diversity. They range from the tiniest single-celled protozoan to gigantic whales, and from immobile sponges to the most acrobatic birds. This diversity is believed to be the result of evolution over an immensely long time. The oldest recognizable fossil remains of animals are about 600 million years old, but they are quite complicated and must themselves be the products of prolonged evolution. Life first appeared in its simplest forms several thousand million years ago.

We do not know how many kinds of animals there are. New kinds are discovered regularly but we cannot say how many remain undiscovered. So far, almost 1.5 million species have been described and named. The vast majority of these are insects (about a million species). Other major groups of animals contain smaller, but nevertheless large, numbers of species. For example, there are about 9,000 species of birds and 4,000 species of mammals.

No book of reasonable size can describe all of the known species of animals but it is possible to arrange animals into groups of more-or-less similar species (believed to be related in evolutionary terms) and to introduce the major groups. This is attempted here.

To be able to discuss animals, names are needed for the different kinds. Most people regard tigers as one kind of animal and lions as another. All tigers look more or less alike. They breed together and produce young like themselves. Male lions have manes and females (lionesses) do not, but they breed together and produce a mixture of lions and lionesses. This popular distinction between kinds of animals corresponds closely to the zoologists' distinction between species. All tigers belong to one species and all lions to another. The rare white tigers look different from ordinary ones but may be born in the same litter and are included in the same species. The now extinct lions of North Africa had distinctive, almost black, manes, but there was apparently nothing but distance to prevent them from mating with the lions of equatorial Africa, and they are put in the same species.

The lion species has different names in different languages (for example, Löwe in German, Simba in Swahili). Zoologists find it convenient to have internationally recognized names for species and use a standardized system of two-word Latinized names. The lion is called *Panthera leo* and the tiger *Panthera tigris*. The first word *Panthera* is the name of the genus (a group of closely similar species) which includes the lion and the tiger,

▲ **Father of classification** Carolus Linnaeus (1707–1778) who established the binomial system of naming animals and plants.

▶ **Different color but the same species.** All forms of tiger belong to the same species. *Panthera tigris*, of which there are eight subspecies. The Indian subspecies (*P. t. tigris*) exists in two quite distinct forms; those showing normal colors ABOVE and a white form BELOW, but both have the same scientific name. The white form was once quite frequent in northern India.

as well as the leopard, Snow leopard and the jaguar. The second word, *leo* or *tigris* indicates the particular species within the genus. The generic name *Panthera* may be used alone, to refer to all the members of the genus. The specific names *leo* and *tigris* should not be used alone, because the same specific name may be used in more than one genus. For example, there is an Australian fish called *Yozia tigris*.

Classification—Lumping and Dividing

It is often necessary to make statements about larger groups of animals; for example, about all the cat-like animals or all the mammals. There is a formal system of classification to make this possible.

Domestic cats are similar to lions and tigers, but not as similar as those species are to each other (for example, they do not roar). They are put in a different genus (*Felis*), but *Felis*, *Panthera* and other cat-like animals are grouped together as the family Felidae. Notice that family names (and names of larger groups) are conventionally printed in roman type, although generic and specific names are printed in *italics*. The flesh-eating mammals (cats, dogs, hyenas, weasels and so on), together with a few plant eaters that seem obviously related

to them (such as pandas) are grouped together in the order Carnivora. These and all the other animals that suckle their young are grouped together in the class Mammalia. Finally, the mammals are included, with all the other animals that have backbones (fish, amphibians, reptiles and birds) and some other animals that seem to be related to them, in the phylum Chordata.

The animals are divided into about 38 phyla (phyla is the plural of phylum), but many of the phyla are very small and obscure. It is conventional to group all of these phyla together in a single animal kingdom but, in this book, it has been thought better to divide the animals into two kingdoms—the single-celled protozoans and the multicellular animals. Most phyla are divided into several classes, most classes into several orders and most orders into several families. These categories, together with genus and species, are the basic units in animal classification. Other categories such as subphylum and super-family are introduced when more elaborate schemes seem necessary.

Classification is a matter of opinion, and differences of detail will often be found between schemes given in different books.

Evolution

The great majority of zoologists believe that animal species have not been created separately, but have arisen by evolution. The most direct evidence comes from fossils, which are the preserved remains (mainly bones and shells) of long-dead animals. Geological studies indicate the ages of the rocks, and fossils outline the history of life. Unfortunately, the fossil record is very incomplete. Generally, only hard parts of animals are preserved, so there are very few recognizable fossils of worms, jelly-

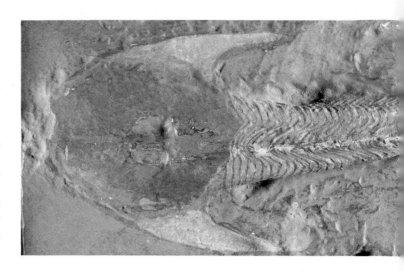

A Classification of Animals

Single-celled Organisms
Kingdom: Protista

Protozoans
Subkingdom: Protozoa

Flagellates, Amoebae
Phylum: Sarcomastigophora
About 18,500 species

Ciliates
Phylum: Ciliophora
About 7,200 species

Sporozoans
Phyla: Apicomplexa
    Labyrinthomorpha,
    Microspora, Ascetospora,
    Myxospora
About 5,600 species

Animals
Kingdom: Animalia

Mesozoans
Subkingdom: Mesozoa
Phylum: Mesozoa
About 50 species

Sponges
Subkingdom: Parazoa
Phylum: Porifera
About 5,000 species

Multicelled Animals
Subkingdom: Metazoa

Sea Anemones, Jellyfish, Corals
Phylum: Cnidaria
About 9,400 species

Comb Jellies
Phylum: Ctenophora
About 100 species

Endoprocts
Phylum: Endoprocta
About 130 species

Rotifers
Phylum: Rotifera
About 1,700 species

Kinorhynchs
Phylum: Kinorhyncha
About 120 species

Gastrotrichs
Phylum: Gastrotricha
About 200 species

Lampshells
Phylum: Brachiopoda
About 260 species

Moss Animals
Phylum: Bryozoa (Ectoprocta)
About 4,000 species

Horseshoe Worms
Phylum: Phoronida
About 11 species

Flatworms
Phylum: Platyhelminthes
About 10,000 species

Ribbon Worms
Phylum: Nemertea
About 800 species

Roundworms
Phylum: Nematoda
About 12,000 species

Spiny-headed Worms
Phylum: Acanthocephala
About 700 species

Horsehair Worms
Phylum: Nematomorpha
About 80 species

Segmented Worms
Phylum: Annelida
About 11,500 species

Priapulans
Phylum: Priapula
About 9 species

Sipunculans
Phylum: Sipuncula
About 320 species

Echiurans
Phylum: Echiura
About 130 species

Beard Worms
Phylum: Pogonophora
About 150 species

Arrow Worms
Phylum: Chaetognatha
About 70 species

Acorn Worms
Phylum: Hemichordata
About 90 species

Crustaceans
Phylum: Crustacea
About 39,000 species

Spiders, Horseshoe Crabs
Phylum: Chelicerata
About 70,000 species

Insects, Centipedes, Millipedes
Phylum: Uniramia
About 1,000,000 species

Water Bears
Phylum: Tardigrada
About 400 species

Tongue Worms
Phylum: Pentastomida
About 90 species

Velvet Worms
Phylum: Onchyphora
About 120 species

Mollusks
Phylum: Mollusca
About 37,000 species

Echinoderms
Phylum: Echinodermata
About 6,000 species

Chordates
Phylum: Chordata

Sea Squirts
Subphylum: Urochordata
About 2,000 species

Lancelets
Subphylum: Cephalochordata
About 20 species

Vertebrates
Subphylum: Vertebrata

Jawless Fish
Class Agnatha

Bony Fish
Class: Osteichthyes
About 21,000 species

Sharks, Skates
Class: Selachii
About 700 species

Amphibians
Class: Amphibia
About 3,080 species

Reptiles
Class: Reptilia
About 6,600 species

Birds
Class: Aves
About 8,805 species

Mammals
Class: Mammalia
About 4,070 species

The above scheme includes all phyla, but many are of such insignificance that they are not discussed further in this volume. It should also be noted that the above scheme is the synthesis of the opinions of many experts on individual groups; it reflects a pattern of modern thought, although other schemes are deemed to be equally valid.

▲ **Reconstructing past life.** LEFT Actual fossil of the extinct fish *Cephalaspis*, which lived in the Silurian period some 400 million years ago. By studying these remains and comparing their form with living fish, it is possible to reconstruct how the animal probably looked RIGHT.

fish and the like. The oldest fossils are very rare and, by the period from which fossils are reasonably plentiful, most if not all of the phyla had already appeared.

The most complete record is of the vertebrates, the animals that have backbones. Fossils show the fish appearing first, then the amphibians, then the reptiles and finally the birds and mammals. The earliest-known amphibians were very like a group of fish that had appeared a little earlier. The earliest-known bird had a reptile-like tail and teeth instead of a bill. These and other details strongly suggest a process of evolution.

Young animals inherit most of their characteristics from their parents. Random variation in the molecules responsible for inheritance, however, produces some new characteristics which have not been inherited but can be passed on by inheritance to subsequent generations. Animals bearing new characteristics that are better fitted to their environment are

Plurals of Animal Terms

Many technical terms in zoology are Latinized words, and are converted from the singular to the plural form according to the rules of Latin grammar. For example, the plural of phylum is not phylums but phyla. Here are some rules:

Words ending "-a" usually have plurals ending "-ae" (for example, trachea (windpipe), tracheae; antenna, antennae).

Words ending "-us" usually have plurals ending "-i" (for example, humerus (upper arm bone), humeri).

Words ending "-um" have plurals ending "-a" (for example, phylum, phyla;

operculum (gill cover), opercula).

Words ending "-is" usually have plurals ending "-es" (for example, metamorphosis, metamorphoses).

Unfortunately, there are awkward exceptions. For instance, the plural of genus is genera. Also, English plural forms are sometimes used (for example, humeruses instead of humeri).

The names of species are never put into the plural: zoologists say *Panthera tigris* both when they are speaking of one individual tiger and when they are speaking of many.

particularly likely to survive and breed, so these characteristics are likely to be passed on. This is the mechanism of natural selection.

The successes of animal breeding strongly suggest that this mechanism should be effective. Humans have bred extraordinarily different kinds of dogs by artificial selection, over many generations, of puppies with desired characteristics. Natural selection may not be as efficient as artificial selection, but it has been in progress for hundreds of millions of years.

A few cases of rapid, small-scale evolution have occurred recently enough to be observed by scientists. For example, resistance to the rat poison Warfarin has been developed among rats in districts where the poison has been used.

Protozoans

Cells are the basic building blocks of which animals are built. The protozoans are the simplest of animals, in the sense that each individual consists of just one cell. The largest are about 2mm long and the smallest about 1μm (a thousandth part of a millimeter), so that microscopes are needed for examining them.

It has been customary to class all the single-celled animals together in a single phylum, but the main groups of protozoans are so distinctly different from one another that it seems better to regard them as separate phyla. Also, some protozoans contain the green pigment chlorophyll and were regarded by botanists as plants, although zoologists claimed them as animals—a quite ridiculous situation. One way to resolve the problem is to regard all single-celled organisms, whether plant- or animal-like, as a separate kingdom (the Protista) distinct from the kingdom Animalia. The protozoans then form a subkingdom containing seven phyla.

The first of the phyla is the Sarcomastigophora, which consists of the amoebas and flagellates. Typical **amoebas** are well known as subjects of biology lessons, but are not very common. They are irregularly shaped blobs of living material, that crawl around on the mud at the bottoms of ponds. As they crawl, they change shape: lobes extend from the body in the direction of crawling, and the cell contents flow into them. There is no mouth or even any fixed point for taking in food, and the animal simply flows around its food and engulfs it. Under high magnification, the cell contents look like transparent, rather lumpy porridge. This may seem to be the ultimate simple animal, but it must be far more complicated than is immediately apparent. The processes of even its simple way of life require exceedingly complicated molecules appropriately arranged within the cell.

The **flagellates** look more complicated and better organized than amoebas, but may well have evolved first. Many of them contain the green photosynthesizing pigment, chlorophyll, and do not need to feed as animals do, but can capture energy from sunlight by the process of photosynthesis. These flagellates are plant-like, but they seem obviously closely related to others that lack chlorophyll and eat food in animal fashion.

The green flagellates (the ones that have chlorophyll) are immensely important as sources of food in seas and lakes. Some small animals feed directly on them, larger animals feed on these small animals and so on, so that even the largest fish and whales depend ultimately on the energy captured from sunlight by green flagellates and other microscopic plants. Similarly, animal life on land depends on the land plants.

The distinctive feature of flagellates is the flagellum, a whip-like extension of the body that can be undulated to propel the animal through the water. Most flagellates have two flagella but some have only one and others have many. Some flagellates have simple round bodies and others have more complicated shapes, some with long projecting spikes. Most look very different from amoebas but some can change back and forth between amoeba-like and flagellate forms, suggesting that the amoebas and flagellates are close relatives.

The next phylum, the **ciliates** (Ciliophora), includes the most complex of all single-celled animals. Instead of a few flagella, they have hundreds of short, bristle-like cilia which act like so many oars, and can row the animals along at speeds of a millimeter or so per second. Some ciliates swim around continuously, eating bacteria and such other particles of suitable food as they encounter. Others spend much or all of their time attached to larger objects and use their cilia to set up water currents that bring food to them. There is a particular point on the body which serves as a mouth, at which food is taken in.

Ciliates play an important role in sewage beds, where bacteria break down the organic waste and are in turn eaten by ciliates. Other ciliates flourish in the rumen (part of the stomach) of cattle. The enzymes that cattle themselves produce are incapable of digesting the cell walls and fibers that are the main organic constituents of grass. Ciliates and bacteria in the rumen digest these materials and reproduce rapidly but are, in turn, digested by the cattle as the food passing through carries them further along the gut. Thus, the cattle get much more benefit from the grass than they otherwise could.

The remaining protozoan phyla are parasitic and are sometimes jointly referred to as **sporozoans**. These parasites live in the bodies of other animals, some of them causing serious diseases. For instance, members of the genus *Plasmodium* cause malaria, and members of the genus *Eimeria* cause the intestinal disease, coccidiosis, of cattle, sheep and poultry. There are parasites in the other groups of protozoans (for example, an amoeba

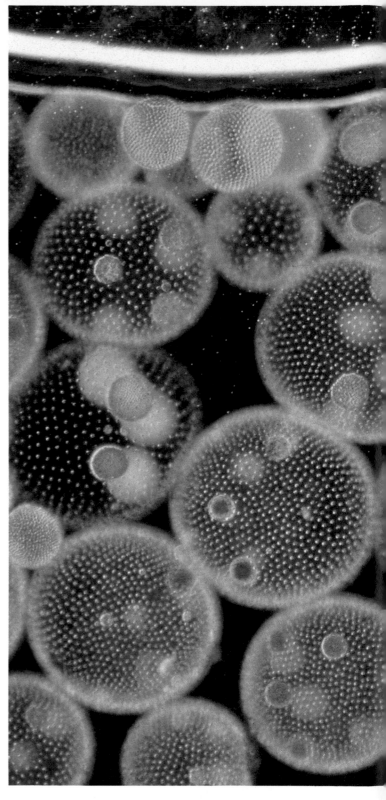

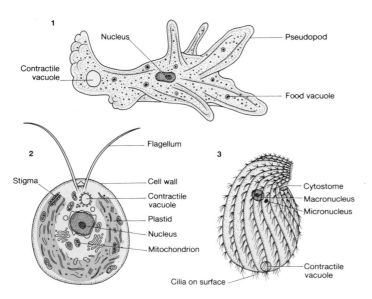

◄ **Protozoans forms** (1) *Amoeba*. (2) *Chlamydomonas*—a flagellate. (3) *Colpoda*—a ciliate.

▲ **Classification conundrum**—a mass of the flagellate protozoans *Volvox*. Each sphere consists of a mass of cells, each just like an individual of other protozoan species. Is it a colony of individuals or a single many-celled individual? Also each cell contains chlorophyll and captures energy by photosynthesis. Some other flagellates lack chlorophyll and feed like animals. Are flagellates animals or plants?

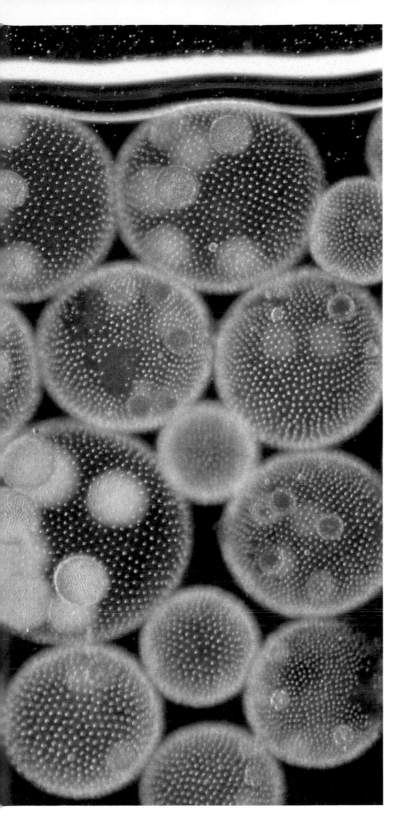

better regarded as a single, many-celled individual. The distinction between single-celled and many-celled structure is not quite as sharp as it might at first appear. Also, the distinction sometimes seems rather trivial, even when it is clear. The nuclei of cells store the information needed for constructing the complex molecules on which life depends. Typical cells have just one nucleus each but some large protozoans have many nuclei. Such protozoans would only require membranes, partitioning the cell contents, to make them many celled.

Animals with Two Layers of Cells

The very simple many-celled animals, such as sponges, jellyfish, sea anemones and corals, all have a central cavity in the body. A single layer of cells covers the outside surface of the body and another single layer lines the cavity. Between them, often forming most of the thickness of the body wall, is a jelly-like substance called the mesogloea. The jelly layer is particularly thick and obvious in the jellyfish.

The **sponges** form the phylum Porifera, within their own sub-kingdom, the Parazoa. They live attached to rocks and other submerged objects both in fresh water and (much more commonly) in the sea. They cannot move around (although some contract their surface pores when they are touched) and may seem more like plants than animals. Their manner of feeding shows that they are animals, however. They do not use light energy to build up foodstuffs as plants do, but capture and ingest such small particles of food as happen to be suspended in the water around them. They get this food by drawing water through their body cavities, in through numerous tiny pores and out through fewer larger ones. The water is driven partly by the beating of flagella and partly by external currents.

Another phylum, the Cnidaria, includes the **jellyfish** (class Scyphozoa), the **sea anemones** and **corals** (Anthozoa) as well as some less well-known animals. Two main body forms are found in the phylum. One is the polyp, exemplified by the sea anemones. The animal is a hollow cylinder with a mouth surrounded by tentacles at one end, and with the other end usually fixed to a stone or plant. The other form is the medusa, exemplified by the jellyfish. These animals are shaped like upside-down bowls and are generally not anchored, but swim freely. The mouth is at the center of the inside of the bowl. Some cnidarians produce polyps and medusae at different stages of their life cycles. For example, jellyfish develop from tiny polyps.

Corals are closely related to sea anemones but lay down masses of stony material (calcium carbonate). Most do not live as separate individuals but as colonies of many polyps attached together. The corals that form reefs have green flagellates inside some of their cells. The flagellates produce food by photosynthesis. Some of this food supports the flagellates but much apparently diffuses out and supplements the diet of the coral.

The bryozoans or **moss animals** look rather like some of the smaller cnidarians, but are considerably more complicated in structure. They are colonies of tiny individuals, rather like cnidarian polyps. They are plentiful in coastal rock pools but are generally inconspicuous, forming tufts of plant-like growth or scab-like layers on rocks and plants. Some can foul man-made structures, for example piers, pilings, buoys and ship's hulls. A few bryozoan species occur in freshwater.

that causes dysentery and a flagellate that causes sleeping sickness), but the sporozoans are all parasitic. Sporozoans spend part of their life cycle inside the cells of their hosts. For example, malaria parasites live inside red blood cells.

Protozoans have become adapted to a great variety of ways of life, but, because each individual is a single cell, they are necessarily small. Only the many-celled animals have evolved to large sizes. The largest animals contain millions of cells.

Some protozoans live in colonies of many individuals, connected together. In some cases it could be argued whether the colony is indeed a group of animals, or whether it would be

Simple Worms and Rotifers

Many cnidarians and all bryozoans live sedentary lives, attached to stones and other objects. In contrast, these simple worms and wheel animalcules or rotifers crawl or at least wriggle.

The **flatworms** (phylum Platyhelminthes) are simple worms with bodies which are, in most cases, flattened like pancakes. Like cnidarians, they have a mouth but no anus. There is a layer of cells on the outside of the body and another lining the gut but, instead of a jelly-like mesogloea, there is a mass of cells between the inner and outer layers. There is no blood system and only a very simple nervous system, but the reproductive system is often extremely complicated with male and female organs in the same individual.

Some flatworms live independent lives, crawling around on the bottoms of ponds, rock pools and so on. A few live on dry land, but many other flatworms are parasites. For example, liver flukes are large flatworms that infect the livers of sheep, cattle and occasionally humans, causing disease. Tapeworms are more peculiar flatworms that anchor themselves in the guts of their hosts and absorb the digested foods around them. They are thin but often very long. Tapeworms up to 12m (40ft) long have been found (as tangled masses) in human guts.

The phylum Nematoda consists of the **roundworms** which are slender worms that are circular in cross-section but do not have the body divided into segments as earthworms do. One of the characteristic features of the nematodes is a thick cuticle that allows the body to bend but prevents it from shortening in the way that earthworms do when disturbed. Enormous numbers of tiny nematodes live between the grains of soil, feeding mainly on bacteria and decaying plant material. Other nematodes parasitize plants and some of them, including the Potato root eelworm, cause troublesome plant diseases. Yet others, some of them quite large, are parasites of animals. They include the hookworms, which live in the guts of their hosts and have a debilitating effect on infected people. It has been estimated that 450 million people are infected, mainly in underdeveloped countries.

Rotifers (phylum Rotifera) are tiny animals which are not

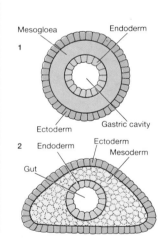

▲ **Sponge on sea floor.** This species is *Polymastia boletiforme* found in the north Atlantic.

▶ **Free-floating or sedentary.** The phylum Coelenterata contains swimming forms such as the jellyfish *Chrysaora hyoscella* ABOVE and colonial sedentary forms such as the Precious coral *Corallium rubrum* BELOW.

◀▼ **Two- and three-layered animals.** (1) Simple animals comprise just two layers of cells separated by a jelly-like mesogloea, eg (a) sea anemones and (b) jellyfish, whereas in three-layered animals (2), the mesogloea is replaced by a central cellular layer (mesoderm), as in (c) roundworms.

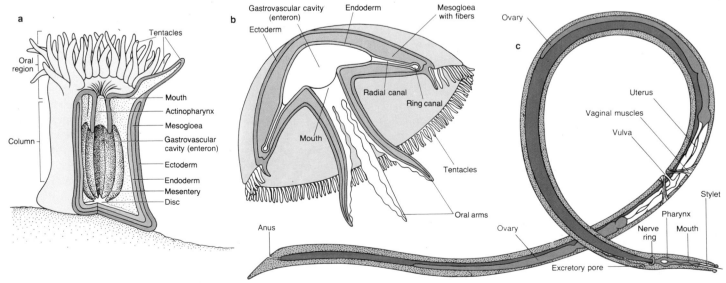

worm shaped but show some resemblance to nematodes in their internal structure. They are similar in size to ciliate protozoans, and depend on cilia for swimming and for setting up feeding currents. Although they are so similar in size to ciliates, their bodies consist of hundreds of tiny cells.

Segmented Animals

The annelids are the earthworms and other segmented worms. The arthropods are the crabs, insects, spiders, centipedes and other animals that are enclosed in a generally hard, jointed cuticle rather like a medieval suit of armor. These two groups are described together because their members consist of segments connected together like the carriages of a railroad train. The segments of earthworms are marked off by grooves in the outer surface of the body. Those of centipedes are separated by joints in the armor plating, and each segment has a pair of legs. In both cases, dissection would show structures repeated in successive segments. For example, almost every segment in an earthworm contains a pair of tubes called nephridia, which function as kidneys.

Railroad trains do not generally consist entirely of identical units. They usually have a locomotive, a guard's van or caboose, and often a dining car. Similarly, segmented animals have some segments, especially ones near the front end, considerably different from the rest. Also, the boundaries between segments may be obscured. It is not obvious that a crab is segmented, until it is turned over.

There are three main orders of Annelida. The Polychaeta includes most of the **marine worms**. Typically, each segment has a pair of paddle-shaped projections, called parapodia, with bundles of bristles on them. Some polychaete worms crawl and swim freely, but others live in burrows at the bottom of the sea. Some have long tentacles for collecting food. The second order is the Oligochaeta, which includes the **earthworms**. They have no parapodia and only a few (often very short) bristles. The third order, the Hirudinea or **leeches**, have no bristles, and have a sucker at each end of the body.

The jointed-limbed animals have generally been grouped as the phylum Arthropoda, but it is now thought this is a group of quite unrelated animals and it may be better to regard each group as a phylum in its own right.

The arthropods include three very large, important phyla, the Crustacea (shrimps, crabs and so on), the Uniramia (insects, centipedes, millipedes) and the Chelicerata (spiders, scorpions and so on).

Nearly all **crustaceans** live in water, although woodlice and a few others live on land. Some, such as crabs and lobsters, crawl around on the sea bed and rarely or never swim. Others are members of the plankton, the assemblage of (generally small) animals and plants that live in the surface waters of lakes and seas. Copepods a few millimeters long are particularly important in the plankton of temperate seas. They feed on green flagellates and other single-celled plants and, in turn, form the principal food of important fishes such as herring and mackerel. Much larger planktonic crustaceans, called krill, are immensely important in the Southern Ocean, as the principal food of the baleen whales. Barnacles are crustaceans that have evolved a protective shell and live attached to rocks or ships.

Land-living Arthropods

Nearly all the insects and spiders spend their adult lives on land but some insects (including mayflies) have young stages that live in water. Most adult insects have two pairs of wings, and can fly, but the Diptera (the "true" flies) have only one pair and some insects (such as worker ants) have no wings. Also, insects have three pairs of legs and most have the body clearly divided into three main sections: the head; the thorax (which bears the legs and wings); and the abdomen. These features distinguish insects from all other arthropods.

Most adult insects have wings but their young stages are wingless. Some insects (for example, grasshoppers) have young stages that look very much like the adults, apart from the lack of wings. Others (for example, flies and butterflies) develop from grubs or caterpillars that look quite unlike the adults. These spend an inactive period, as a pupa, while making the drastic change to the adult form.

Insects are small. Most of them weigh less than 1g (0.035oz) and only a few giant tropical bugs and beetles weigh more than 10g (0.35oz). Nevertheless, the insects are phenomenally successful. About three-quarters of all known species of animals are insects, and many insects are extremely important to humans. Some (such as locusts) are serious agricultural pests. Some suck the blood of humans and other animals and transmit diseases such as malaria and yellow fever (transmitted by mosquitoes) and sleeping sickness (transmitted by tsetse flies). Other insects bring great benefits by pollinating flowers or by preying on pests and keeping them in check.

Spiders and scorpions have four pairs of legs and no wings. Their bodies have only two main sections, the prosoma (which corresponds in function to the head and thorax together of

▶ **Worm types** TOP LEFT Body plan of an earthworm, showing the regular external segmented structure, but with some internal segmental variation. TOP RIGHT A fan worm *Sabella pavonina*, showing the tentacles extended during feeding.

◀ **Weaving ants** (*Oecophylla smaragdina*) holding leaves together to form a nest, while secretions from the larvae inside are used to stick the leaves together. Insects such as ants, bees and termites have complex social systems.

▶ **Crustacean body plan.** External and internal structure of a lobster, which has a basic segmented form although both internally and externally the segments have different structures and functions.

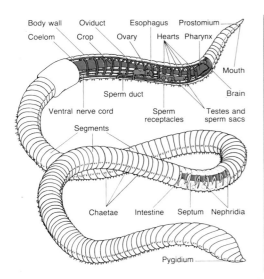

insects) and the opisthosoma (which corresponds to the abdomen). Scorpions have the prosoma and opisthosoma obviously divided into segments, but spiders do not. Mites have round bodies with no obvious segments and without even an obvious division between prosoma and opisthosoma. Another confusing feature of mites is that, although the adults have four pairs of legs like other arachnids, they have young stages with only three.

Scorpions and spiders are predators, feeding on insects and other prey. Mites have much more varied habits. Enormous numbers of tiny mites live in the soil, feeding on decaying plant material. Other mites feed on living plants, and some of them are important agricultural pests. Yet others live as parasites on the skins of larger animals, especially mammals and birds. The large ones, called ticks, feed by sucking their hosts' blood.

Mollusks

Mollusks (phylum Mollusca) have soft bodies, but many of them have hard, rigid shells. The ones with shells include snails and clams, and those without include **slugs** (although some have a rudimentary shell) and octopus. They differ very widely in shape and way of life, but they are grouped together because they are built to a common plan. Each has a head, a muscular foot and a visceral mass that contains the guts. There is a mantle cavity open to the outside environment, usually containing gills (called ctenidia). The central nervous system consists of a few pairs of ganglia linked by connecting nerves. Most mollusks have a tongue-like organ, called a radula, covered with teeth like a carpenter's rasp.

The most primitive living mollusks (apart from the rare monoplacophorans) are the **chitons** (class Polyplacophora). These are flattened marine animals that attach themselves to

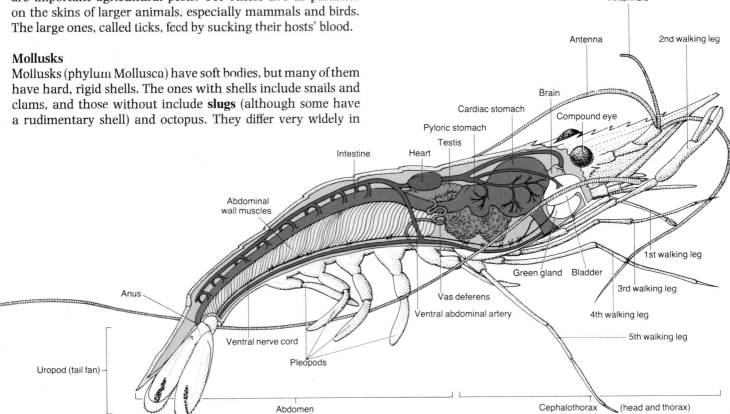

rocks by means of large feet, on which they can crawl. They are protected by a shell made of eight overlapping plates. They feed by using the radula to rasp the surface film of algae off rocks. The mantle cavity is a groove between the foot and the visceral mass, running round the animal under the edge of the shell.

The gastropods (class Gastropoda) are the various kinds of **snail** and **slug**. Most have large, coiled shells, big enough to contain the whole body. When the animal retires into its shell, the tough, muscular foot is the last part to be drawn in, so it is left blocking the shell opening. It often carries a hard operculum that can close the shell like a door, leaving the animal very well protected. Gastropods that live in the sea or on shores have gills in their mantle cavities, but the land snails and slugs and most of the freshwater snails have no gills: their mantle cavities have evolved into lungs, and they breathe air. Many gastropods feed on plants but some prey on other animals.

The bivalve mollusks (class Bivalvia) are the **clams**, **mussels** and the like. They live sandwiched between two shells, one on each side of the body. These shells are hinged together along the animal's back. They can be opened to allow the foot to emerge or shut ("like a clam") to enclose and protect the animal. Clams do not crawl on their feet like chitons and snails, but many of them use their feet for burrowing in sand or mud. Their mantle cavities contain huge ctenidia that serve more as food collectors than as gills. Cilia on the ctenidia draw water through the mantle cavity where it is filtered, removing suspended particles of food such as single-celled algae and fragments of decaying organic matter. Bivalves are plentiful on the sea floor and play an important role in the ecosystem, feeding largely on dead plankton that sinks from above. Their sedentary lifestyle gives them little need for complex sense organs, and there is no distinct head.

In contrast, cephalopod mollusks (class Cephalopoda: **squids**, **octopus** and so on) are active animals with highly developed eyes, and with the ganglia of the head enlarged to form a complex brain. The foot has become a ring of tentacles, long in octopus but relatively short in squids. Octopus spend most of their time on the bottom of the sea, grabbing crabs and other prey with their tentacles. Squids swim around, pursuing prey such as fish. They can swim fast using "jet propulsion," by squirting water out of the mantle cavity. In turn, squid and octopus are food for other animals including humans.

Echinoderms

The members of the phylum Echinodermata are the **starfish**, **sea urchins**, **sea lilies** and the like. All of them live in the sea. They have hard ossicles (small, bone-like, calcified nodules) embedded in their body walls. They have a unique system of fluid-filled tubes, the water vascular system, which connects to the tube feet (tiny suckers on stalks that project from the surface of the body). They have no distinct head, and no brain. Finally (and most obviously), they have five-fold symmetry. Starfishes (class Asteroidea) and brittlestars (Ophiuroidea) have five arms, each with a double row of tube feet. Sea urchins (Echinoidea) and sea cucumbers (Holothuroidea) have no arms, but their tube feet are still arranged in five double rows. Sea urchins have the ossicles in their body walls joined together to form a rigid case, called a test.

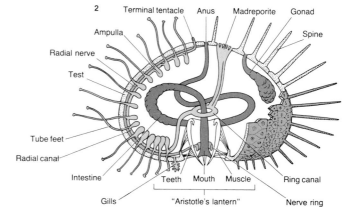

▲ **Sea urchin body plan** showing the main internal organs.

▶ **Massed squid.** A shoal of the squid *Loligo opalescens* that have come together to spawn near the shore in California.

▼ **Cuttlefish body plan** showing the main internal organs.

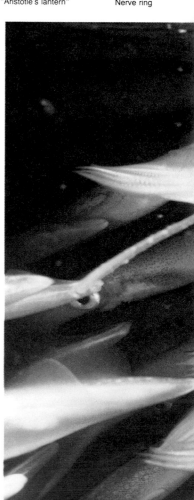

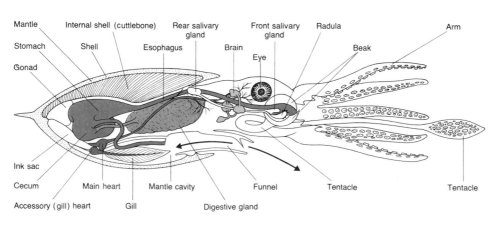

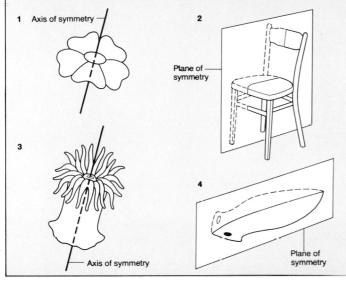

Symmetry in Animals

Animals show two main kinds of symmetry. Radial symmetry is the symmetry of a flower (1) in which the petals are all identical. Bilateral symmetry is the symmetry of a chair (2) which could be cut into two halves that were mirror images of each other. Cnidarians, both polyps (3) and medusae, are more-or-less radially symmetrical. Flatworms (4) and most other more advanced animals (including humans) are more-or-less bilaterally symmetrical. However, the partitions inside a sea anemone are not strictly radially symmetrical, and the human heart is asymmetrical.

1 Axis of symmetry

2 Plane of symmetry

3

Axis of symmetry

4 Plane of symmetry

Most sea lilies (Crinoidea) live on long stalks, standing up from the sea floor. Most other echinoderms crawl around on their tube feet, as if on hundreds of tiny legs. Echinoderms are important scavengers in the sea, feeding largely on particles of decaying organic matter. Many of the starfish, however, are predators, attacking bivalve mollusks and other invertebrates.

Animals with Backbones

The phylum Chordata includes all the vertebrate animals—the fishes, amphibians, reptiles, birds and mammals. Classed with them are some much simpler marine animals, commonly called protochordates. Three main characteristics are shared by all the chordates.

1 They have a hollow nerve cord running along the dorsal surface (the back). Such nerve cords contrast with those of arthropods and annelid worms, which are solid and ventral (they run along the belly).

2 Chordates have a notochord, a slender rod close under the nerve cord, during some stage of their life. It is a sort of primitive backbone, present in embryos of all chordates but replaced by the vertebral column in adult vertebrates.

3 Chordates have gill slits perforating the throat. Fish have gills in them. Higher vertebrates have gill slits during embryonic stages but lose them before becoming adult.

In addition to these features, vertebrates have a characteristic, complex brain protected by a skull, and most of them have a well-developed vertebral column.

There are two groups of protochordates, the **sea squirts** and their relatives (subphylum Urochordata) and the **lancelets**

(subphylum Cephalochordata). Both groups are filter feeders, like bivalve mollusks. Typical sea squirts are simple animals enclosed in a tough cellulose bag with two openings. The water they filter enters by one opening and leaves by the other. They have huge numbers of gill slits (with openings that are hidden and protected by the bag), but adults have no hollow nerve cord and no notochord. They develop, however, from tiny tadpole-like larvae that show these chordate features.

The best-known lancelets are the species of *Branchiostoma*, commonly called amphioxus. They are a few centimeters long and look rather like semitransparent eels, but they have no proper brain, no skull and no vertebral column.

Fish

Fish are aquatic vertebrates that have fins but no legs. They are not treated as a single group in formal classifications, but as several distinct classes within the subphylum Vertebrata.

The most primitive belong to the so-called class Agnatha, which consists of fish that have not evolved jaws. The oldest fossil vertebrates belong to this group, and so do the modern **lampreys** and **hagfish**. Lampreys are eel-shaped fish which breed in fresh water and spend their adult life either there or in the sea. Their larvae are filter feeders like the amphioxus. The adults of some species do not feed but simply breed and die. Those of other species are parasites that feed on the blood of other fishes. The adults of all species have muscular suckers round their mouths that serve to anchor them to stones or to attach them to the fish whose blood they suck. Lampreys in aquaria sometimes remain attached to the same prey fish for several days. Hagfish are also eel shaped but have no sucker. They live in the sea, spending much of their time buried in mud. They feed partly on the corpses of dead fish and partly on worms and other invertebrates. It is now felt that the lampreys and hagfish are only very distantly related so grouping them as a class Agnatha is losing favor.

A much larger class, the Selachii, includes the **sharks** and **rays**. Most of them are fairly large, and the Whale shark (*Rhincodon typus*) is believed to reach a maximum weight of 40 tonnes. Typical sharks are notorious predators, capable of biting hunks of flesh out of large prey, but the Whale shark feeds by straining plankton from the sea water that passes through its gills. Rays are flat-bodied relatives of the sharks with wing-like fins. Most of them live and feed close to the sea bottom.

By far the largest class of fish is the class Osteichthyes, the bony fish. These have skeletons made of bone, in contrast to the selachians and modern agnathans, which have skeletons made of cartilage (gristle). Most of them have a bladder of gas in the body cavity: this may be either a lung used for breathing air or (more often) a swim bladder that serves only to give them buoyancy. The **bony fish** are divided into three groups. The lobe-finned fish (crossopterygians) are extinct apart from the modern coelacanth, *Latimeria*, but it was from them that the amphibians and eventually all the other land-living vertebrates

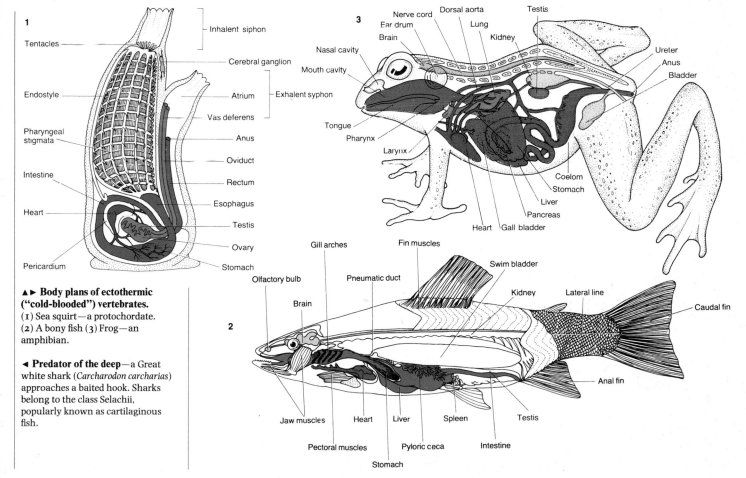

▲▶ **Body plans of ectothermic ("cold-blooded") vertebrates.** (1) Sea squirt—a protochordate. (2) A bony fish (3) Frog—an amphibian.

◀ **Predator of the deep**—a Great white shark (*Carcharodon carcharias*) approaches a baited hook. Sharks belong to the class Selachii, popularly known as cartilaginous fish.

evolved. The lungfish (dipnoans) use lungs to breathe air as well as gills to breathe water. They seem to be a dead end in evolution, but they are particularly interesting because they provide hints about how ancestral animals may have made the transition from water to land. The few surviving species live in Africa, Australia and South America. Finally, the ray-finned fish (actinopterygians) include the largest group of bony fish, the teleosts, and a few primitive relatives such as the sturgeons.

The vast majority of modern freshwater and marine fish are teleosts. Most of the fish in a fishmonger's shop and nearly all those in aquaria belong to this group. They have fins that can open and close like fans, or undulate to drive subtle swimming maneuvers. They include such oddities as the flatfish (Pleuronectiformes), which lie on one side of the body and have both eyes on the other, and the bizarre seahorses (*Hippocampus* etc), as well as fish of more ordinary shape. Some can breathe air as well as water, and mudskippers (*Periophthalmus*) leave the sea to shuffle around on land. Teleosts live in a wide variety of habitats, from mountain torrents to depths of several kilometers in the oceans. As a source of food for humans, they are more important than any other wild animals, and fish farming is an increasingly important industry.

Amphibians

The amphibians (class Amphibia) evolved from fish and gave rise to all other land-living vertebrates. The earliest amphibians lived about 350 million years ago and had the general shape of modern newts, but their skeletons were rather different and they may not have had the moist skin that is characteristic of newts and other modern amphibians. Fossil footprints show that they walked like newts, with their feet splayed well out on either side of the body. Some of these early amphibians grew as large as modern crocodiles.

Modern amphibians are all relatively small. They include the **newts** and **salamanders**, the tailless **frogs** and **toads** and the legless, burrowing **caecilians** of the tropics which resemble worms. Typically, they spend their adult life largely on land, breathing air by means of lungs but also depending in part on diffusion of gases through their moist skin. They lay eggs (frogspawn, for example) in water and their young stages (tadpoles) live in water, breathing water by means of gills. The change from tadpole to adult involves a dramatic metamorphosis.

Reptiles

The reptiles (class Reptilia) include the lizards, snakes, turtles and crocodiles, and many extinct groups such as the dinosaurs. In contrast to most amphibians, which lay small eggs in water, reptiles lay much larger eggs on land. Reptile eggs have shells, similar to birds' eggs, but the shell is, in many species, flexible instead of rigid. Oxygen diffuses through pores in the shell to supply the respiratory needs of the developing embryo. Young reptiles, shaped much like the adults, hatch from the eggs so there is no need for any dramatic metamorphosis. Reptiles have dry horny skin, quite unlike the moist skin of amphibians. This makes them less liable to dry up, and better able to survive in dry conditions.

Turtles and **tortoises** have shells which are usually rigid boxes, made of plates of bone covered with the horn-like

material that is known as tortoiseshell. The land-living tortoises and the freshwater turtles (terrapins) have feet which are well formed for walking, although the terrapins also use them for swimming. The marine turtles have flippers that enable them to swim gracefully, but they can only shuffle clumsily on the beaches where they lay their eggs.

Lizards have long tails, like newts and early amphibians, and stand with their feet well out on either side of the body. Some have lost their legs in the course of evolution. **Snakes** have also lost their legs, and another characteristic feature is that they have so many freely movable joints in their skulls that they are able to swallow extraordinarily large prey. They pacify their prey by constriction or (in poisonous snakes) by injecting venom as they bite.

The **crocodiles** are the only survivors of a large group of reptiles that included the dinosaurs and the flying pterosaurs. The birds evolved from the same group.

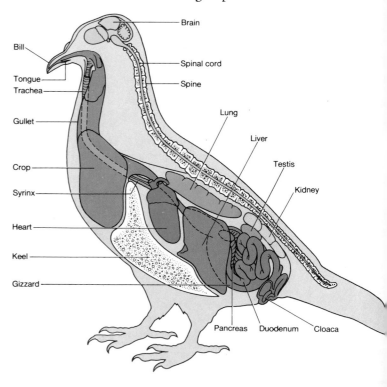

▲ **Python devours gazelle.** The enormity of the meal for this Rock python (*Python sebae*) will probably mean that it will not need to eat for many weeks, or even months, because of its low rate of metabolism.

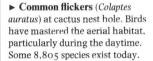

► **Common flickers** (*Colaptes auratus*) at cactus nest hole. Birds have mastered the aerial habitat, particularly during the daytime. Some 8,805 species exist today.

◄ **Bird body plan** showing the main internal organs.

Birds

Birds (class Aves) are the only large animals that commonly fly by day (insects are small and bats generally fly by night). Consequently, they are by far the most conspicuous of the wild animals that most people see near their homes. Birdwatching always seems to be the most popular of all branches of natural history.

Bird flight was made possible by the evolution of feathers, but feathers seem to have evolved first for a different function — as heat insulation. Birds (and mammals) keep their bodies warmer than their usual surroundings, by means of heat released from foodstuffs by the chemical processes that are called metabolism. Birds and mammals are described as endotherms, meaning that the heat that keeps them warmer than

their surroundings is generated within them. Some reptiles become just as warm by basking in the sun, but they are called ectotherms to indicate that they can be warmed substantially only by heat from outside the body. To supply the energy needed for their faster metabolism, birds and mammals need about five times as much food as fish, amphibians and reptiles of equal weight.

The insulating layer of feathers on birds restricts heat losses to an acceptable level. Its effect depends on the air trapped by the feathers, just as the heat-insulating effect of a woollen jersey depends on the trapped air rather than on the wool itself. Bird embryos would require enormous rates of heat production to keep their bodies at adult temperatures, because they are small. (Similarly a small coffee pot cools faster than a large one.) Birds have to sit on their eggs, to keep the developing embryos at the appropriate temperature.

As well as being endothermic, birds and mammals resemble each other in having very large brains—typically about 20 times as heavy as in ectothermic vertebrates of equal body weight. This has permitted the evolution of very complex patterns of behavior.

Birds' wings are drastically modified fore legs, given the necessary area by large, stiff feathers. They are no longer suitable for walking, and birds hop or run on their back legs. Similarly, members of the extinct group of reptiles from which birds and dinosaurs both evolved ran on their hind legs only.

The earliest known bird is the fossil form *Archaeopteryx*, from the age of the dinosaurs, about 150 million years ago. Impressions in the rocks show that it had feathers and wings like those of modern birds, but many details of its skeleton were still reptile like. For instance, its jaws had teeth instead of a bird-like bill.

Modern birds are numerous and successful, but remarkably uniform in design. The differences between, for example, the hooked bills of the birds of prey, the strong crushing bills of the seed-eating finches and the long probing bills of many shore birds are often stressed but these are, however, differences of detail. The structure of the body is far more uniform than in reptiles or in bony fish.

The one group of modern birds that stands clearly distinct from the rest is the ratites: the kiwi, ostrich, emu and a few others. Like young chickens, they have strong legs, fluffy feathers and tiny wings, and they cannot fly. It has been suggested that they evolved by becoming adult while retaining juvenile features, a process called neoteny. Most of them are much larger than flying birds. Male ostriches weigh about 80kg (176lb) but the largest flying birds (various swans, pelicans and bustards) weigh, only 10 to 16kg (22 to 35lb).

Mammals

The mammals form the class Mammalia. Like birds, they are large-brained endotherms, but they rely on fur instead of on feathers for heat insulation. They also resemble birds and differ from amphibians and most reptiles in walking with their feet directly under the body, not sprawled out on either side. Their most characteristic feature is that mothers secrete milk and suckle their young.

Mammals evolved from reptiles, and seem to have appeared about 200 million years ago. At the beginning of their history it is difficult to be sure which fossils should be classed as reptiles and which as mammals because the breasts and fur that distinguish mammals from reptiles are not preserved in fossils. Throughout the age of the dinosaurs the mammals remained quite small and apparently unimportant but, when the dinosaurs became extinct, the mammals began to flourish as they do now.

The most primitive living mammals are the monotremes of Australasia: the **Duck-billed platypus** and the **echidnas**. They lay eggs like reptiles but suckle their young like other mammals. Platypuses curl round their eggs to keep them warm but female echidnas carry their eggs around in a pouch on the belly.

The **marsupials** are more advanced. Most of them live in Australasia, where the kangaroos are their best-known representatives, but the American opossums are also marsupials. They do not lay eggs but give birth to tiny young which attach themselves to their mother's nipples and remain attached during a long period of growth and development. Many marsupials have a pouch that encloses the nipples, keeping the attached young safe and warm. The Australasian mar-

▼▲► **Types of mammal.** There are three main types of mammal alive today. The monotremes, such as the Short-beaked echidna (*Tachyglossus aculeatus*) BELOW are the most primitive and lay eggs. Marsupials, such as the Eastern gray kangaroo (*Macropus giganteus*) RIGHT are more advanced, but give birth to very poorly developed young that have to be nurtured in a pouch. Placental mammals, such as the giraffe (*Giraffa camelopardalis*) ABOVE retain young within the womb to a much later stage of development and are the most successful mammals.

supials have taken up a remarkable variety of ways of life. The kangaroos are large grazers. The marsupial "mice" are shrew-like animals that feed largely on insects. The Tasmanian "wolf" or thylacine (*Thylacinus cynocephalus*, probably extinct) was a dog-like carnivore. There are even marsupial equivalents of moles and anteaters.

The great majority of modern mammals are included among the eutherian or **placental mammals**. They retain the young in the womb to a much later stage of development than marsupials do. For example, sheep give birth five months after copulation to 6kg (13lb) lambs, but large kangaroos give birth one month after copulation to "joeys" that weigh less than 1g.

The eutherian mammals are divided into a considerable number of orders. The order Insectivora includes the most primitive of them, and also the smallest of terrestrial mammals: the smallest shrews weigh as little as 2g (0.07oz). The hedge-hogs, and the Madagascan tenrecs, also belong to this order. The order Chiroptera consists of the bats, the only mammals capable of flight as distinct from mere gliding. This group contains the smallest mammal—the recently discovered Kitti's hog-nosed bat which weighs only 1.5g (0.05oz). The order Carnivora (Fissipedia) consists of dogs, cats, bears, weasels and other mainly flesh-eating mammals. The Pinnipedia (seals) and Cetacea (whales) are large aquatic mammals with flippers instead of legs. The order Rodentia has more species than any of the other orders. It consists of fairly small, mainly plant-eating mammals with chisel-like front teeth. Mice, squirrels, beavers and porcupines all belong to this order, but rabbits belong to a separate, quite unrelated order, the Lagomorpha. The orders Artiodactyla and Perissodactyla are the ungulates, the hoofed, plant-eating mammals. Artiodactyls (pigs, hip-popotamuses, camels, deer and antelopes) have a principal pair of toes, equally well developed, on each foot but perissodactyls (horses, rhinoceroses and tapirs) have just one central toe which is stronger than the rest. The Proboscidea are the elephants, the largest land animals. The order Primates includes the lemurs, monkeys, apes and humans.   RMCNA

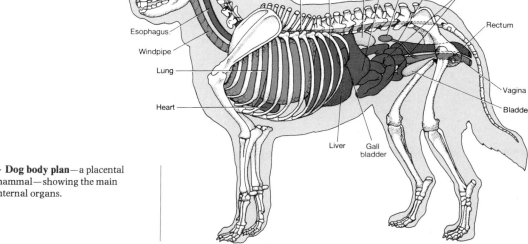

▶ **Dog body plan**—a placental mammal—showing the main internal organs.

Brain · Spinal cord · Kidney · Pancreas · Ovary · Ureter · Stomach · Small intestines · Esophagus · Rectum · Windpipe · Lung · Vagina · Bladder · Heart · Liver · Gall bladder

Molecules and Cells

THE staggering diversity of shape, size and organization of living things seems to diminish as we peer down the microscope. The more powerful the microscope, the more it appears that all organisms are built from standardized parts. The basic unit which makes up all life forms is the cell which has been likened to a discrete bag of gray, jelly-like material, called protoplasm, surrounded by a membrane and, in the case of plants, by a cellulose cell wall. But, as might be expected, the detailed structure of the cell is hardly so simple!

Advances in the techniques of looking at the detailed architecture of cells and for examining the chemical transformations and information processing of cells have led to a view of the cell radically different from that held only a few decades ago. The cell can no longer be thought of as a bag of chemicals in a thick syrup, or even as a plum pudding of subcellular structures. Cells are organized and specialized to a degree that biologists are only beginning to understand. Cellular structure and organization are crucial determinants of cellular function, and the organization of subcellular structures is as important an adaptation as the more easily seen adaptations discussed elsewhere.

Most remarkable about the varieties of cellular organization is the effective use of standardized parts: it may be estimated that animals contain fewer than 200 cell types, each containing fewer than 20 kinds of functional units (organelles).

◄ **Tissues within a blowfly larva**—a light micrograph showing the major nerves, ganglia (nerve cell clusters), muscle cells and tracheoles (air ducts).

Sizes and types of cells. . . Units and measures. . . The chemistry and energy of cells. . . Cell membranes. . . The insides of cells. . . Nucleus, mitochondrion, endoplasmic reticulum, cytoskeleton. . . Cell division. . . Cilia and flagella. . . Small molecules and giant molecules. . . Proteins, nucleic acids, polysaccharides. . . Types of protein. . . Enzymes and enzyme action. . . The genetic alphabet. . . Test tube genetics. . . Viruses and jumping genes. . .

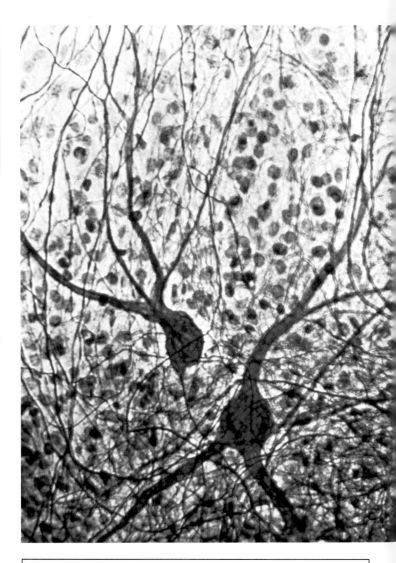

ALL organisms are composed of cells. Some organisms consist of only a single cell. Others, like most of the animals described here, are composed of very many cells: humans, for example, are built from some 10 million million cells. Every cell contains a variety of smaller structures (organelles), each of which makes a special contribution to the maintenance and function of the cell. Similarly, each cell makes a special contribution to the whole organism. Thus, a multicellular organism is a community of cooperating cells.

Most animal cells are approximately the same size. Nature keeps to the same bricks, whether she builds a large house or small. The diameter of a typical animal cell is 10 to 20μm. A light microscope can be used to examine structures as small as 1μm. An electron microscope, however, can be used to observe structures that are 1,000 times smaller. A few highly specialized cell types, such as a bird's egg, are large enough to be seen without a microscope.

The relatively small size of the cell permits it to regulate its own internal environment, to take in food and oxygen, to excrete wastes, and to develop the ability to perform specialized tasks different from other cell types. A human is estimated to be made up of about 200 cell types that are recognizably different from one another. Most of these cells are variants of four main types: those which form continuous layers over the external and internal surfaces of the body are called epithelial cells; the cells which make materials, such as bones and tendons, for the internal support of the body are known as connective cells; those which are responsible for movement and work are the muscle cells; and the cells which carry messages within the brain and from the brain to other parts of the body and vice versa are the nerve cells. Red blood cells carry oxygen through the blood stream; white blood cells recognize and destroy foreign invaders; and germ cells (eggs or sperm) transmit information from one generation to the next. Striking differences in the appearance of different cells are also found in the wide variety of single-celled protozoans and in the specialized cells of plants and of fungi. But the total number of recognizably different cell types is far less than the total number of recognizably different organisms.

The Chemistry and Energy of Cells

Organisms and cells need energy to live. Animals obtain their energy by harvesting the chemical energy stored in the food they eat. Chemical compounds in food are broken down and rearranged to give both energy and the materials needed to build cellular structures and molecular machinery. These transformations are accomplished by a set of chemical

Units and Measures

Basic SI (Système International) Units

length	meter (m)
mass	kilogram (kg)
time	second (s)
electric current	ampere (A)
temperature	kelvin (K)
amount of substance	mole (mol)
luminous intensity	candela (cd)

Some Conversion Factors

1 kilometer (1km) = 0.62 miles (0.62mi)
1 meter (1m) = 39.37 inches (39.37in)
1 centimeter (1cm) = 0.394 inches (0.394in)
1 millimeter (1mm) = 0.0394 inches (0.0394in)
1 kilogram (1kg) = 2.202 pounds (2.204lb)
1 gram (1g) = 0.0353 ounces (0.0353oz)

The Metric System of Length

1 meter (1m) = 100 centimeters (100cm) = 1,000 millimeters (1,000mm) = 1,000,000 micrometers (1,000,000μm) = 1,000,000,000 nanometers (1,000,000,000nm)

1,000 meters (1,000m) = 1 kilometer (1km)

The colors of the photographs result from
either special stains applied to the tissues
or patterns produced by the light used.

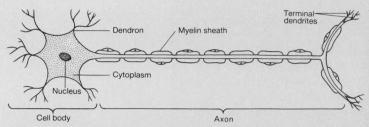

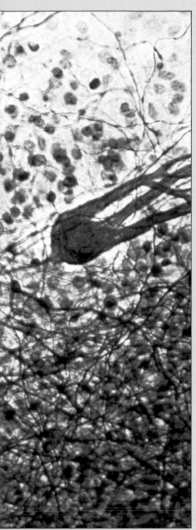

◀▲ **Nerve cells (neurons)** LEFT from the spinal cord of a mouse; ABOVE diagram
of a motor nerve cell.

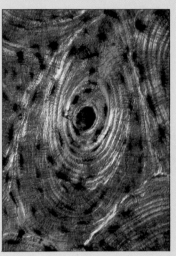

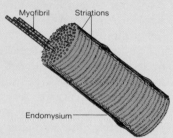

◀▲ **Connective tissue.** Human bone LEFT
showing the layered (lamellar) structure of
Haversian systems, each with a central canal.
ABOVE Cells of areolar tissue—a form of
connective tissue.

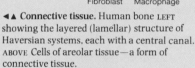

▲▼ **Muscle tissue.** A mass of smooth muscle
cells ABOVE from the duodenum of cat.
BELOW Structure of a striated muscle fiber.

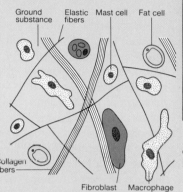

▲▼ **Germ cells.** Diagram of sperm ABOVE and an electron micrograph of a
mass of sea urchin sperms surrounding an egg before fertilization BELOW.

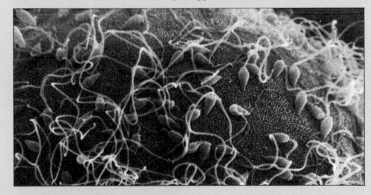

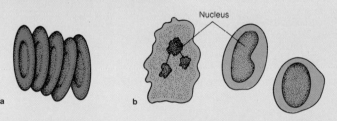

▲▼ **Blood cells.** Diagram of (a) red and (b) white human blood cells ABOVE and
as appearing under a microscope BELOW.

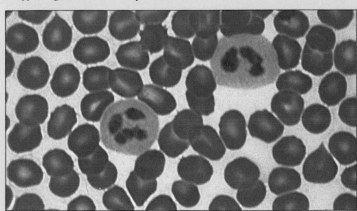

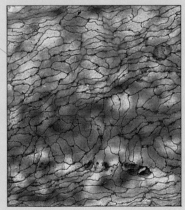

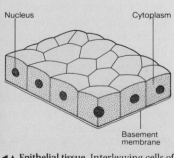

◀▲ **Epithelial tissue.** Interleaving cells of
squamous epithelium with the plasma
membrane enhanced LEFT and diagram
of columnar epithelium ABOVE.

reactions, that take place inside cells, and which are collectively called metabolism.

Of all the millions of chemical reactions that might be possible for the molecules of a cell to be involved in if they were in a test tube, only a limited number actually occur in cells. These reactions occur because they are specifically helped along by special substances, called catalysts, which speed up chemical reactions without themselves being consumed by the reactions. The catalysts which are involved in biochemical reactions are known as enzymes. Each enzyme is a large molecule that binds specifically to a specific molecule that is going to be chemically changed. The molecule that is bound to an enzyme is usually much smaller than the enzyme molecule and is called the enzyme's substrate. Although the substrate then undergoes a chemical change—a rearrangement of its atoms— enzymes are not affected in any permanent way and may be used over and over again. Some enzyme molecules are recycled in this way thousands of times per second.

All organisms store energy in a single kind of molecule called ATP (adenosine triphosphate). The energy stored in the ATP contained within a cell may be released by certain enzymes, which convert ATP into another molecule called ADP (adenosine diphosphate).

The harnessing of energy from food into ATP is accomplished by a relatively small number of chemical reactions common to cells from plants and animals, and even to many bacteria. All cells, in fact, from those of bacteria to elephants or redwood trees, contain a set of enzymes that enables them to extract energy from glucose (blood sugar) in a series of steps called glycolysis or fermentation. Since this universal process does not require oxygen, it is often referred to as anaerobic metabolism. The fact that all cells use ATP to store energy and have the same set of enzymes to perform glycolysis is strong evidence that all organisms are descended from the same ancestor. In the presence of oxygen, still more energy can then be extracted from the products of glycolysis (aerobic metabolism).

The Active Boundaries of Cells

The inside of a cell is separated from the outside by a boundary called the cell membrane. If there were no such boundary, the inside of a cell would have the same chemical composition and microscopic make up as the outside. The membrane thus serves as a fence to keep the inside of a cell in and the outside out. Specific channels within the membrane serve as gates which allow the passage of certain chemicals, including mineral salts needed for the functioning of cellular machinery, molecules that serve as food, and signals such as hormones that allow cells from different parts of the body to communicate with one another.

Most chemicals move through the membrane (and within the cells) by a slow bouncing of molecules, in a process called diffusion. Molecules diffuse to produce a uniform distribution of each kind of molecule so that they always move from a higher concentration to a lower concentration. In many cases, however, a substance is present in a higher concentration inside a cell than outside (or vice versa); here molecules or atoms are actually pumped through the cell membrane. This process is called active transport because the cell uses part of

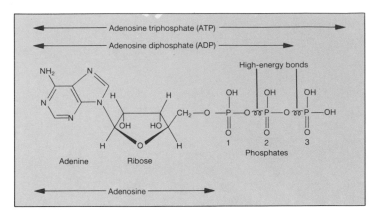

▲ **The chemical of life**—adenosine triphosphate (ATP) is the universal energy source of living cells. Just as the energy stored in a tightly coiled spring is released to drive a clockwork motor, the energy stored in ATP is made available when it is converted to ADP (one phosphate less). This energy is then used for cell maintenance, growth and movement.

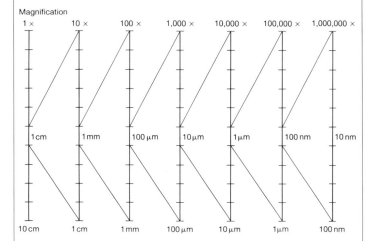

▲ **The sizes of biological objects.** A series of scales reducing by factors of ten to indicate the size terminology used in biology.

▼ **How enzymes work.** Enzymes attach to substrate molecules, literally like a lock and key; in this complex the energy required to split the substrate molecule is very low. When the products are released the enzyme molecule is free to work on another substrate molecule.

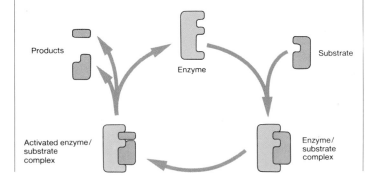

◀ **Getting material** in and out of cells. (**1**) Phagocytosis where materials to be engulfed are enveloped by part of the cell membrane. Digestive enzymes may be released into the pinched-off vacuole containing engulfed food. (**2**) Exocytosis where enzymes may be released or waste food items eliminated.

◀ **Moving chemicals** in and out of cells. (**1**) Diffusion: chemicals move through the membrane from areas of high concentration to those of low concentration. This is a passive process, that is, it requires no energy. (**2**) Active transport: chemicals move through the membrane from areas of low concentration to high concentration, a process that requires energy to be expended.

its energy from ATP to achieve a difference between inside and outside.

Cells may also actively reach into their surroundings to fence off a small particle or a bit of fluid. The cellular extensions that perform this operation are called pseudopods ("false feet"). A captured particle or an enclosed fluid droplet is then brought into the cell often to be digested. For some single-celled animals such as the amoeba, this engulfing process or phagocytosis ("cell eating") is a major source of nutrition. In multicellular organisms, phagocytosis is the means by which scavenger cells rid the organism of bacteria or other troublesome invaders. Some cells put phagocytosis into reverse gear to export materials that the cell has made. In this case the process is called exocytosis.

Thus, the cell membrane is not merely a passive fence but rather it is an active participant in the life of a cell. The membrane regulates the internal environment, actively takes in materials from outside, and also provides signals that allow the cells of a multicellular organism to recognize one another.

The Insides of Cells
Scientists used to think that the inside of cells was simply made up of a special but homogeneous substance called protoplasm. In the nineteenth century, however, improved microscopes and the new dyes developed for the textile industry, which can be used to stain the different structures in a cell to increase their contrast, showed that cells had unexpectedly complex internal architecture. The interior of a cell is by no means homogeneous. Instead, cells contain many organelles ("little organs") each of which performs a specialized function. In the last 30 years the development of the electron microscope has allowed cell biologists to study the structure of many previously unseen organelles.
The nucleus. The largest organelle of the cell is the nucleus which is usually a nearly spherical structure positioned near the center of the cell. The nucleus is the cell's "director." It contains the plans for the complex apparatus of the cell. Like many other organelles, the nucleus is surrounded by a membrane (the nuclear membrane) composed of a double thickness of the same kind of membrane material that surrounds the whole cell. Some material from the nucleus can diffuse or be transported into the rest of the cell, which is called the cytoplasm, through pores in the nuclear membrane. Special molecular machinery copies the genetic instructions in the nucleus into information-carrying molecules, called messenger RNAs. These molecules move to the cytoplasm, where the plans stored in them are used to build new cellular materials. In this way, the cell nucleus directs the construction of the rest of the cell.

The cells of all animals, plants, fungi, and protozoans contain a nucleus and other organelles bounded by membranes. These organisms are called eukaryotes ("true nuclei"). Bacteria and blue-green algae, however, do not contain nuclei or internal membranes. These more primitive organisms are therefore called prokaryotes ("before nuclei").

The nucleus of each cell in a plant or animal contains more than the plans for the construction, maintenance and functioning of that individual cell. It also contains all the plans for the whole organism. Only some of these instructions, however, are carried out in each cell. Animals (as well as plants and fungi) contain many cells. All the cells of a multicellular organism arise from the division of a single cell—the fertilized egg. During the growth and development of an organism, cells become distinct from one another in their external appearance, their internal organization and their contribution to the working of the whole organism. Despite this differentiation of cells, all the information in the nucleus of each cell is passed on to its daughter cells. This information is called genetic information because it is passed from generation to generation of organisms and from generation to generation of cells. Germ cells, that is, sperm and eggs, carry information to the next generation.

Genetic information is located in the chromatin ("colored matter") of the nucleus. During cell division, chromatin is seen to be organized into a number of chromosomes ("colored bodies"—they are colored when stained with a dye). Human cells, for example, have 46 chromosomes, each of which serves as a kind of file drawer of genetic information. To ensure that information is passed on precisely to daughter cells when a cell divides, the chromosomes participate in an elaborate ballet called mitosis, during which each chromosome splits into two daughter chromosomes, with each daughter cell getting one copy of each original chromosome. Before the next cell division, each chromosome duplicates itself so that it will contain two copies for distribution.

The many cells of a multicellular organism all derive from a single cell formed by the fertilization of an egg by a sperm. During the development of the organism, the chromosomes of the fertilized egg are duplicated and distributed by mitosis so that essentially all cells have the same genetic information. The germ cells, however, must contain only half as many chromosomes as the other cells of the body, otherwise the number of chromosomes would be doubled during fertilization. This necessary halving of the chromosome number is possible because nearly all the genetic information in a cell is present in two copies. With the exception of two sex chromosomes, which are different in males and females, all chromosomes are present in two copies, or homologs. Thus, the 46 chromosomes of a human cell consist of 22 homologous pairs plus two sex chromosomes. In females the two sex chromosomes are homologous and are called X chromosomes. In males the two sex chromosomes differ and are called X and Y chromosomes. During the development of the germ cells, the two homologs of each pair are separated in an alternative chromosomal dance called meiosis. Each human sperm or egg thus contains 23 chromosomes instead of 46. When sperm and egg come together at fertilization, the number of chromosomes again becomes 46. Thus, the genetic plans stored in the chromosomes are passed on from generation to generation by meiosis and fertilization and from a cell to its daughter cells by mitosis (see also Reproduction and Development).

Mitochondria. The cytoplasm of a eukaryotic cell contains several types of organelles surrounded by membranes. The most conspicuous of these are the mitochondria (singular mitochondrion). These are structures about the size of a bacterium, typically $0.5 \times 5\mu$m, and filled with folded membranes. Mitochondria are the power plants of a cell. They are responsible for most of a cell's synthesis of ATP.

The mitochondria of all eukaryotes contain enzymes that further process the partially degraded food molecules that is first produced in glycolysis. The set of reactions used in this processing is called the Krebs cycle after its principal discoverer, Sir Hans Krebs. In the mitochondria, the products of the Krebs cycle combine with oxygen to produce energy, which is immediately stored in ATP molecules. The overall process of combination of food molecules with oxygen is called respiration; it yields far more energy in the form of ATP than anaerobic metabolism does.

Other cell compartments. Membranes not only surround cells, nuclei and mitochondria. They also form internal boundaries within cells. The cytoplasm contains an elaborate network of membranes folded into sheets, sacs and tubes. This network, called the endoplasmic reticulum, serves a number of functions, including the synthesis of fatty substances, called lipids, the distribution of some materials from the nucleus (whose outer

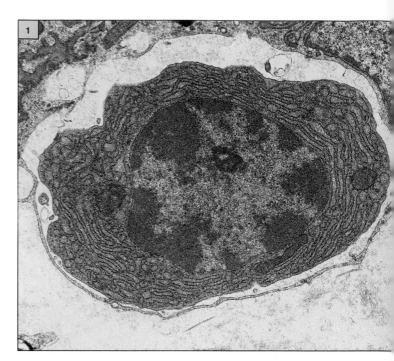

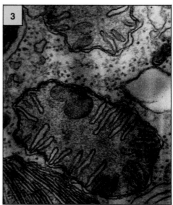

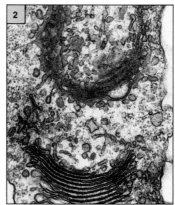

membrane is continuous with the endoplasmic reticulum), and the synthesis of enzymes and other molecules destined for secretion to the outside of the cell. Another membranous structure, the Golgi body, also participates in the formation of the secreted sacs of material. Some materials that are to be secreted by a cell are made on the endoplasmic reticulum and packaged by the Golgi body into sacs of membranes. These sacs then fuse with the plasma membrane, and their contents are dumped outside the cell.

In addition to the system composed of the endoplasmic reticulum, Golgi body and nuclear membrane, the cytoplasm also holds other small sacs that are surrounded by membranes. Some of these, called lysosomes, contain enzymes that break down food or cell debris, including materials taken in by phagocytosis. Digestion within cells is confined to these isolated compartments. This compartmentation protects the machinery of the cells from unwanted self-destruction, which would occur if the digestive enzymes were mixed with the rest of the cell's contents.

The cytoskeleton. In addition to an extensive system of membranes, animal cells contain a system of structural supports

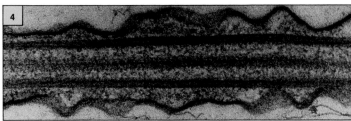

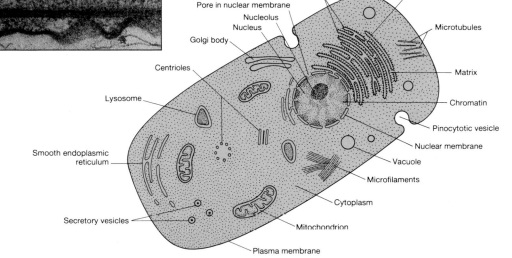

► **Internal structure** of an animal cell showing the main organelles.

◄▲► **Structures,** as seen through an electron microscope, within animal cells. (1) Complete cell. (2) Golgi bodies which produce secretions: one (top) is shown in cross section, the other is in transverse section. (3) Mitochondria, within which chemical energy is generated. (4) Microtubules which make up the internal cellular skeleton. (5) Rough endoplasmic reticulum— "rough" because it is covered in ribosomes—the small dots; these structures are included in the production of proteins and other molecules.

Labels on diagram: Ribosomes; Pore in nuclear membrane; Nucleolus; Nucleus; Golgi body; Centrioles; Lysosome; Smooth endoplasmic reticulum; Secretory vesicles; Rough endoplasmic reticulum; Microtubules; Matrix; Chromatin; Pinocytotic vesicle; Nuclear membrane; Vacuole; Microfilaments; Cytoplasm; Mitochondrion; Plasma membrane

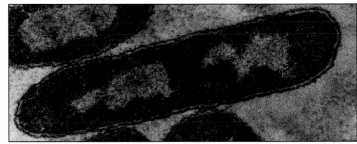

▲ **Bacterial cell** as revealed by the electron microscope. This type of cell, known as prokaryotic, does not have a distinct nucleus.

called the cytoskeleton. The cytoskeleton not only provides internal support for the cell, but it is also the machinery for movement and changes of cell shape. The cytoskeleton is composed principally of three kinds of very thin fibers which can be seen only with the electron microscope: microtubules, with a diameter of 25nm; microfilaments (or actin filaments), with a diameter of 7nm; and intermediate filaments, with a diameter of about 10nm. Almost all animal cells contain all three kinds of filaments. The layout of filaments establishes and stabilizes the shape of a cell and can also produce directed movement. Thus, the separation of chromosomes during mitosis and meiosis is powered by the microtubules of the spindle fibers that attach to the chromosomes.

Different kinds of cells have different arrangements of the cytoskeleton. In muscle, for example, filaments of actin, a contractile protein, are assembled together with enzymes and other structures so that energy stored in ATP may be converted into the mechanical work of muscle contraction. A similar contractile arrangement is found in the contractile fibers, or myonemes, of protozoans. Another way of producing movement by cells makes use of special assemblies of microtubules, cilia, and flagella. Cilia and flagella are hair-like projections which can propel protozoans or sperm cells through a liquid medium or can move liquid over surfaces such as those of the lung or the gut.

The cytoskeleton gives shape to cells and is responsible for cell movement. In addition, elements of the cytoskeleton also appear to be responsible for the overall internal organization of the cell, anchoring many organelles and other structures.

Advances in microscopy, particularly the development of the electron microscope, have led cell biologists to realize that the internal architecture of cells is far more complex than previously suspected. Just as the observed diversity of organisms is much greater than the diversity of cell types, however, the diversity of cell types is much greater than the diversity of organelles. Cell specialization results largely from differences in the ways in which more-or-less standard organelles are arranged.

Small Molecules and Giant Molecules

The ultimate level at which the architecture of life must be understood is chemical. The stuff of cells, like that of all other matter, is made of molecules which, in turn, are composed of atoms. At the molecular level the differences between all forms of life almost disappear. Going one step further, to the atomic level, living things are indistinguishable from non-living, because atoms are atoms whatever they comprise. The specialness of life does not lie in a unique chemistry, but in the way a relatively small number of molecules are organized to form the structures of cells and organisms.

The kinds of atoms which make up living organisms are much fewer than those of the non-living world. More than 99 percent of the matter of life is composed of only six kinds of atoms: hydrogen, carbon, nitrogen, oxygen, phosphorus and sulfur. Other kinds of atoms are found in smaller amounts, but they are also necessary for life. These include sodium, magnesium, chlorine, potassium, calcium, and another dozen or so elements. Most of the chemical characteristics of organisms derive from the unique properties of the carbon atom. Carbon atoms can combine with other atoms (including other carbon atoms) in many ways to give a wide variety of molecules with diverse shapes, sizes and chemical properties. Carbon-containing substances (compounds) are so central to the chemistry of organisms that nineteenth-century chemists named the chemistry of carbon compounds organic chemistry. Molecules containing carbon atoms are still called "organic" molecules despite the fact that most organic molecules are never found in organisms. Although carbon atoms form more different kinds of compounds than all other kinds of atoms combined, only a small number of these are used by organisms.

The molecules of life. The organic molecules used by organisms fall into two broad classes: small molecules usually containing fewer than 50 atoms, and giant or macromolecules, each composed of thousands (or even millions) of atoms. Despite their complexity, macromolecules are put together in a simple way—they are all composed of a few kinds of small molecules linked together in chains.

Cells contain three kinds of macromolecules. Proteins are the most important structural and functional units of cells. Nucleic acids, including DNA (deoxyribonucleic acid) and RNA (ribonucleic acid) store and carry out genetic instructions. Polysaccharides are used by animal cells for relatively long-term energy storage and in some places as structural or protective material.

Each kind of macromolecule is built from a few small molecules: proteins from 20 different kinds of amino acids; DNA and RNA each from four different kinds of nucleotides; and polysaccharides mostly from a few different kinds of sugars. Polysaccharides and the sugars from which they are built, together with a variety of related molecules, are all called carbohydrates because they contain the equivalent of one molecule of water for each carbon atom.

In addition to carbohydrates, proteins, and nucleic acids, cells contain another class of organic molecule, the lipids. Lipids are oily or partially oily molecules which tend to avoid water. They are employed by cells to build the membranes that form both the cells' external boundaries and their internal compartments. Lipids also serve to store energy and to provide insulation, perhaps the most dramatic example being the blubber of a seal or a Polar bear.

Universal Propulsion—Cilia and Flagella

Some animal cells can propel themselves through a liquid, and others can push liquid over their surfaces by using the whipping movements of fine, thread-like projections, called cilia and flagella (singular cilium and flagellum). The cells that line the respiratory tract and the lungs have more than one thousand million cilia per square centimeter of surface. These cilia continuously push fluid with suspended dust particles and dead cells up from the lungs to the mouth, where they are swallowed and eliminated.

Cilia are typically $0.25\mu m$ in diameter and $10\mu m$ long, although they may also be much longer. They are found in most animal species, as well as in some lower plants. All cilia have the same basic design: two single microtubules (thin, cylindrical tubes) surrounded by nine double microtubules. The hollow rods of the microtubules in turn are assembled from two relatively small globular proteins. Each of the microtubules extends the whole length of the cilium. The microtubules are held together in the cilium by other proteins. Some proteins link adjacent tubules of the outer nine, while others make up spokes that attach to the center pair of tubules. The entire cilium is covered by an extension of the cell membrane. A cilium bends back and forth because the microtubules slide along each other, breaking and remaking their contacts with the other proteins.

Flagella in animals are just long cilia (up to $200\mu m$ long), with the same "9 + 2" design. In the flagellum of a sperm cell the basic design is slightly changed, with nine additional stiff fibers surrounding the "9 + 2" arrangement of microtubules. Some bacteria also have flagella but these are completely unrelated to the flagella of animal cells. Bacterial flagella work more like propellers than like whips. They provide the only example of the use of a wheel by organisms.

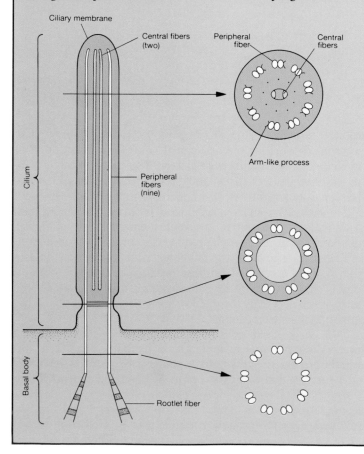

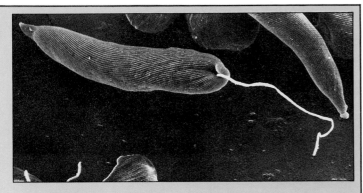

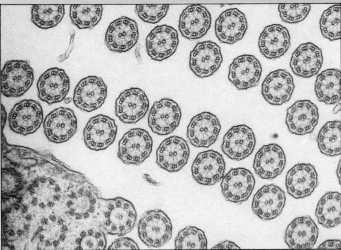

▲ **Structure of cilia** and basal bodies (bottom left) as revealed in cross section by electron microscopy.

▲ **A single flagellum** TOP is all the propulsive power required by many single-celled animals, such as this *Euglena*, to move them through their watery habitat.

◄ **Cilium structure,** showing the arrangement of fibers at different levels.

▼ **How a cilium works.** (1) The active stroke in which fluid is driven over the surface of the cell, followed by (2) the recovery stroke where resistance is kept to a minimum.

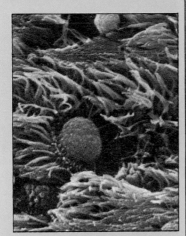

▲ **The mass of cilia** in the bronchial tubes of mammals moves fluid across the surface.

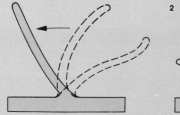

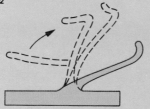

Proteins contribute to the life of organisms and cells by providing structural supports inside and outside cells and by functioning as molecular machines that transform chemicals, produce work and operate cell communication. The ability of a protein to fill these roles depends upon its three-dimensional shape. Proteins come in two major shapes: long, thin fibrous proteins, and nearly spherical globular proteins. Both globular and fibrous proteins are composed of unbranched chains, usually 100 to 1,000 amino acids long. Often two or more such chains can associate to form a more complex protein. Vertebrate hemoglobin, the red oxygen-carrying protein of the blood, for example, is composed of two pairs of identical chains—two chains 141 amino acids long, and two chains 146 amino acids long. The four chains assemble together to form a compact, almost spherical protein about 5.5nm in diameter. Globular proteins can further assemble into still more complicated structures such as microtubules.

The most abundant protein in vertebrate animals is collagen, a fibrous protein that holds cells together in skin, tendons and blood vessels, and gives strength to all connective tissue in the body. Hair, fingernails and horns are made from another fibrous protein, keratin. Most proteins in a cell, however, are globular. The most important of these are the enzymes, of which there are probably a few thousand different kinds in every organism.

Organelles and cell membranes are formed by the association of protein molecules with other kinds of molecules. Cell membranes, for example, are about half protein and half lipid. The gates and pumps that regulate the internal environment of cells, and many of the signals that allow cells to recognize one another are formed by proteins embedded in the lipid part of the membrane.

The way in which a protein interacts with other molecules is determined by the three-dimensional folding of the chains of amino acids. This folding depends, in turn, on the particular sequence of amino acids in each chain. In a given environment the three-dimensional structure of a protein is totally determined by its sequence of amino acids. Most proteins appear to keep a fixed structure within the regulated environment of a cell, but some proteins respond to chemical changes in the cell by changing their shape and the way in which they interact with other molecules in the cell. When a cell starts mitosis, for example, changes in the cellular environment trigger the globular protein tubulin to assemble into the microtubules of the spindle fibers.

Globular proteins are often specialized for recognizing and binding to other molecules. Part of the final structure formed by folded protein chains provides a surface that fits ("complements") another molecule in the way a lock complements the proper key or the way the inside of a glove fits a hand. All enzymes are globular proteins. The molecular mating of an enzyme and its specific substrate can speed up a particular chemical reaction by thousands or even millions of times. The enzyme accomplishes this by bringing together two molecules to react with one another or by straining the chemical bonds that hold together the atoms of the substrate molecule. This speeding up of specific chemical reactions by enzymes determines the chemistry of a cell.

Of the millions of reactions that are possible for the molecules of a cell, the only ones that occur rapidly enough to be significant are those catalyzed by enzymes. The total chemistry of a cell depends, therefore, on the ability of protein chains with specific amino acid sequences to fold themselves into active enzymes.

Each protein has evolved so that it can perform its particular function. The evolution of life depended on the possibility of passing on the ability to make proteins of a given sequence from one generation to the next.

The Genetic Alphabet

Proteins furnish cells with molecular versions of generators, engines and support beams. These determine the appearance, the chemistry and the physiology of each cell. The ability of a protein to serve its role in the cellular economy is determined by its amino acid sequence. The major questions of molecular genetics are: how is the exact amino acid sequence of each protein stored?; how are instructions transmitted to daughter cells?; and how are instructions interpreted by the cell's machinery?

The sequence of amino acids in a protein chain may be compared, for example, to the sequence of letters in an English word. Just as 26 different letters are used to compose English words, 20 amino acid "letters" are used to make up protein "words." Genetic information, however, is not stored in protein words themselves. Rather, each word is recorded in the chromosomes as a corresponding word in another language, the language of DNA. The sequence of amino acids in each protein chain is stored in a corresponding sequence of nucleotides in DNA. Each single protein "word" has a corresponding DNA "word," called a gene, so that each gene contains the information for a single protein chain. This information is encoded in a sequence of the four different nucleotides that make up the chains of DNA and has to be "translated" before the actual proteins are made (see later).

Genetic information stored in DNA must not only be converted to protein sequences, it must also be passed on to daughter cells. Each cell of a multicellular animal contains all

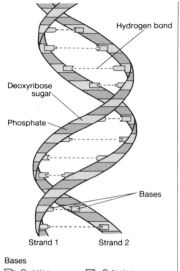

Bases
- ▭ Guanine
- ▭ Adenine
- ▭ Cytosine
- ▭ Thymine

▶ **Bacterium spewing out its chromosomes.** This *Escherichia coli* bacterium has been treated so that its chromosome strands have been forced from the broken cell wall.

◀ ▼ **Structure of DNA,** diagrammatically represented LEFT. The two ribbons symbolize the two phosphate/sugar chains and the horizontal symbols the pairs of bases holding the chain together. BELOW the same molecule but showing individual atoms represented by colored spheres: hydrogen: yellow, oxygen: red, nitrogen: blue, (carbon atoms are not included).

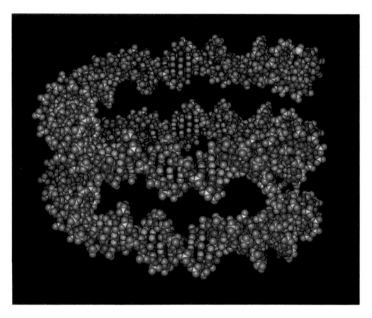

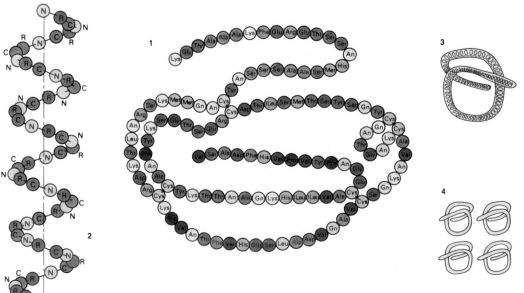

◀ **Assembly of large molecules from small.** Proteins have four levels of organization: (1) the primary structure comprising the sequence of amino acids in a polypeptide chain (shown here for the enzyme ribonuclease); (2) the secondary structure comprising the helical coiling of the polypeptide chain; (3) the tertiary structure comprising the bending or folding of each polypeptide chain; and (4) the quaternary structure comprising the relationships of the individual polypeptide chains in a complex protein.

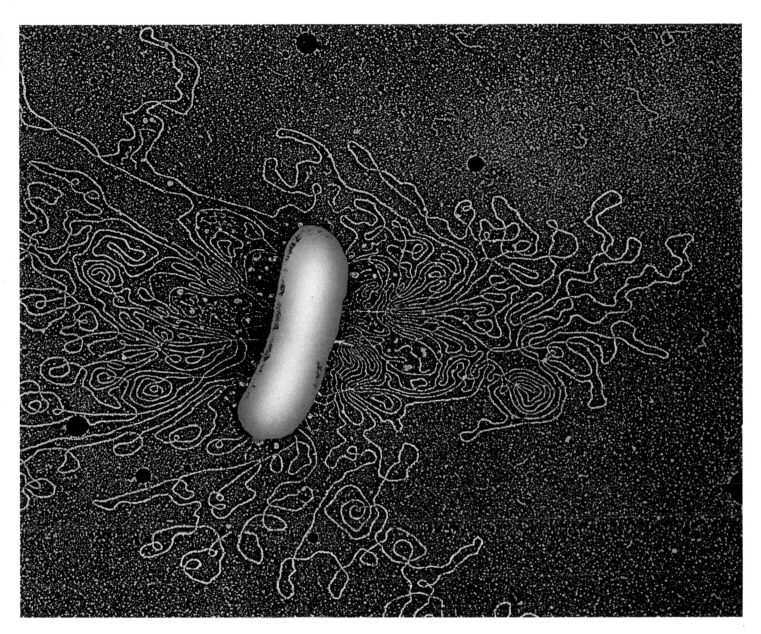

the genetic information of that animal—not just the information needed for that cell. Before each cell division, the genetic information in DNA must be duplicated in preparation for mitosis.

In any one cell, only part of the total genetic information is used. Thus, different kinds of cells interpret different parts of the genetic plans and make different sets of proteins. The kinds of proteins in a cell give each cell its special character. Besides the plans for the amino acid sequences of every protein chain, therefore, DNA must contain instructions for the regulation of protein synthesis. These instructions must specify when and where each type of protein is to be made.

DNA. Long molecules of DNA, each containing thousands of genes, associate with proteins in the nucleus to form chromosomes. In the life cycle of a cell, DNA must participate in two distinct processes—duplication of information for distribution to daughter cells and conversion of this information into the structure of proteins. DNA must be duplicated in the nucleus

of cells before mitosis can begin. The molecular structure of DNA is adapted to produce replicas of itself through the arrangement of its component nucleotides.

Each DNA molecule is composed of two strings of nucleotides. The four nucleotides are abbreviated A, T, G and C, after the distinctive part of the nucleotide, the nitrogen-containing bases adenine, thymine, guanine, and cytosine which are attached to sugar-phosphate chains. The two strands of DNA are wound around each other to form a double helix. The nucleotides of one strand exactly complement those of the other strand. Whenever the nucleotide A appears in one strand, the nucleotide T appears in the second. Similarly, G is always paired with C. The complementary nature of the two strands of DNA is the basis of the exact doubling of the genetic material before cell division. When DNA replicates, each strand directs the assembly of a new strand with the complementary sequence. When replication is complete, each of the two original strands is paired with a new strand and the two new DNA

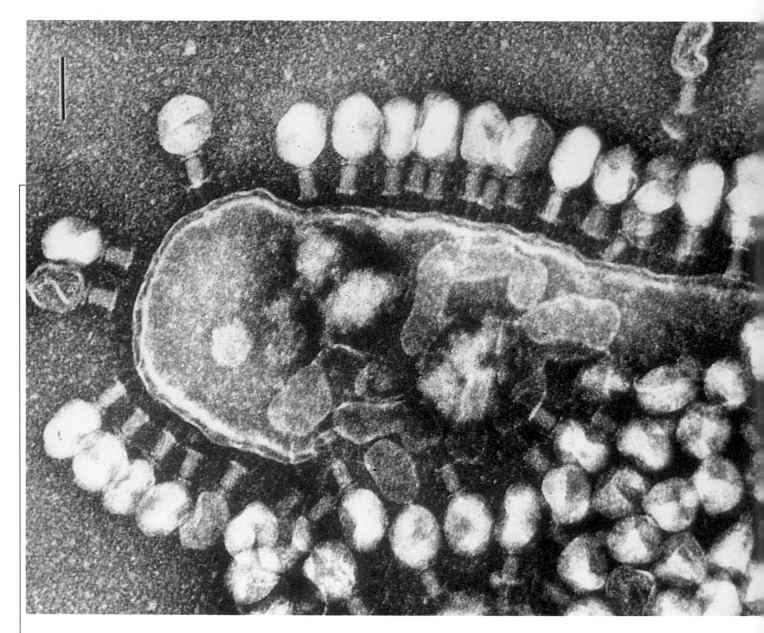

Viruses and Jumping Genes

Cells are the smallest units of life. The machinery of cells can be taken over, however, by molecular parasites called viruses. A virus is a small package of genes. It can attach to a cell, inject its own genes into the cell, and change the cell's entire program. Infection of a cell with certain viruses results in the destruction of the cell: the genes of the virus direct the cell's machinery to make components for new viruses instead of the materials needed for the cell's normal maintenance and growth. After enough virus material is produced, the cell bursts and hundreds of new virus particles are released.

Other viruses are more subtle. They manage to redirect the cell just enough to produce new viruses without the cell being destroyed. They may even just arrange to have their own genes duplicated along with the cell's genes. The most insidious viruses are those that alter the cell's machinery in such a way that the cells become cancer cells. It is not known whether most human cancers are caused by viruses, but it is certain that many

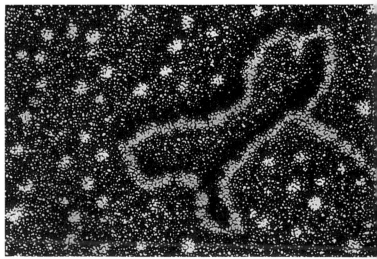

molecules have exactly the same sequence as the original double helix.

Translation of the information stored in the nucleotide sequence of DNA into the amino acid sequences of proteins is more complex than DNA replication. Protein synthesis occurs in the cytoplasm, away from the DNA. Information from DNA must, therefore, be converted into a form that can be carried to the organelles that assemble protein chains, the ribosomes. These assembly machines are composed of a few dozen kinds of proteins associated with a few molecules of RNA. Other RNA molecules, called messenger RNAs, carry information from DNA to the ribosomes.

Like DNA, RNA molecules consist of long strings of nucleotides. But instead of A, G, C and T, RNA contains A, G, C and U (the base uracil) as its four-letter alphabet. The language of RNA is thus a "dialect" of the DNA language. The transfer of information from DNA to RNA is called transcription. While DNA contains two nucleotide chains, RNA usually contains only one. Moreover, the backbone of RNA uses ribose (a five-carbon sugar) instead of deoxyribose (another five-carbon sugar), making it less stable than DNA.

Messenger RNA molecules are not as long as DNA molecules. While the DNA molecules of each chromosome contain thousands or tens of thousands of genes, each messenger RNA molecule in any animal cell usually contains information for only a single protein chain. In general, only part of the information of DNA is converted to protein in a single cell type so that the conversion of DNA into gene-sized pieces of RNA aids in the selective expression of individual genes in different cell types.

Once a messenger RNA molecule enters the cytoplasm, ribosomes attach to it and begin to translate from nucleic acid language into protein language. They read from one end of the messenger RNA to the other, three nucleotides at a time, since each sequence of three nucleotides in the messenger RNA corresponds to a particular amino acid. The amino acids are then assembled by the ribosomes into the sequence dictated by the messenger RNA. The amino acids are linked together to give the protein chain whose exact sequence has been stored in the DNA, virtually unchanged through thousands of cell generations.

Test-tube Genetics

In the last 30 years, the mechanisms of molecular information processing by cells have become understood in such detail that it is now possible to study many steps in the test tube. It has even become possible to synthesize a few genes by purely chemical methods, that is, outside the cells. Molecular biologists have also found ways of cutting and splicing DNA to produce large amounts of particular DNA sequences and combinations that do not occur in nature. The new DNA sequences produced by these scientific techniques are called recombinant DNAs.

Scientists can now isolate individual genes from DNA and use these genes to reprogram bacteria to make human proteins. The proteins so far produced include a number that are medically significant, such as the protein hormone insulin, which normal people produce in the pancreas, but which many diabetics need to obtain by injection to reduce the levels of sugar in the blood and urine.

Specific isolated genes have also been inserted into early embryos of fruit flies and mice so that the genetic instructions of whole multicellular organisms can be altered. Recombinant DNA technology has become the basis of a new industry based on the genetic reprogramming of bacteria to make particular products. The technology also gives biologists powerful new tools with which they can examine how animals develop and function.

AJT

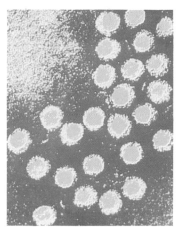

▲ **Producers of disease.** Viruses, such as those of Hepatitis A, are hardly life—they are simply packets of genetic material that attack and take over the machinery of cells.

◄ **Enemies of bacteria.** Special viruses (bacteriophages or "phages,") attack bacteria.

▼ **Added genetic material.** An electron micrograph of a piece of bacterial chromosome (left) to which has been added additional DNA (the stem and loop on right)— a so-called transposable element.

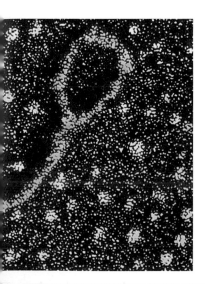

viruses can cause cancers in animals. These viruses change the properties of individual cells by inserting their own genes into the cell's DNA. Cells that are "transformed" in this way no longer respond to the signals in their environment that regulate their growth. They keep dividing when normal cells would stop. Such cells may grow into tumors that eventually kill the host animals.

The genes of a cancer virus can move back and forth between a virus package and the DNA of the host cell. Scientists have recently discovered that other genes can also move about. A gene that makes bacteria resistant to penicillin, for example, may be carried on a special piece of DNA that can be transferred from one bacterium to another. Such genes called transposable elements—may either be inserted into the DNA of a bacterium or may be carried along as an independent piece of DNA. The possibility that antibiotic resistance can be transferred from one bacterium to another is a major medical problem because this ability can very rapidly make an antibiotic ineffective.

Many animals contain genes that can move from one location among the chromosomes to another. Viruses probably evolved by the jumping of a few genes out of a cell's DNA into an independent particle surrounded by a protein coat. Jumping genes have also provided new arrangements of genes on the chromosomes of cells. This process has probably been an important source of variation during evolution.

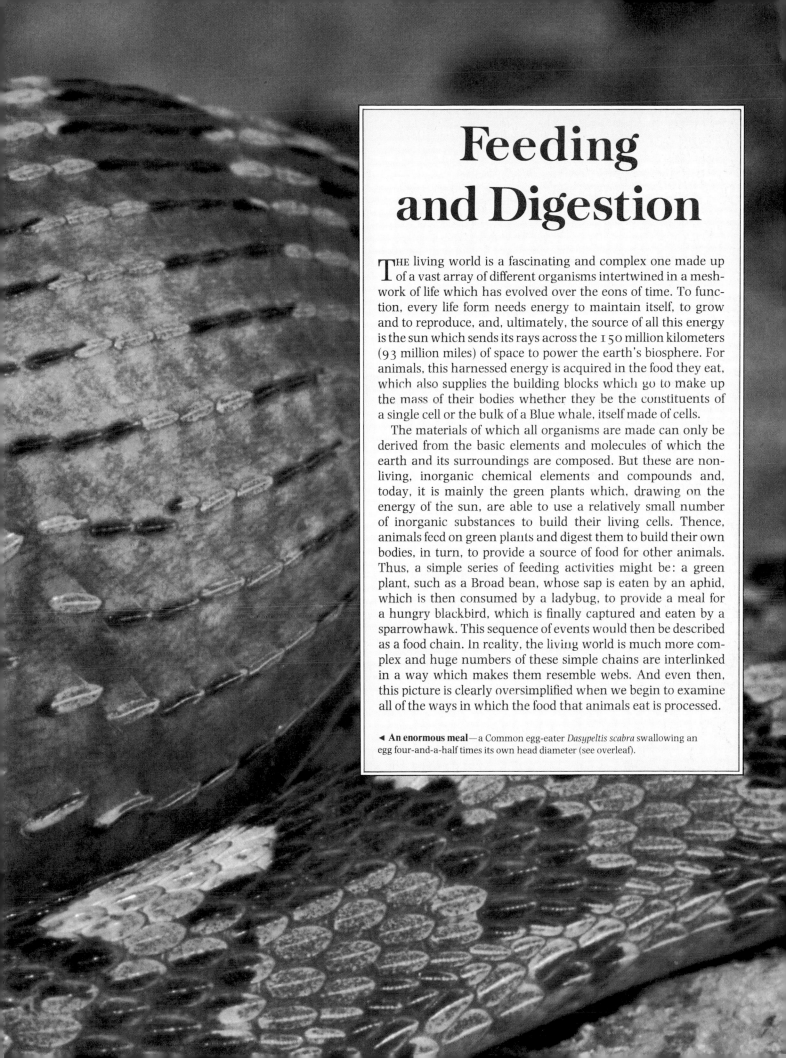

Feeding and Digestion

THE living world is a fascinating and complex one made up of a vast array of different organisms intertwined in a meshwork of life which has evolved over the eons of time. To function, every life form needs energy to maintain itself, to grow and to reproduce, and, ultimately, the source of all this energy is the sun which sends its rays across the 150 million kilometers (93 million miles) of space to power the earth's biosphere. For animals, this harnessed energy is acquired in the food they eat, which also supplies the building blocks which go to make up the mass of their bodies whether they be the constituents of a single cell or the bulk of a Blue whale, itself made of cells.

The materials of which all organisms are made can only be derived from the basic elements and molecules of which the earth and its surroundings are composed. But these are non-living, inorganic chemical elements and compounds and, today, it is mainly the green plants which, drawing on the energy of the sun, are able to use a relatively small number of inorganic substances to build their living cells. Thence, animals feed on green plants and digest them to build their own bodies, in turn, to provide a source of food for other animals. Thus, a simple series of feeding activities might be: a green plant, such as a Broad bean, whose sap is eaten by an aphid, which is then consumed by a ladybug, to provide a meal for a hungry blackbird, which is finally captured and eaten by a sparrowhawk. This sequence of events would then be described as a food chain. In reality, the living world is much more complex and huge numbers of these simple chains are interlinked in a way which makes them resemble webs. And even then, this picture is clearly oversimplified when we begin to examine all of the ways in which the food that animals eat is processed.

◄ **An enormous meal**—a Common egg-eater *Dasypeltis scabra* swallowing an egg four-and-a-half times its own head diameter (see overleaf).

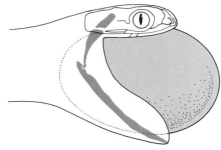

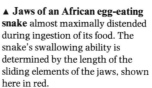

Food chains. . . Adaptations to feeding. . . Filter feeders. . .
Symbiosis. . . Chewing the cud—rumination. . . Microbial
fermentation. . . Feeding on flesh—carnivores. . . Feeding on
fluids. . . Parasites and parasitism. . . Digesting food. . .
Vitamins. . . Digestive enzymes. . . Enzyme adaptations. . .
Essential minerals. . . Timing enzyme secretion. . .

L IFE depends upon the balance between building organic material from carbon dioxide, water and minerals, and its ultimate breakdown into the initial constituents. Green plants are able to synthesize organic compounds from inorganic starting materials using sunlight as a source of energy—they are known as autotrophic organisms. Animals and most bacteria are heterotrophic organisms, that is they break down organic materials to provide carbon and most of their own organic constituents. Some bacteria may also act as synthesizers, however, using energy from chemical processes.

Plants, animals and bacteria interact mutually, as well as with their non-living environment, to form communities of living organisms. These communities are organized in food chains or food webs, built up of the plants, the plant eaters or herbivores and the carnivores which feed on the flesh of other animals. To a large extent, therefore, the community patterns are determined by who eats whom.

The relationships between the living organisms and their food is a theme evolution has varied infinitely, but the diversity unfolds within unifying frameworks, Typically, food chains have only three or four levels—plants, herbivores and first and second order carnivores, the top carnivores returning to their basic constituents by bacterial decomposition after their death.

▲ **Jaws of an African egg-eating snake** almost maximally distended during ingestion of its food. The snake's swallowing ability is determined by the length of the sliding elements of the jaws, shown here in red.

▼ **Methods of filter feeding**
(1) Filtration by means of setae in a copepod maxilla. The setae and their bristles make the copepod maxillae look like filters, and the maxillae were generally believed to filter food particles, such as planktonic algae, from the water. In recent years, however, it has been shown that the water does not pass through the maxillae, which rather move the water by acting as paddles. (2) Filtration by means of mucous nets—cross section of the body of a sea squirt. Sea squirts pass a current of water from the pharynx to the atrial cavity by means of cilia lining the perforations of the pharyngeal wall. The passing water is intercepted by a net of mucus

which is continuously produced by the endostyle and carried across the pharynx by means of ciliary tracts. In the dorsal lamina other ciliary tracts roll the sheets with filtered food particles into a string that passes through the esophagus down into the stomach. (3) Filtration by means of ciliary water currents in a mussel gill (a) from side (b) in cross section. At the entrance to the interfilamentary spaces the through currents cross the surface currents produced by cilia along the frontal face of the filaments. Where the two flow systems meet, suspended particles in the through currents are exposed to viscous forces that tend to move the particles into the surface currents. This implies capture of the particles, which the surface currents carry directly to the mouth and down the esophagus.

▶ **Sifting the seas,** individual polyps on a gorgonian coral extract minute food items from the surrounding water.

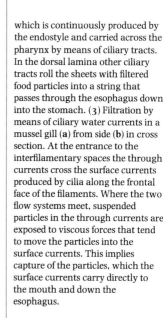

▼ **Food for filter feeders.** A range of microscopic aquatic plant life (phytoplankton), as revealed by a light microscope.

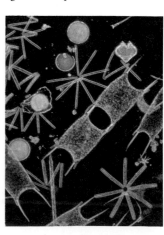

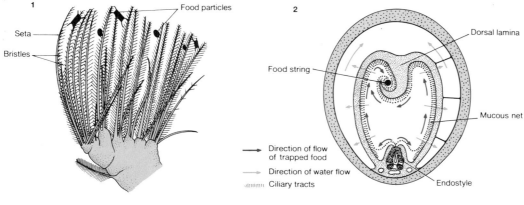

1
Food particles
Seta
Bristles

2
Dorsal lamina
Food string
Mucous net

→ Direction of flow of trapped food
→ Direction of water flow
⌇ Ciliary tracts

Endostyle

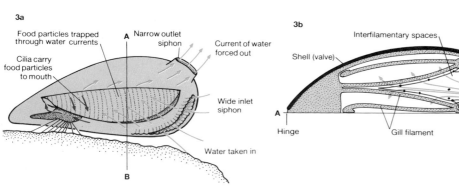

3a
Food particles trapped through water currents
A Narrow outlet siphon
Cilia carry food particles to mouth
Current of water forced out
Wide inlet siphon
Water taken in
B

3b
Interfilamentary spaces
Shell (valve)
Mantle
A   B
Hinge   Gill filament   Marginal food groove

Filter Feeding

The characteristics of the food chains depend largely upon the difference in size between the food and its consumer, especially between the plants and the herbivores. In the oceans and larger lakes, plant life is dominated by tiny, microscopic, single-celled algae, the phytoplankton, floating freely in the water. Seaweeds, and other larger plants, are restricted to the shallow, coastal waters. The concentration of phytoplankton usually amounts to less than 1mg of organic matter per liter of water. Therefore, animals that live on phytoplankton are presented with a highly dilute diet of food particles that are so small that they cannot be sensed and seized individually. Thus, to graze on phytoplankton, it is implied that the animal must process the water that surrounds it through filters that retain suspended particles including the phytoplankton.

Typically, filter feeders process the water continuously, independently of the concentration of food and other particles in the water. The efficiency with which the filters retain particles suspended in the water depends upon the size of the particles and not upon their food value. Usually particles down to some few micrometers (thousandths of a millimeter) are retained and eaten.

Water processing and filtration may be carried out by means of tiny, thread-like cilia, as in mussels and many other animals, or bristle-like setae, as in many planktonic crustaceans. Sea squirts propel the water by ciliary activity and filter it through nets built of fine mucous threads. The mucous net acts as a mechanical filter which retains particles that are too large to pass the meshes. Also, the filters in mussels and in copepods have been said to function as mechanical sieves—mussels sieving particles out of the water by means of rows of cilia and copepods by means of bristles on the setae of the feeding appendages. In fact, the filters do not work like a sieve; the feeding structures function under physical conditions that are now only beginning to be understood.

A fluid is characterized by the physical properties of inertia, or the tendency to remain at rest or in uniform motion unless acted upon by an external force, and viscosity, that is, the property which resists internal flow. The Reynolds number is an estimate of the ratio of inertial to viscous forces in a particular

► **Rasping at the surface**—section through the front part of the body of the mollusk *Vema ewingi* showing the principal structure of the radula apparatus ("rasping tongue") and the muscles controlling the complex movements of the radula. When feeding, the radula protrudes through the mouth and rasps up algae and organic debris on the substrate. This feeding mechanism has occurred throughout molluskan evolution and is seen in present-day snails and slugs. This species belongs to a group once believed to have become extinct some 350 million years ago, but a similar living species was recently discovered. FAR RIGHT Electron micrograph showing "teeth" on the radula of a Giant land snail.

◄ **Fermentation tanks.** Many large herbivores, such as these African elephants (*Loxodonta africana*), have been likened to giant fermentation tanks on legs, because the plant material they eat has to be broken down by bacterial fermentation in their guts. INSET An electron micrograph of plant cells showing the cellulose cell walls—the basic food material of herbivores which cannot be broken down by any of the enzymes that mammals produce. Bacteria and protozoans in the gut break them down.

◄ **Specialized herbivores,** such as this koala (*Phascolarctos cinereus*) BELOW, have digestive systems that can cope with poisonous chemicals produced by plants, in this case eucalyptus trees.

▼ **Digestive tract** of a ruminant herbivore.

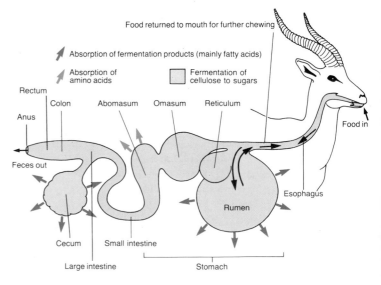

Food returned to mouth for further chewing

↗ Absorption of fermentation products (mainly fatty acids)

↗ Absorption of amino acids

☐ Fermentation of cellulose to sugars

Rectum

Colon

Abomasum

Omasum

Reticulum

Anus

Food in

Feces out

Esophagus

Rumen

Cecum

Small intestine

Large intestine

Stomach

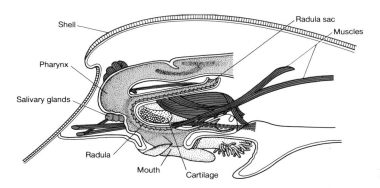

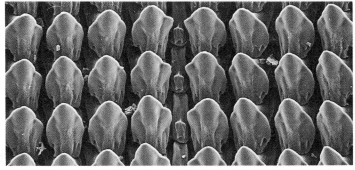

flow situation. In the case of the water in which filter feeders function, this number is low, that is, the viscous forces dominate and the fluid behaves like a syrup. Under these conditions, water does not seem to flow between the rows of cilia or setae which are supposed to function as filters and, instead, these structures move the water itself. New hypotheses to explain the way in which filter feeding actually works are currently being developed based on low Reynolds number fluid mechanics. It does seem, however, that the particles are captured by mechanisms other than that of physically intercepting the particles suspended in the water which passes the filter.

Feeding Associations in Water—Symbiosis

Many aquatic animals have established close associations or symbioses with their food organisms, the single-celled plankton algae. Symbiosis is remarkably common among protozoans, sponges, coelenterates and mollusks. In fresh waters, the symbionts of sponges and other animals are various species of green algae whereas, in the sea, one species of dinoflagellate, *Gymnodinium microadriaticum*, predominates. This flagellate is found in all reef-building corals as well as in several other groups of coral reef inhabitants, including the giant clams and most sea anemones.

The symbiotic algae live and multiply inside the cells of their host. Until recently, it was believed that the host harvested the crop by digesting the algae, but it turns out that the relationship between host and symbiont is far more sophisticated. When *Gymnodinium microadriaticum* lives outside the host it behaves like a normal phytoplankton alga, closed off from the environment by a practically impermeable cell wall. Inside the host cell the structure and properties of the alga's cell membrane change, and it becomes permeable to the products of photosynthesis, sugars and amino acids, which pass into the tissues of the host. In return, the symbiotic algae receive ammonia produced by the host, use it to synthesize amino acids and thus establish a recycling system of nitrogen between host and algae. Probably in some way the host controls the growth, division and therefore the number of symbiotic algae. The host appears to be able to recognize aged or defective algae, which are then expelled, as are other indigestible materials.

Symbiosis between animals and algae in coral reef habitats appears to be a highly successful adaptation for solving nutritional problems in nutrient-poor tropical seas. Photosynthetic production by the symbiotic algae of a coral reef may be several times higher than that of the phytoplankton production close to the reef.

Chewing the Cud—Rumination

The higher plants on land grow to large size, and animals that feed on grasses, herbs and leaves have no difficulties in spotting the plants on which they graze or browse. The food is sometimes hard to digest, or even eat. The living cells in higher plants are encased in thick cell walls built of cellulose and other polysaccharides to give them rigidity. Most animals cannot digest these materials because they lack the necessary enzymes. Further, higher plants have often developed protective means against consumers, varying from toxins to thorns. In fact, only a small part of the primary production on land is eaten, and most vegetation simply dies and begins to decompose under the action of a variety of enzymes from the ubiquitous bacteria and other soil microorganisms. During this process the plant material, including cellulose and other indigestible substances, is converted into microbial mass, bacteria, protozoans and fungi, which can be eaten and digested by animals. Thus, the microbial activity converts those parts of the primary production that is not accessible to most animals into matter of high nutritional value for the rich fauna that feeds in the soils of fields and forests or on the sediments of coastal waters and lakes.

In the presence of oxygen the microbial decomposition proceeds to the complete oxidation of the materials on which the microorganisms live. Under anaerobic conditions (ie in the absence of oxygen), the microorganisms will ferment their substrate and convert most of the structural polysaccharides into small organic molecules. Such anaerobic conditions prevail in the digestive tracts of larger animals, where the anaerobic microbial breakdown has resulted repeatedly in the establishment of symbiotic associations between herbivores and decomposing microorganisms. Digestion by means of symbionts may be considered the major adaptation in the utilization of plant food among terrestrial animals.

Microbial fermentation is probably characteristic of the large intestine of mammals and of large animals generally, not just herbivores. These fermentation processes produce volatile fatty acids, such as acetic acid and propionic acid, which are absorbed from the intestine into the blood. Fermentation may be of great importance in the utilization of food even in such unspecialized feeders as the pig and the rat. In these animals one-fourth to one-third of ingested plant fibers may be digested by means of microbial fermentation.

Many herbivores have specialized the fermentation chambers of the digestive tract by enlargement of the large intestine and cecum. The Green turtle, the ptarmigan, the dugong and

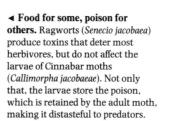

◀ **Food for some, poison for others.** Ragworts (*Senecio jacobaea*) produce toxins that deter most herbivores, but do not affect the larvae of Cinnabar moths (*Callimorpha jacobaeae*). Not only that, the larvae store the poison, which is retained by the adult moth, making it distasteful to predators.

▶ ▼ **Carnivores come in all shapes and sizes.** The more expected scene of a lion (*Panthera leo*) and prey ABOVE RIGHT, contrasts with the marine cone shell (*Conus geographus*) which engulfs its fish prey whole BELOW. Flesh is richer in nutrients than plant material and carnivores tend to eat less often than herbivores.

the horse and its relatives are examples. In other herbivores, such as rabbits and hares, both the large intestine and the stomach serve as fermentation chambers. The rabbit has also attracted interest because of its habit of eating its own feces. It produces two types of fecal pellets: one, the well-known hard, day type, and the other soft type formed in the cecum and expelled during the night. The latter are picked up by the animal directly from the anus and eaten. These pellets, which consist mainly of bacteria, are retained in the stomach to serve in the fermentation of carbohydrates and the formation of lactic acid.

Symbiont-aided digestion has reached its highest development in the ruminants and other groups of ruminant-like animals. Animals that ruminate include the cattle, sheep, goats, antelopes, giraffes, deer, camels, llamas, hippopotamus, sloths, and kangaroos. Large-scale symbiont digestion of cellulose and other insoluble and resistant polysaccharides needs space and is time consuming. The digestive tracts of animals that have adopted this feeding habit are therefore equipped with greatly expanded sections in which the voluminous mixture of microorganisms and food is stored for the long periods needed to break down the plant material (often several days). In ruminants, the rumen serves as the fermenting chamber. In cattle its capacity amounts to about 15 percent of the body mass.

The ruminants owe their name to their habit of returning some of the content of the rumen to the mouth for further chewing. This chewing increases the surface area of the food exposed to the action of the digestive enzymes in the rumen. In the mouth the repeated returns of the rumen contents further mix the cud with large amounts of saliva. The saliva is rich in bicarbonate, which serves to neutralize the fatty acids produced by the fermentation.

The initial stages in the breakdown of the food in the rumen are carried out by digestive enzymes secreted by the micro-

organisms. The enzymes split the variety of polysaccharides, including cellulose, into simple sugars. These sugars are largely absorbed by the microorganisms and fermented into fatty acids which constitute the host's share of the carbohydrates in the food.

The proteins in the food are also split by digestive enzymes secreted by the microorganisms, which also absorb most of the liberated amino acids to use for their growth and multiplication. The protein, however, is not lost to the ruminant. When the microorganisms themselves pass further down the digestive tract and reach the abomasum, or stomach proper, they are attacked by the host's own enzymes and digested. Thus, the microorganisms represent a most important source of protein to the host.

Digestion by means of symbionts endows the host with other advantages. The rumen microorganisms are able to reuse the products of excretion, ammonia and urea, for the synthesis of proteins. Moreover, they synthesize many vitamins, especially those of the B group, thereby reducing the dietary vitamin requirements. The price of digesting food by means of symbionts depends both upon the energetic cost of maintaining the microbial population and the efficiency with which this population utilizes the food.

Feeding on Flesh—Carnivores
Herbivores spend a great deal of time feeding. Animals which graze on plankton algae feed almost continuously, and grazers of higher plants often spend most of their waking hours eating. Continuous eating by filter-feeding animals may be looked upon as a consequence of the highly dilute state of the food particles, while the protracted periods of grazing on higher plants may be related to the indigestibility and bulkiness of the food. In herbivores, therefore, feeding, digestion and absorption of the food mostly proceeds simultaneously. By contrast, most carnivores take distinct meals, and feeding is followed in time

by digestion and absorption of the food as it passes along the intestinal tract. The intervals between meals vary in duration depending upon the numbers and size of prey. Predators may be adapted to feed on prey that may be available only at long and irregular intervals. Carnivores which feed on prey that is scarce may be able to cope with and swallow much larger animals. Some deep-sea fish can swallow prey much larger than themselves.

A characteristic feature of carnivorous feeding is the specialized teeth for dealing with flesh. Such specializations are particularly conspicuous within the mammalian order Carnivora, from which arose the concept of carnivores as contrasted with herbivores. The mammalian carnivores include dogs, wolves, foxes, bears, ferrets, badgers, otters, hyenas and the cats which may be large, such as lions and tigers, or small, such as the European wild cat and its close relative, the domestic cat. Common to them all are the well-developed canine teeth, suited for grasping and tearing the prey, and the back teeth, the molars and the premolars, shaped for cutting rather than for chewing and grinding.

Many animals feed on both animal and vegetable matter— they are omnivorous. Most primates, including humans, belong to the omnivores, as do pigs and rats. In agreement with the diverse nature of their food, the omnivores lack the highly specialized feeding structures and digestive tracts, so common in herbivores and carnivores.

Feeding on Fluids
Blood in animals, and cell sap and nectar in plants, as well as a variety of exudates and secretions are foods for animals that suck or pump the fluids into their digestive tracts. Most fluid feeders are invertebrates, especially insects, spiders and scorpions and leeches. Two main types of fluid feeding can be distinguished. In one type, freely accessible fluids, such as nectar, exudates of decaying matter and secretions and excretions

of plants and animals are used, and the animal simply sucks up the fluid. The other type of fluid feeder exploits internal fluids, such as cell sap and blood, using mouth parts that combine piercing with sucking, as in the mosquitoes and ticks. Animals which feed on blood prevent it from clotting by injecting an anticoagulant into the wound made by their piercing mouth parts. By their very nature, blood and other fluids are watery, so that, effectively, they are bulky foods. Moreover, blood-sucking animals typically take meals at long intervals, in some cases only once in a lifetime! When only one meal is taken it can be very large. Thus, a female tick stores blood in the digestive tract amounting to about 200 times its own body mass during the seven or eight days the meal lasts, before the tick drops from the host. This corresponds to an increase in weight from about 2mg to about 400mg.

Parasites and Parasitism

It seems a short step from visiting a source of fluid to feed to a life in permanent contact with the fluids. When these fluids are blood and body fluids, or the content of an intestinal tract, parasitic relationships are established. At the establishment of parasitic life the surrounding fluid presumably is ingested through the mouth, but uptake of small organic molecules through the external surface of the parasite may evolve as adaptations to the high concentrations of the molecules present, especially in the contents of digestive tracts. Thus, it is important to discover whether it is the intestine or the body surface of a parasite which is the main site of absorption.

The ascarids, including the Common roundworm in the human intestine, suck in the intestinal content through the mouth, and uptake through the surface seems to be insignificant. In other roundworms, such as filariids living as parasites in the blood and tissue of vertebrates, uptake through the surface predominates. Trematodes, including flukes and other parasites of blood and tissue, both ingest the food and absorb small organic molecules through the surface. Other helminth worms, such as the tapeworms, lack an intestinal canal altogether and feed exclusively by absorbing food, digested by the host, through the body wall.

It might seem a major evolutionary innovation to establish properties in the integument that are ordinarily thought of as specializations of the intestine—the ability to absorb small organic molecules as well as inorganic ions. This ability seems to be a general feature of cell membranes, however, rather than a specialization of the intestinal cells. Also, the integument of soft-bodied marine invertebrates is capable of absorbing organic molecules, such as glucose and amino acids, which may be present in the surrounding water.

The ability to transport the molecules across the cell membrane into the cell is associated with the development of protrusions of the cell membrane, the microvilli. Microvilli can increase the surface area of the cell by as much as 25 times, thereby greatly enhancing the absorbing capacity of the surface. Microvilli cover the integuments of marine invertebrates as well as of parasites.

Successful parasitism depends upon the survival of both host and parasite. No wonder, therefore, that parasite life histories reflect complex interplays between parasite and host, with

▲▼ **Sap suckers.** Aphids are among the many species of insects which obtain their food by sucking sap from plant tissues. Shown here ABOVE are Rose aphids (*Macrosiphum rosae*) clustered around a rose stem. BELOW The proboscis of aphids (1) is pushed into the plant veins and sap sucked out. The apparent external simplicity of the proboscis hides a complex series of layers (2).

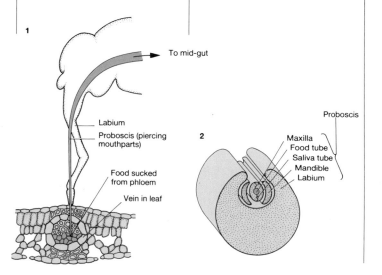

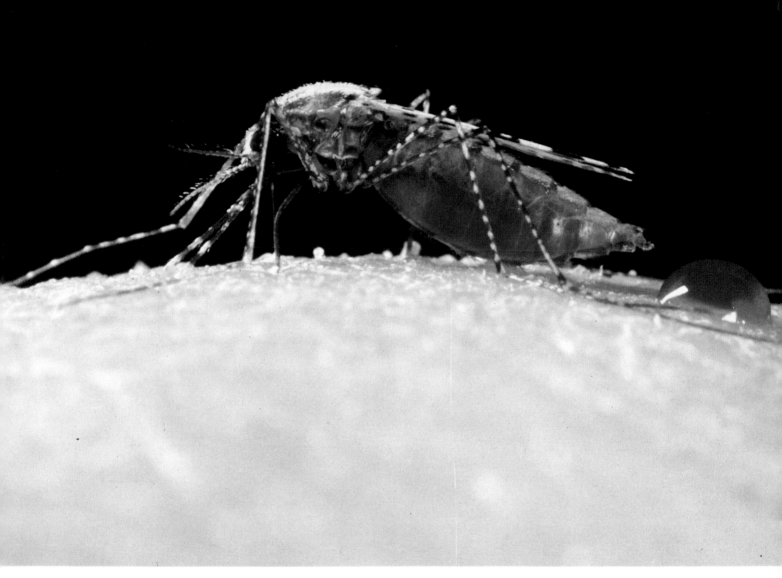

▲ **Blood meals** may be obtained in different ways by parasites. Mosquitoes (*Anopheles stephensi*) are external parasites which use their sharp proboscis to penetrate the hosts' skin and suck out blood. The actual loss of blood is minimal. The main problem is that such parasites may convey to the hosts other pernicious pathogens, such as malaria in the case of mosquitoes.

mutual defense mechanisms as recurring themes. Parasites inhabiting the intestinal tract must defend themselves from being digested, although it is not yet fully understood how they achieve this. Tapeworms appear to secrete substances that deactivate the protein-digesting enzymes, trypsin and chymotrypsin. Such "anti-enzymes" have been isolated and purified from another intestinal parasite, *Ascaris*. But protection against digestion also depends upon retaining an intact integument. Parasites are digested not only when they die, but also when the integument of the living worm is damaged.

When parasites in the blood and tissues first enter the body, they are exposed to the immune system of the host. The immune system protects the organism against foreign substances, viruses, bacteria and other organisms, including parasites, by producing antibodies against the invading antigens, and by activating the macrophages which can eat and destroy the invading organisms.

When an organism is invaded for the first time by parasites, an immune defense is lacking. During the time the immune

system builds up, the invading parasites may manage to become established within the body by developing means of protecting themselves against the immune defense mechanisms which the host has mobilized. One way is to coat themselves with host antigen. Such host-disguised parasites go unrecognized by the host's defense mechanisms, including attack from macrophages. If the organism becomes exposed again to the parasite, however, (for example, the bilharzia blood flukes which burrow through the skin of people who wade in an infested river), the immune system may effectively act upon the invaders to prevent reinfection. Thus, the immunological interplay between host and parasite may serve to establish a balance and to prevent overcrowding with parasites that may endanger the life of the host.

Digesting Food

The bulk of most foods is made up of giant molecules that animals cannot utilize directly as sources of energy or for synthesis of new cell constituents. Therefore, the first step in the treatment of food consists of splitting these giant molecules into smaller molecules: proteins into amino acids, carbohydrates into monosaccharides (sugars) and lipids into fatty acids and glycerol. The splitting of the macromolecules is performed by means of digestive enzymes. These enzymes may act either inside cells (intracellularly) or outside cells (extracellularly) according to the organization of the digestive system.

Most multicellular animals possess a digestive tract in which digestion may occur inside the cells lining the digestive tract, outside cells in the lumen of the tract or both. Presumably digestion within the cells is the primitive condition, taken over from the unicellular protozoans. Coelenterates (jellyfish, corals) and many flatworms (turbellarians, flukes) may serve as examples of animals in which intracellular digestion represents a primitive condition. In other groups, digestion is essentially completed in the lumen of the digestive tract before absorption takes place. Examples are the crustaceans, insects, cephalopods (cuttlefish, octopus), tunicates (sea squirts), and all fish, amphibians, reptiles, birds and mammals.

The fact that filter feeding is often associated with intracellular digestion suggests that the type of food has an influence on the type of digestion that takes place. Thus, intracellular digestion is typical of microphagous animals, including bivalves. Fluid feeders may also develop intracellular digestion. The tick, which took a meal of blood amounting to 200 times its own volume, starts by reducing the volume four or five times by absorbing and excreting water. At the same time, the cells in the strongly extended intestinal wall rapidly multiply, to phagocytize (take in) and digest the intestinal content.

Extracellular digestion differs markedly from intracellular digestion in the high degree of specialization of the intestinal tract. Thus, different regions of the tract may be specialized for food uptake, storage, digestion and absorption (which often overlap) as well as formation and evacuation of feces. This functional differentiation is most advanced in vertebrates.

Digestive enzymes. The same types of digestive enzymes are present throughout the animal kingdom, and they may act inside the cell producing the enzymes, as in intracellular digestion, or after being secreted into a digestive tract. Three main types of digestive enzymes can be distinguished: carbohydrases splitting carbohydrates; peptidases splitting proteins; and esterases splitting lipids.

The most widely distributed carbohydrates are built up from glucose. They include cane sugar, starch and cellulose, which

Vitamins and their Functions

In terms of food and feeding mechanisms, animal nutrition is diverse but, at cellular and biochemical level, there is little diversity. In terms of energy sources (proteins, lipids and carbohydrates) and specific substances (essential amino acids, vitamins and minerals), the basic nutritional requirements of animals are very similar. Throughout the animal kingdom the same types of enzymes are responsible for the digestion of the food, for the metabolic breakdown of the absorbed organic molecules and for the synthesis of new macromolecules.

The enzymes are proteins, but many metabolic enzymes require non-protein components for their function. These components may be small organic molecules, vitamins, or inorganic ions.

Thus, vitamins are organic nutrients which are required in small amounts in the food for proper function and growth of the organism. Vitamin deficiencies result in various types of disease which may threaten life. There is little obvious connection between the known biochemical roles of the vitamins and the enzymes of which they are constituents on the one hand and the diverse structural and functional symptoms of deficiencies on the other hand. These symptoms are mainly known from humans and laboratory animals.

Vitamins are divided into the water-soluble and the fat-soluble types. Both groups are present in most foods but particular sources of the water-soluble vitamins are vegetables, whole-grain cereals, fruits and meat, and of fat-soluble vitamins, dairy and egg products and fish oil.

Water-soluble vitamins	Deficiency symptoms
thiamine	muscle weakness and wasting; lack of co-ordination; beriberi
nicotinamide	dermatitis; diarrhea; mental deterioration; pellagra
riboflavin	sores on lips; dermatitis of the face; anemia
folic acid	anemia; weight loss; weakness
ascorbic acid	bleeding gums; loose teeth; anemia; emaciation; scurvy

Fat-soluble vitamins	
vitamin A	night blindness; abnormal keratinization of the skin
vitamin D	deficiently calcified and deformed bones; rickets

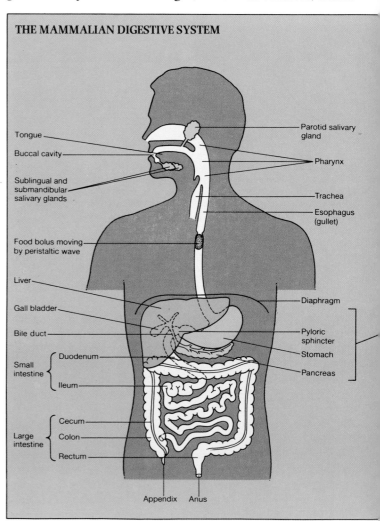

THE MAMMALIAN DIGESTIVE SYSTEM

Tongue
Buccal cavity
Sublingual and submandibular salivary glands
Food bolus moving by peristaltic wave
Liver
Gall bladder
Bile duct
Small intestine { Duodenum, Ileum
Large intestine { Cecum, Colon, Rectum
Parotid salivary gland
Pharynx
Trachea
Esophagus (gullet)
Diaphragm
Pyloric sphincter
Stomach
Pancreas
Appendix   Anus

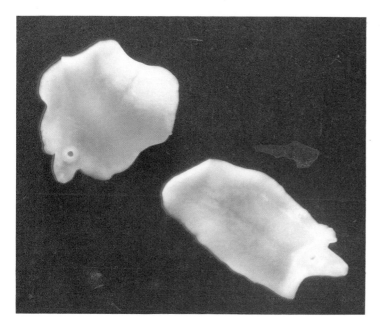

▲ **Intestinal parasites**—sheep liver flukes (*Fasciola hepatica*). These flukes live in the bile ducts of their hosts, attached to the wall by suckers sited at the front end. They feed on blood sucked from the bile duct wall.

is the main component of the cell walls of higher plants. A great number of carbohydrate-splitting enzymes exist. These enzymes are characterized by their great specificity towards their substrate. Practically each carbohydrate requires its own enzyme to be split into its basic sugars. If the enzymes are missing in the digestive tract of the animal, the carbohydrates will pass through intact unless microorganisms equipped with the enzymes are present. This is the basis for the symbiont-aided digestion of cellulose.

Proteins are built up from amino acids by means of so-called peptide bonds. Therefore, the enzymes which split these bonds are termed peptidases. Peptidases are grouped into families of chemically related enzymes. One group, the pepsins, requires a highly acid medium, at *p*H about 1 to 2, to be optimally active. The pepsins are secreted in the stomach of most vertebrates, from fishes to mammals, along with hydrochloric acid to produce the required acidity. The peptidases of the intestinal tract, trypsin and chymotrypsin, are optimally active in neutral or slightly alkaline conditions.

The esterases are the least specific of the digestive enzymes, and various esterases may split a variety of fats and other lipids into the constituent fatty acids and alcohols.

Enzyme adaptations. The composition of enzymes in the digestive tract of animals reflects, in a general sense, the

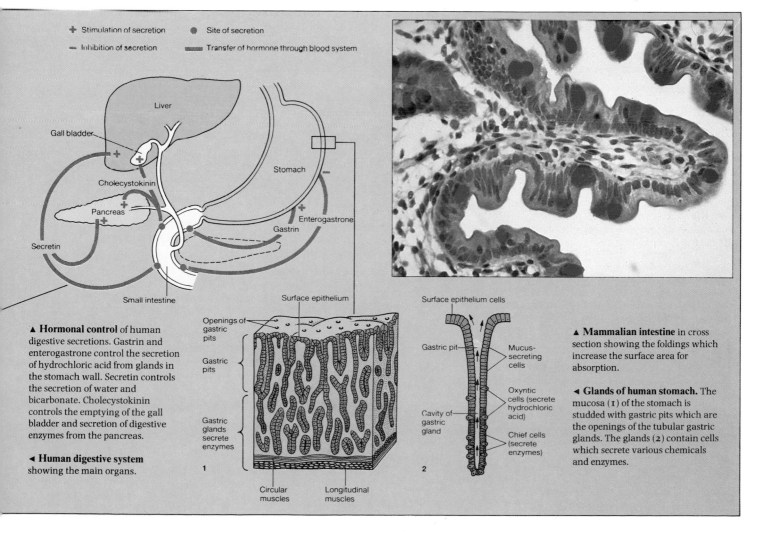

▲ **Hormonal control** of human digestive secretions. Gastrin and enterogastrone control the secretion of hydrochloric acid from glands in the stomach wall. Secretin controls the secretion of water and bicarbonate. Cholecystokinin controls the emptying of the gall bladder and secretion of digestive enzymes from the pancreas.

◄ **Human digestive system** showing the main organs.

▲ **Mammalian intestine** in cross section showing the foldings which increase the surface area for absorption.

◄ **Glands of human stomach.** The mucosa (**1**) of the stomach is studded with gastric pits which are the openings of the tubular gastric glands. The glands (**2**) contain cells which secrete various chemicals and enzymes.

composition of their normal diet. Carbohydrases are often found to dominate in the digestive tract of herbivorous animals, peptidases in the tracts of carnivores, and all groups of digestive enzymes appear to be fairly equally represented in omnivorous species, including humans and the pig. Thus, the composition of enzymes in the digestive juices of animals is largely genetically determined, and adapted to the kind of food eaten. But the enzyme composition may also adapt to changes in the composition of food. A striking example of such an enzyme adaptation is found in the amylase of human saliva.

Amylase is a carbohydrase which splits starch to sugar. The amylase activity was found to differ among the Tswans of Bechuanaland (who eat a predominantly carbohydrate diet), the Bushmen from the Kalahari Desert (who eat a diet rich in protein) and Europeans (living on a mixed diet). Amylase activities, expressed in parts per milliliter of saliva, amounted to 248, 22 and 101, respectively. These values did not vary significantly over a period of months on constant diets. On the other hand, an activity of 95 parts, that is, the level of the Europeans, was found in the saliva of five Bushmen who had been held as court witnesses for three months and who had lived on a mixed diet during that time.

The lactose (milk sugar)-splitting enzyme, galactosidase, represents another type of enzyme adaptation. The enzyme is present in the digestive tract of suckling infants and the young of mammals, where it splits the lactose into the absorbable sugars, glucose and galactose. In the absence of the enzyme, the lactose in the milk cannot be digested and absorbed, and diarrhea ensues. Normally, the secretion of lactase stops

Essential Minerals and their Functions

Bulk elements	Concentration	Main actions
calcium	2.0% of body mass	99 percent in bone and teeth, 1 percent in soft tissue; essential for transport of ions and organic molecules across cell membranes, contraction of muscles, excitability of nerves
phosphorus	1.0%	80–85 percent in bone and teeth, in chemical combination with calcium as the mineral apatite, component of cell membrane macromolecules, nucleic acids (DNA and RNA), energy-rich adenosine triphosphate
potassium	0.35%	predominant intracellular cation; essential in impulse conduction in nerves and muscles
sulfur	0.25%	constituent of some amino acids; chondroitin sulfate in cartilage, and some vitamins (eg, thiamine)
sodium	0.15%	predominant extracellular cation; essential for transport of glucose and amino acids across cell membranes
chlorine	0.15%	predominant extracellular anion; constituent of hydrochloric acid secretion in stomach, activator of amylase in saliva and pancreatic juice
magnesium	0.05%	60 percent in bone; essential for muscular

Secretions, Control Mechanisms and Enzyme Actions in the Mammalian Digestive Tract

ORAL CAVITY
Secretions. *Saliva* especially from paratoid, sublingual and submaxillary glands.
Mechanisms of Control. Nervous control especially through parasympathetic secretory nerves.
Enzymes. *a-Amylase* splits starch and glycogen to dextrins and maltose.

STOMACH
Secretions. *Gastric juice* mainly composed of hydrochloric acid from parietal cells and pepsin from chief cells.
Mechanisms of Control. Nervous: vagus secretory nerve for hydrochloric acid and pepsin secretion. Hormonal: *gastrin* from antral mucosa stimulates hydrochloric acid secretion; *enterogastrone* from duodenal mucosa inhibits gastric secretion and motility.
Enzymes. Pepsin splits proteins and polypeptides.

SMALL INTESTINE
Secretions. *Pancreatic juice* composed of water and salts, especially bicarbonates and enzymes. Intestinal secretion "*succus entericus*" from intestinal crypts and villus cells.
Bile composed of water and solids, especially bile salts.
Mechanisms of Control. Nervous: vagus secretory nerve for enzymes. Hormonal (predominant): *secretin* from intestinal mucosa stimulates secretion of water and salts and increases volume of bile, but not output of bile salts; *cholecystokinin* stimulates secretion of enzymes and contraction of gall bladder wall and emptying of its contents into small intestine. Chemical: bile salts are important substances in increasing bile secretion.

Enzymes.
In pancreatic juice:
Lipase splits triglyceride fat molecules into free fatty acids, diglyceride, monoglyceride, and glycerol.
a-Amylase splits starch and glycogen to dextrins and maltose.
Trypsin splits proteins and polypeptides.
Chymotrypsin splits proteins and peptides.
Carboxypeptidases split free amino acids from dipeptides.
Ribonuclease and *deoxyribonuclease* split RNA and DNA to nucleotides.

In succus entericus:
a-Glucosidase splits maltose and other a-glucoside sugars, eg sucrose.
Oligo-1 6-glucosidase splits branching dextrins derived from amylopectin and from glycogen.
β-Galactosidase splits lactose, mainly in suckling young.
Aminopeptidases split free amino acids from dipeptides.
Dipeptidases split dipeptides into free amino acids.

In bile:
Bile does not contain enzymes, but the bile salts are important in the digestion and absorption of lipids.

▶ **Human digestive systems vary.** Because of the basic differences in diets, the digestive enzymes produced by this Bushman woman are quite likely to be different in some respects from those produced, for example, by Europeans.

		contraction and excitability of nerves and muscles
iron	0.005%	constituent of oxygen-transporting proteins (hemoglobin in blood and myoglobin in muscles) and some metabolic enzymes
zinc	0.002%	constituent or activator of many of both digestive and metabolic enzymes
copper	0.00015%	constituent of many enzymes and the oxygen-transporting protein hemocyanin (mollusks, crustaceans)
iodine	0.00004%	constituent of thyroid hormones
manganese	0.00003%	activator of several enzymes

The constituents of food can be divided into organic nutrients and inorganic nutrients, the minerals. The minerals serve a variety of functions in animals. The essential minerals are probably common to all animals but their identity and the amounts needed have been studied mainly among laboratory animals, especially in the rat and chicken. The minerals may be required in such small amounts that they are difficult to detect but, with improved chemical analytical techniques, trace elements are still being added to the list of essential minerals. It is customary to distinguish between minerals that are required in relatively large amounts, the bulk elements, and the trace elements. But there is no sharp delineation between the two groups. The amounts of essential minerals decrease gradually over many orders of magnitude. By definition, trace elements are present in the body in concentrations smaller than 1 in 200,000. Iron occupies a transitional position.

with weaning. Simultaneously, children and young become intolerant towards lactose and, therefore, towards milk. Tolerance persists, however, in most members of the milk-drinking human populations in North America, Europe and certain areas of Africa. Within these populations, the continued secretions of lactase after weaning seems to be genetically determined, the gene for lactose tolerance being dominant. It seems, however, that tolerance can be acquired, that is, secretion of lactase can be resumed if lactose (milk) is added to the diet of individuals who do not drink milk after weaning.

Timing enzyme secretion. Animals that feed continuously also digest their food more-or-less continuously. In other animals a non-continuous, coordinated secretion of the digestive juices occurs in response to feeding. In the vertebrates, complex regulatory mechanisms ensure that the digestive secretions enter the lumen of the digestive tract in the proper amounts and at the proper times.

Saliva is secreted from glands in the mouth to lubricate the food and thus to assist in its easy passage through the esophagus during swallowing. The saliva of some vertebrates contains amylase which aids in the digestion of starch. The secretion of saliva is generally coordinated with the intake of food. Smell and taste of the food stimulate secretion of saliva through a nervous reflex. It is well known that conditioned reflexes resulting in salivary secretion are easily established. Such conditioned reflexes can be stimulated by sounds or visual signals presented simultaneously with food.

In the stomach different kinds of cells secrete pepsin and hydrochloric acid. Together, the two secretions constitute the main components of the gastric juice. Much the same stimuli that result in nervous stimulation of the salivary glands also cause prolonged secretion of gastric juices from the gastric glands. Conditioned reflexes are also easily established for gastric secretion; this was first demonstrated by Pavlov in dogs. In addition to the nervous control, gastric secretion is also controlled by the secretion of the hormone, gastrin, in one part of the stomach. It is liberated into the blood when pepsin starts to break down proteins in the swallowed food. Gastrin, which also stimulates the secretion of hydrochloric acid, reaches other parts of the stomach by the blood circulation.

The digestive enzymes of the intestine originate mainly from the pancreas, but also from the cells lining the intestine. Ingestion of food leads only to moderate secretion from the pancreas, and the nervous control of the secretion plays a minor role. Prolonged and profuse secretion of pancreatic juice only starts when food passes from the stomach into the intestine. The mechanism of secretion is similar to the hormonal mechanism of the stomach. Products of digestion stimulate secretion of hormones from the intestine to reach the pancreas and other parts of the digestive tract by way of the blood circulation. It has long been known that the hormones control the secretions of pancreatic juice and its composition, as well as the emptying of the gall bladder into the intestine. Work in recent years has, however, greatly extended our knowledge about hormones originating in the intestinal tract. The hormones are all peptides, and they appear in families of chemically related molecules, but the physiological functions of most of them are incompletely understood.   CBJ

Food for All
Animal feeding types

Animal foods and feeding mechanisms probably represent the most diverse of all areas of animal physiology. It constitutes a rich field for exploration of adaptive mechanisms. Practically every type of organic matter can be utilized as food, and it is obtained by a diversity of mechanisms determined by the kind of animal and nature of the food. A widely used classification of feeding types divides animals into three groups according to the size of the food they consume. The microphages feed on food that is of small size compared with the animal itself, whereas the macrophages take large-sized food. Most microphages are filter feeders. The third group includes the feeders on fluids and dissolved food, such as blood, nectar, cell sap and secretions. Subdivisions of the major groups are based on the types of mechanisms which the animals use to acquire their food.   CBJ

◄▼► **Feeding techniques** of a selection of animals. (**1**) Moose (*Alces alces*) grazing on vegetation in a lake; this species is a macrophagous herbivore. (**2**) Goshawk (*Accipiter gentilis*) and captured prey; this bird is a macrophagous carnivore (or predator). (**3**) Common genet (*Genetta genetta*) and prey; this mammal is a macrophagous carnivore. (**4**) St Andrew's cross spider (*Argiope aetherea*) with fly caught in web; although spiders catch large prey they inject digestive juices into the victim which dissolve its body tissues that the spider then sucks up; spiders are thus defined as fluid feeders. (**5**) Greater flamingos (*Phoenicopterus ruber roseus*) feeding; even though they are large animals, the diet of flamingos comprises minute organisms which they filter from water; they are thus microphagous filter feeders. (**6**) Gulf fritillary (*Dione vanillae*) sucking nectar from a flower; butterflies are fluid feeders. (**7**) Squid (*Loligo* species) with captured fish; these mollusks are equipped to catch large prey and are thus macrophages.

Feeding Mechanisms

Microphages

pseudopods	radiolarians, foraminiferans
cilia	ciliates, sponges, fanworms, bivalves, amphibian tadpoles
mucous nets	several gastropods, sea squirts, lancelets
setae and similar filtering structures	water fleas, copepods, Basking shark, some teleosts, flamingo, baleen whales

Macrophages

mechanisms for swallowing the surrounding medium (mud, sand, earth, etc)	sea cucumbers, sea urchins, lugworms, earthworms
mechanisms for seizing prey	amoebae, jellyfish, corals, most non-mammalian vertebrates, some mammals
mechanisms for seizing and masticating prey, and for biting, rasping, grazing, etc often combined with mastication of food	snails, slugs, cuttle-fish, squids, octopus, crustaceans, insects, lampreys, hagfish, some birds and most mammals

Feeders on fluids and dissolved food

mechanisms for sucking fluids	flukes, roundworms, leeches, parasitic copepods, several groups of insects (lice, butterflies, moths, mosquitoes, bees, fleas), arachnids (scorpions, spiders, mites and ticks), young of mammals
mechanisms for absorbing dissolved food through the external surface	many parasites (the protozoans that cause sleeping sickness and malaria, tapeworms, filariid worms, bilharzia fluke), marine soft-bodied invertebrates

Gas Exchange and Circulation

W^E humans, like other animals, usually take breathing for granted—it occurs without any conscious involvement whatsoever. Indeed, the only times we are usually aware of our respiratory functions are when they become difficult or impaired either through strenuous exercise or through damage or disease in the system. We know that we will die if breathing stops for more than a few minutes, but why? What is breathing for and how does it take place?

◄ **Living in water but breathing air** have their problems. This Water spider (*Argyroneta aquatica*) builds its own bubble of air below the surface to which it retreats when it needs air.

The energy of life... The color of gas transport... Oxygen and carbon dioxide... Transport of respiratory gases... Bulk transport and diffusion... Why are gills, lungs and blood needed?... Gas exchange in water... Gas exchange in air... Gas exchange and transport in insects... Air exchange in lungs... Bird lungs... How fast is oxygen consumed... Diving animals... Blood circulation... Hearts... Arteries and veins...

LIVING organisms need a constant supply of energy to maintain their bodies, to grow and move and finally to reproduce themselves. Plants are capable of capturing the energy of sunlight to build up chemical compounds which are then used as energy sources. Animals rely on obtaining these compounds, which are mainly carbohydrates, fats and proteins, more directly by eating plants or other animals.

Energy is most economically derived by a series of metabolic reactions called oxidations which occur in most, if not all, the cells of the body under the control of enzymes. Oxidative metabolism of this sort requires a constant supply of oxygen (O_2) and removal of end products which are mainly carbon dioxide (CO_2) and water. The amounts of oxygen required and of carbon dioxide produced are roughly equivalent. The relationship is often referred to as the respiratory quotient and can be expressed by the formula $RQ = \dfrac{\text{volume of } CO_2 \text{ produced}}{\text{volume of } O_2 \text{ consumed}}$
The RQ varies slightly depending on whether fats, proteins or carbohydrates are being oxidized but it usually results in values around 0.8, that is 8ml of carbon dioxide are produced for every 10ml of oxygen consumed.

In some cells, and occasionally in whole organisms, when the oxygen supply is restricted for any reason, energy can be derived from the breakdown of organic compounds in fermentation reactions resulting in the production of end products such as lactic acid, pyruvic acid or alcohol. Anaerobic metabolism of this sort, however, taking place in the absence of oxygen, has an energy yield of only one tenth to one twentieth of that derived from the oxidative processing of equivalent amounts of organic substrate. It is not surprising, therefore, that most animals rely extensively on oxidative metabolism and that the movement of oxygen into and carbon dioxide out of the body cells is essential for the maintenance of life. The uptake of oxygen and the release of carbon dioxide, at the levels of both the cells and the whole organism, is known as respiration. It is the mechanism by which the respiratory gases are exchanged between organism and environment as well as those by which they are transported between the gas exchange surface (for example, gills or lungs) and the cells of the body that are considered here. The gases move between three different media (air, water or body fluid, and blood) during these processes, so that the properties of each of the three media will be examined.

Transport of Respiratory Gases

Two distinct processes are involved in moving oxygen and carbon dioxide between the environment and cells. The first of

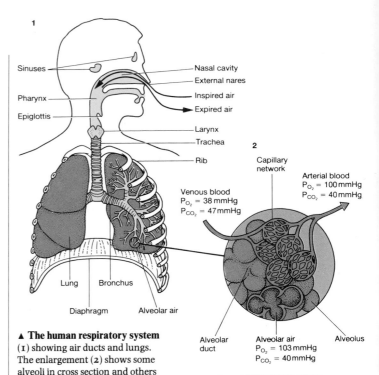

▲ **The human respiratory system** (1) showing air ducts and lungs. The enlargement (2) shows some alveoli in cross section and others surrounded by blood vessels. Each alveolus is supplied by capillary networks.

P_{O_2} = partial pressure oxygen
P_{CO_2} = partial pressure carbon dioxide

▼ **Types of gas exchange surface.** (1) Body surface with underlying blood supply. (2) Evaginated expansion of the body surface forming a gill. (3) Invaginated expansion of the body surface forming a lung.

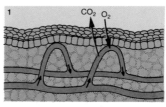

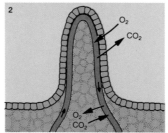

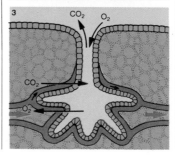

► **Oxygen and carbon dioxide concentrations**—the relationships between partial pressure and concentration of (1) oxygen and (2) carbon dioxide in the three respiratory media—air, water and blood. Concentrations can be expressed in a variety of ways; one that is commonly used is to give the volume of either oxygen or carbon dioxide in a liter of medium. The differing abilities of blood, gas and water to take up oxygen are illustrated here by considering the concentrations found in the three media at an oxygen partial pressure of 100mm mercury. At this partial pressure mammalian blood would contain 200ml of oxygen per liter, a gas mixture such as alveolar air 132ml/l and fresh water only 4ml/l. Blood is said to have a high capacity for oxygen and water a low one. Blood has an even higher capacity for carbon dioxide. As a result, oxygen and carbon dioxide can be transported in bulk at flow rates of blood that are reasonably low. (See also box p62).

these is a bulk transport process in which the medium containing the respiratory gases is actively pumped from one location to another. The pumping of air in and out of the lungs of terrestrial animals, of water through the gills of aquatic animals and of blood between gas exchange surfaces and tissues all fall into this category. Oxygen and carbon dioxide molecules are carried in each medium in different ways. In air they are simply components in a gas mixture, in water or in body fluids they occur as substances in solution and in blood they are found in chemical combinations with blood pigments (see box p62).

Although these differences affect the number of molecules contained in one liter of medium (the concentration), the principles by which they are transported by bulk movement of the medium remain the same in all cases. The molecules of gas are moved from place to place like passengers in a train. The quantity of gas transferred in a given time depends on the number of molecules carried (the number of passengers per train) and the flow rate of the medium (the number of trains completing the journey in the given time).

The second process involved in gas movement is that of diffusion, which depends on gas molecules spreading out from regions where they are close together to less densely occupied regions. Ultimately, diffusion leads to a completely uniform distribution of the molecules concerned. It goes on in gas mixtures and in solution and it is a very much slower process than the bulk transport mechanisms (convection). Diffusion is responsible for transferring the respiratory gases between air and blood, or water and blood, within the gas exchanger and, at the tissue level, between blood and the enzyme systems inside cells. In very small animals diffusion may be the only process necessary to transport gases over the entire distance between the environment and cells.

In many ways, diffusion is analogous to the transfer made by the individual travelers on foot from bus to train or from train to house during the course of a complete journey. The travel analogy is less than perfect, however, because the mechanisms which determine the direction of movement are different. People travel in order to arrive at some definite destination even though they may depart from a poorly populated, rural situation and arrive at a crowded sports stadium. The respiratory gases, on the other hand, rely on simple physical principles so that they always move from regions where there are high levels of each gas to those where the levels are lower. A convenient way to determine the tendency to move is to measure what is called the partial pressure of a gas. All gases behave as though they move down partial pressure gradients, that is, from regions of high to regions of low partial pressure. Clinical and experimental investigations rely heavily on accurate measurement of the partial pressures of respiratory gases in all media and this can now be achieved.

In a gas mixture, the partial pressure of any component gas is the pressure that would be measured in a closed, constant-volume system if all the other component gases were somehow removed. The total pressure exerted by a mixture is the sum of all the partial pressures contributed by the component gases, each contribution depending simply on the percentage of the total volume occupied by that gas.

Thus, inspired air, expired gas and alveolar gas (the gas found in the final divisions of the mammalian lung) are all mixtures of three main gases—oxygen, nitrogen and carbon dioxide. There is an additional gas, water vapor, which behaves exactly like other gases and has a partial pressure depending on the humidity and the temperature. After allowing for water vapor, the partial pressures of component gases can be simply

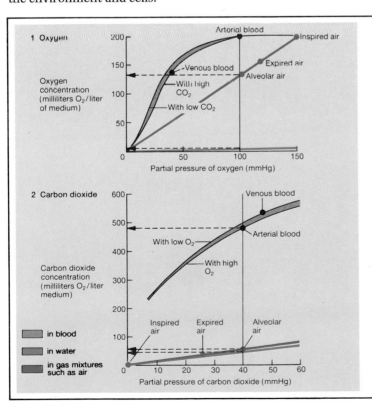

Partial Pressures of Gases and Percentage Composition in the Mammalian Lung

Atmospheric pressure is assumed to be 1 atmosphere (= 760mm Hg), water vapor pressure to be 47mm Hg (the value at 100 percent humidity and 37°C/98.7°F in all cases).

		Partial Pressure (mm Hg)	Percentage Composition by Volume
Inspired Air	Nitrogen and other inert components	563.1	78.98
	Oxygen	149.7	20.99
	Carbon dioxide	0.2	0.03
	Total	**713.0**	**100.0**
	Water vapor pressure	47.0	
	Atmospheric pressure	**760.0**	
Expired Air	Nitrogen and other inert components	568.3	79.7
	Oxygen	118.4	16.6
	Carbon dioxide	26.4	3.7
	Total	**713.0**	**100.0**
	Water vapor pressure	47.0	
	Atmospheric pressure	**760.0**	
Alveolar Air	Nitrogen and other inert components	570.4	80.0
	Oxygen	102.7	14.4
	Carbon dioxide	39.9	5.6
	Total	**713.0**	**100.0**
	Water vapor pressure	47.0	
	Atmospheric pressure	**760.0**	

calculated as percentages of the total pressure remaining.

When gas mixtures are in contact with liquids such as water, body fluids or blood, the component gases will diffuse into or out of the liquids depending on the direction of the partial pressure gradients until, at equilibrium, the partial pressure of each gas is the same in the liquid as it is in the gas phase with which it is in contact. For example, in the alveoli, which are the thin-walled structures in the mammalian lung through which gas exchange occurs, oxygen diffuses from alveolar gas into blood and carbon dioxide diffuses in the reverse direction. Venous blood, coming from the tissues and flowing through the lung, is thereby converted to arterial blood in which the gas partial pressures are about the same as those found in alveolar gas. In fact, the equilibrium between alveolar gas and arterial blood is never quite complete, especially with respect to oxygen, because there are slight inefficiencies in the way the lung works. These inefficiencies are greater in diseased lungs. After the arterial blood has been pumped by the heart from lungs

◄▼ **Simple unventilated lungs** occur in a number of animal groups, including the land snails BELOW. These animals are too large for gases to diffuse in and out of the body surface, but they are small enough that no pumping mechanism is required to get the gases to and from the lungs. Shown LEFT is a tropical snail *Strophoscheilus oblongus*; note that the tentacles are kept erect by blood pressure.

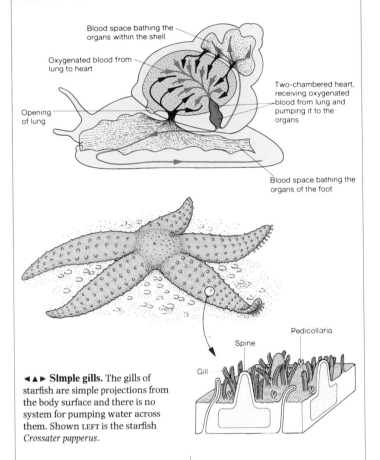

Blood space bathing the organs within the shell

Oxygenated blood from lung to heart

Opening of lung

Two-chambered heart, receiving oxygenated blood from lung and pumping it to the organs

Blood space bathing the organs of the foot

◄▲► **Simple gills.** The gills of starfish are simple projections from the body surface and there is no system for pumping water across them. Shown LEFT is the starfish *Crossater papperus*.

Pedicollaria

Spine

Gill

▼ **Because they are thin and flat,** aquatic flatworms, such as this *Pseudoceros* species, are able to exchange respiratory gases through their body surface and do not require lungs and a blood circulation system.

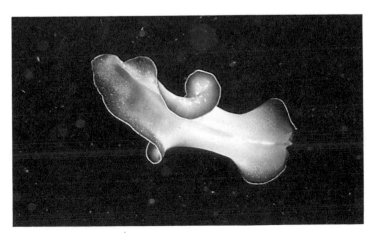

to tissues the reverse process occurs. The oxygen diffuses out of the blood because the partial pressure of oxygen in the cells where oxygen is used is lower than it is in the blood. Carbon dioxide diffuses in the opposite direction because it is constantly being produced in the cells and the direction of its partial pressure gradient is from cells to blood. Thus, arterial blood is converted to venous blood.

Diffusion tends to proceed, therefore, until the partial pressure of a respiratory gas is the same throughout a gas mixture and any liquids in contact with that mixture. However, the actual amounts of oxygen or of carbon dioxide (that is, the number of molecules) that are then present in a given volume of gas or liquid are quite different.

There are important consequences of the difference in oxygen capacities of water and air. Because water contains much less oxygen than air does, an aquatic animal will need to breathe larger quantities of water than its terrestrial counterpart will need to breathe of air, to satisfy its oxygen requirements. In fact water, with its low oxygen capacity, high density and very low rates of gas diffusion, is a very difficult medium in which to breathe and exchange respiratory gases, as compared to air. Aquatic animals show many special adaptations of their respiratory organs to overcome these difficulties.

Why are Gills, Lungs and Blood Needed?

In small animals, the supply of oxygen and the removal of carbon dioxide can be satisfactorily maintained by the process of diffusion because the body surface is relatively large compared to the body volume, and none of the metabolizing regions is far from the surface. As animals increase in size, the volume of metabolizing material (proportional to the cube of the linear dimensions) increases more rapidly than the surface area (proportional to the square of the linear dimensions), so that, eventually, the body surface alone can no longer satisfy the requirements for gas exchange. In addition, some parts of the metabolizing organism become more and more remote from the gas exchanging surface and diffusion distances within the animal's body become very long. Simple calculations show that the oxygen partial pressure of the external medium would have to be impossibly large to serve the realistic oxygen requirements of roughly spherical animals with a radius greater than 1mm. Some animals avoid these limitations if their body is a series of thin, folded sheets (as in sea anemones) or if they are very flat, as in flatworms.

The problems caused by the restricted surface area of large and more solidly constructed animals have been overcome by the development of specially expanded regions of the body to form gas exchangers such as gills or lungs. In general, gills are found in aquatic animals and are outward expansions of the body surface. They vary in structure from simple cylindrical or flap-like protuberances seen in worms and starfish to the complicated and finely divided systems found in crabs, lobsters, octopus and fish. In air, the finest divisions of a gill surface tend to collapse because of lack of the support offered by water. Thus, the overall gill area is reduced and the gas exchange system becomes ineffective. Air-breathers have developed lungs, which are infoldings within the body and so are supported by surrounding tissues. They are found in terrestrial animals such as land snails, amphibians, reptiles, birds and mammals. At their simplest, lungs are sac-like invaginations with walls that are not folded although they are well supplied with blood vessels. In many animals the exchange area is greatly increased, as it is in the mammal, for example, by an enormous expansion of the lung surface at the end of a complicated but highly organized system of branching tubes.

In many gills and lungs, particularly the more advanced and finely divided types, active ventilation is necessary. Water or air is pumped over the exchanging surface by breathing movements executed by a wide variety of different mechanisms. Pumping is necessary because gills are often protected within gill chambers with restricted openings, and lungs have even more restricted connections with the environment because of their infolded structure. In both cases, diffusion processes would not be adequate to bring oxygen to, and carry carbon dioxide from, the exchanging surface.

The second great problem in large animals, that of limitations to diffusion within the bulk of the body itself, is usually overcome by using blood as a gas-transporting medium even in animals with quite simple gas exchangers.

The performance of most gas exchangers depends on both an effective ventilation with air or water and an equally effective perfusion with blood flow. In air-breathing animals, the ratio of volume of air breathed to blood pumped is very roughly one to one. In aquatic animals, however, where the oxygen concentration of the environment is so much lower, the ratio of water breathed to blood pumped increases to 10 to one or to even higher values. An important feature of the way in which gas exchange and transport systems work is that extraction of the oxygen from air or water passing through the exchanger or from blood passing through the tissues is never total. Expired air or water still contains quite a lot of oxygen, as does venous blood. It is the difference in gas concentrations between inspired and expired medium, or between arterial and venous blood that, together with the rate of flow, determines how much oxygen or carbon dioxide is exchanged and transported.

If an animal remains for some time in a steady state, either

of rest or of activity, an equilibrium is quickly established in which the reactions involved in energy production in the cells consume the same amount of oxygen and produce the same amount of carbon dioxide as that which is exchanged in the gills or lungs. As an example, the diagram gives a set of values for a resting, 70kg (155lb) man. Physiologists prefer to study such steady state situations because the relationships are simple and relatively easy to investigate. Unfortunately, they are seldom seen in nature because most animals are more or less active for most of their waking lives. Indeed, the cellular needs for

▲ **External gills** of the mudpuppy (*Necturus maculosus*).

▼ **Gas exchange in humans**—diagrammatic representation of the gas exchange and gas transfer system. The values are typical of a resting 70g (155lb) man. The blood is actively pumped around the body from gas exchanger to cells and back. Thus, diffusion pathways are restricted to very short distances, either between external medium and blood in the gills or lungs, and between blood and cells in the tissues.

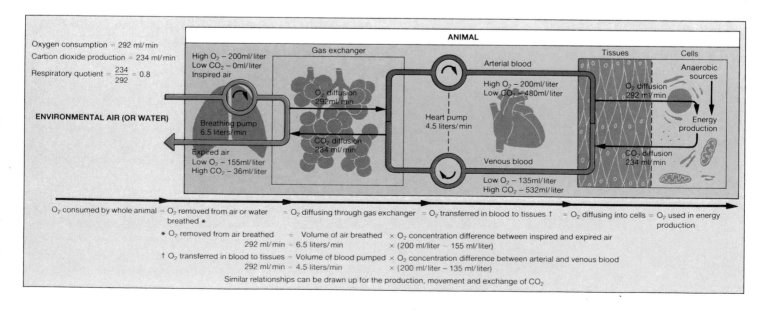

Oxygen consumption = 292 ml/min
Carbon dioxide production = 234 ml/min

Respiratory quotient = $\frac{234}{292}$ = 0.8

ENVIRONMENTAL AIR (OR WATER)

ANIMAL

Gas exchanger

High O₂ – 200ml/liter
Low CO₂ – 0ml/liter
Inspired air

Breathing pump
6.5 liters/min

O₂ diffusion
292ml/min

Expired air
Low O₂ – 155ml/liter
High CO₂ – 36ml/liter

CO₂ diffusion
234 ml/min

Arterial blood

High O₂ – 200ml/liter
Low CO₂ – 480ml/liter

Heart pump
4.5 liters/min

Venous blood

Low O₂ – 135ml/liter
High CO₂ – 532ml/liter

Tissues   Cells

Anaerobic sources

O₂ diffusion
292 ml/min

Energy production

CO₂ diffusion
234 ml/min

O₂ consumed by whole animal = O₂ removed from air or water breathed * = O₂ diffusing through gas exchanger = O₂ transferred in blood to tissues † = O₂ diffusing into cells = O₂ used in energy production

* O₂ removed from air breathed = Volume of air breathed × O₂ concentration difference between inspired and expired air
292 ml/min = 6.5 liters/min × (200 ml/liter – 155 ml/liter)

† O₂ transferred in blood to tissues = Volume of blood pumped × O₂ concentration difference between arterial and venous blood
292 ml/min = 4.5 liters/min × (200 ml/liter – 135 ml/liter)

Similar relationships can be drawn up for the production, movement and exchange of CO₂

GAS EXCHANGE IN WATER – GILLS

By use of many types of gills, aquatic animals have solved the problems of gas exchange in water. Shown below are some of the types that have evolved.

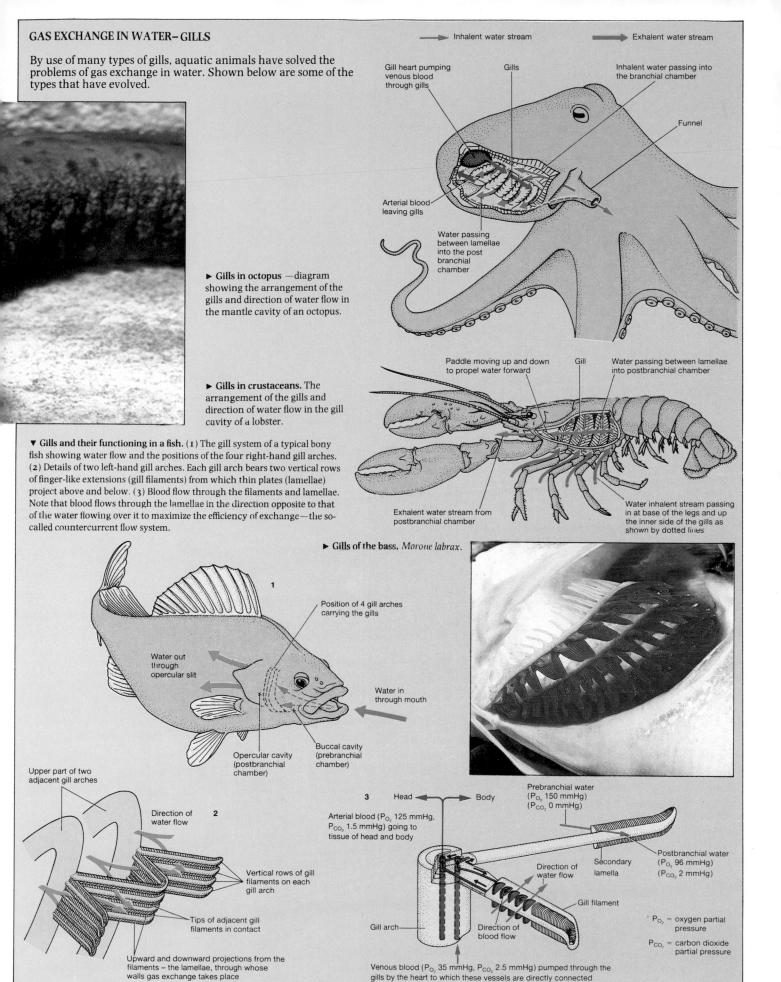

Inhalent water stream ➡️   Exhalent water stream ➡️

Gill heart pumping venous blood through gills

Gills

Inhalent water passing into the branchial chamber

Funnel

Arterial blood leaving gills

Water passing between lamellae into the post branchial chamber

► **Gills in octopus** —diagram showing the arrangement of the gills and direction of water flow in the mantle cavity of an octopus.

► **Gills in crustaceans.** The arrangement of the gills and direction of water flow in the gill cavity of a lobster.

Paddle moving up and down to propel water forward

Gill

Water passing between lamellae into postbranchial chamber

Exhalent water stream from postbranchial chamber

Water inhalent stream passing in at base of the legs and up the inner side of the gills as shown by dotted lines

▼ **Gills and their functioning in a fish.** (1) The gill system of a typical bony fish showing water flow and the positions of the four right-hand gill arches. (2) Details of two left-hand gill arches. Each gill arch bears two vertical rows of finger-like extensions (gill filaments) from which thin plates (lamellae) project above and below. (3) Blood flow through the filaments and lamellae. Note that blood flows through the lamellae in the direction opposite to that of the water flowing over it to maximize the efficiency of exchange—the so-called countercurrent flow system.

► **Gills of the bass,** *Morone labrax.*

Position of 4 gill arches carrying the gills

1

Water out through opercular slit

Water in through mouth

Opercular cavity (postbranchial chamber)

Buccal cavity (prebranchial chamber)

Upper part of two adjacent gill arches

Direction of water flow

2

Vertical rows of gill filaments on each gill arch

Tips of adjacent gill filaments in contact

Upward and downward projections from the filaments – the lamellae, through whose walls gas exchange takes place

3   Head ← → Body

Arterial blood (P_{O_2} 125 mmHg, P_{CO_2} 1.5 mmHg) going to tissue of head and body

Prebranchial water (P_{O_2} 150 mmHg) (P_{CO_2} 0 mmHg)

Direction of water flow

Secondary lamella

Postbranchial water (P_{O_2} 96 mmHg) (P_{CO_2} 2 mmHg)

Gill filament

Gill arch

Direction of blood flow

Venous blood (P_{O_2} 35 mmHg, P_{CO_2} 2.5 mmHg) pumped through the gills by the heart to which these vessels are directly connected

P_{O_2} = oxygen partial pressure

P_{CO_2} = carbon dioxide partial pressure

energy, in some circumstances, can outstrip the capacity of exchange and transport systems to supply oxygen. Anaerobic energy sources (using no oxygen) then become important as they do, for example, in muscles during very strenuous exercise. Anaerobiosis causes the build-up of what is called an oxygen debt with the accumulation of byproducts, such as lactic acid, in both cells and blood stream. These substances are removed by oxidation and the debt is paid off when the high level of activity comes to an end and the supply systems are able to cope again with the needs of oxidative metabolism.

Gas Exchange in Water

The difficulties inherent in aquatic gas exchange are overcome in most advanced gill systems, such as those of octopus, lobsters and fish, by a number of interesting adaptations. The first of these is the development of pumping systems to produce a more-or-less continuous water flow over the gills in one direction, with water being taken into the system at one opening and leaving at another. This means that energy is not expended in accelerating and decelerating considerable quantities of water which, being a relatively dense medium, is difficult to pump through the gills. The pumping mechanisms range from

▲ ► **High flyers.** The unique respiratory system of birds enables them to respire at the very high rates needed for flight. Instead of consisting of the usual pockets (alveoli), the lungs have tubes (parabronchi) running through them. The large air sacs are not directly involved in gas exchange, but serve as reservoirs for the air that is pumped through the lungs. Whooper swans (*Cygnus cygnus*) ABOVE have been seen at high altitudes, where an efficient respiratory system is particularly necessary because of the low levels of oxygen.

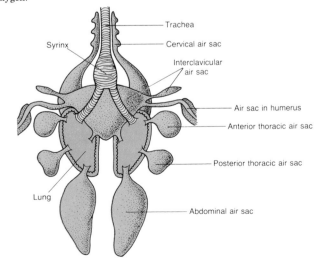

the pulsations of the muscular walls of a chamber called the mantle cavity in octopus, through the beating of a paddle-like appendage in lobsters to the rhythmic expansion and contraction of the mouth and gill cavities in bony fish.

These breathing movements bring the water stream into close contact with the finely divided surfaces of the gills. In fact, the gills present an almost continuous barrier between the inhalant (prebranchial) and exhalant (postbranchial) streams, so that water has to pass through the gaps between the lamellae, the finest divisions of the gills, where gas exchanges actually take place. Thus, diffusion distances for gases dissolved in the water are kept to an absolute minimum, overcoming the difficulties posed by the very slow diffusion of gases in solution.

A final adaptation, seen in many gill systems, is an arrangement of blood vessels which ensures that blood flow within the gill lamellae occurs in a direction opposite to the flow of water around their outer surfaces. This counter-current system makes for a more complete exchange of gases between the lamellae and the environment because oxygen and carbon dioxide partial pressure gradients are maintained along the whole length of the exchange surface. The effect of this arrangement is that the arterial blood leaves the gill with a higher

oxygen partial pressure than that of the exhalant water stream. In other types of exchange system, such as the mammalian lung, the oxygen partial pressure of arterial blood can, at best, come to equal that of alveolar air and is always substantially lower than that of expired air.

Gas Exchange in Air

Air is of much lower density than water and contains much more oxygen so that the design of lungs and their ventilating mechanisms is quite different from that of gills. In general, continuous and unidirectional ventilation is not necessary. Air is usually pumped in and out of the same opening to the environment in an alternating, so-called tidal, flow. In addition, diffusion rates are much higher for gas mixtures than they are for gases in solution. The ventilation stream does not then have to come into close contact with the exchanging surface. In fact, during normal breathing in the mammalian lung, no air movement can be detected in the final divisions of the complex series of branching tubes, such is the vast increase in total cross-sectional area as one passes from tracheae, through bronchi and bronchioles, to alveolar ducts. Diffusion is the dominant mechanism responsible for moving oxygen and carbon dioxide between the bronchioles and alveoli.

Even in lungs, the final stages of exchange, between the moist lining of the alveoli and the hemoglobin situated within the erythrocytes (red blood cells), take place with the respiratory gases in solution in tissue fluid. Diffusion rates will be very low and so the barrier between alveolar gas and blood needs to be reduced to the minimum, even though the alveoli and the pulmonary capillaries are each lined by a layer of cells. The extraordinary reduction in the thickness of these layers, and in the overall distances for diffusion in solution, presents some unique problems for the maintenance and support of the internal structure of lungs, which are insubstantial and fragile structures that have many of the characteristics of a collection of small bubbles. The presence of material known as surfactant, in the thin layer of fluid lining the alveoli, is important in stabilizing the alveolar structure of all vertebrates. Surfactant has some detergent-like properties and lowers the surface tension of the alveolar lining, so that the small alveoli do not empty into the larger ones as would happen with a collection of bubbles in close contact with one another. The absence of surfactant in premature babies causes the respiratory difficulties from which they often suffer (commonly called respiratory distress syndrome).

Although a few lungs, such as those of land snails, rely entirely on the process of diffusion for gas renewal, most others, including all the vertebrate lungs, are actively ventilated. The mechanisms for doing this are varied. The most primitive, seen in amphibians, are based on pumping movements of the buccal cavity which is the space just inside the mouth containing the openings of both nostrils and the glottis. The buccal pump is almost certainly an evolutionary development of the gill-ventilating mechanism seen in fish. It depends on up and down movements of the buccal floor which, with appropriately timed movements of the nostrils and glottis, force gas into or allow gas to escape from the lungs. More advanced mechanisms for ventilation rely on changing lung volumes directly by moving structures around the lungs themselves, rather than by using an anatomically distinct buccal pump. Turtles and tortoises, with bodies that are enclosed in fairly rigid boxes, move regions of the limbs and pectoral and pelvic girdles in order to change pressures around the lungs. Most other reptiles and all mammals use a costal pump, however, in which the rib cage is swung in and out to change lung volume and so cause inspiration and expiration. The mammals also use a diaphragmatic pump. The diaphragm is a dome-shaped sheet of muscular tissue below the lung. When the muscle contracts, the dome flattens increasing the lung volume, causing air to enter the lung (inspiration). When the muscle relaxes the lung volume decreases and air is expelled from the lung (expiration).

Bird lungs are different from those of other air-breathing vertebrates. They are relatively solid structures, through which run a large number of parallel, cylindrical tubes known as parabronchi. Perforations in the walls of the parabronchi open into air capillaries surrounded by the pulmonary blood capillaries and it is through these very thin capillary walls that the gas exchange takes place. Such a structure can change in shape and volume only slightly. Breathing movements (largely of the breast bone or sternum) make air move through the system

► **Giraffe browsing.** Giraffes (*Giraffa camelopardalis*) need exceptionally high blood pressure to get blood up the neck to the brain.

by altering the volumes of a number of thin-walled air sacs which are connected to the bronchi. The pathway that the air follows through the total system has recently been worked out. The evidence suggests that it takes two breathing cycles to move a body of gas through the complete pathway. The mechanisms underlying this complicated system are not fully understood, nor are the reasons for the evolution of a system which differs so markedly from that of mammals entirely clear. Some birds, however, are capable of quite extraordinary feats of endurance and of flight at high altitudes where atmospheric pressure (and, therefore, the partial pressure of oxygen) is extremely low. Well-authenticated radar and visual observations have recorded a flock of Whooper swans migrating from Iceland to Britain at an altitude above 8,200 m (27,000ft), and a flock of curlews has been seen at 10,000 m (33,000ft). The summit of Everest at 8,848 m (29,105ft) is only just within the altitude range of a few, exceptional people breathing air without the assistance of breathing apparatus.

Gas Exchange and Transport in Insects

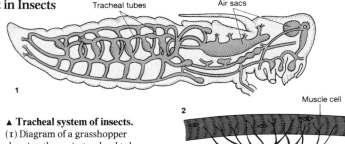

Tracheal tubes   Air sacs

One large and very successful group of terrestrial animals, the insects, relies on a system of gas exchange and gas transport which is fundamentally different from that seen in the majority of other animals. The system consists of many small, gas-filled tubes, called tracheae, that branch throughout the body. The tracheae are supported by rings of thickened cuticle and are connected to the outside air by a restricted number of small openings, the spiracles. At the other end of the branching system, the tracheae eventually divide to form the very finest, unsupported tubes, called tracheoles, about 0.001mm in diameter, that carry gas directly to the individual cells of the body. Insect gas exchange is, therefore, completely independent of a circulatory system for internal gas transport.

The ends of the tracheoles, which can even extend into the interior of some large, active cells, such as those of muscles, are lined with a small amount of liquid. Thus, the respiratory gases are in solution during the final stage of the gas exchange process, over the very short distance between tracheoles and cells. Throughout the rest

▲ **Tracheal system of insects.** (1) Diagram of a grasshopper showing the main tracheal tubes and air sacs. (2) Detail of final divisions of a tracheal tube. The walls of the finest branches do not contain supporting rings.

▼ **Spiracles.** Air enters an insect's body through small pores called spiracles. Those of the Pine hawkmoth (*Hyloicus pinastris*) larva are bright orange.

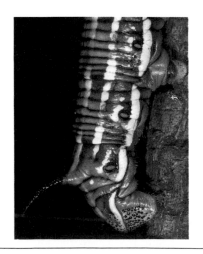

Muscle cell

Fluid filled region of tracheoles

Tracheolar cell

Air filled region of tracheoles

End of tracheal branch with thickened supporting rings

of the system, gas renewal depends upon the diffusion of respiratory gases in the gas phase. Measurements based on a moth caterpillar, weighing 3.5g and about 6cm (2.4in) long, show that the average length of a tracheal tube from spiracle to cells is 6mm (0.24in), and the cross-sectional area of all the tracheae added together is 6.7sq mm (0.01sq in). The oxygen requirements of the animal (0.31ml/g/h) could be met by diffusion alone in a system of this size with a partial pressure gradient as small as

10mm mercury. If these calculations are soundly based, the partial pressure of oxygen in the cells of even quite large insects will be higher than that found in mammals.

In some of the larger insects, the major tracheal tubes are actively ventilated by breathing movements made, in the main, by the abdomen. These can be seen quite clearly if an animal, such as a locust, is observed closely. The movements alternately compress and expand a series of air sacs, which are simply thin-walled expansions of the tracheal tubes, so forcing air in and out of the system. Opening and closing of the spiracles are often synchronized with the breathing movements so that, in some cases, a directional flow of air can be produced—in at some spiracles and out at others.

Even though the tracheal system is very efficient, there is no doubt that it is one factor which imposes a limit to body size in insects. Insects seem unable to attain lengths greater than 15cm (6in) because of problems of ventilation, diffusion and structural design within the tracheal system—a fact not often appreciated by some writers of science fiction!

How Fast is Oxygen Consumed?

The metabolic rate of an animal and, therefore, the rate at which it consumes oxygen is subject to a number of internal and external influences. Obviously, the availability of oxygen is very important and can become a limiting factor for air breathers at high altitude and for water breathers in shaded, tropical pools or in polluted rivers and streams where oxygen levels are very low. Oxygen consumption also depends on the size and the type of animal as well as on the level of activity at the time the consumption is measured. Thus, the oxygen consumption *per gram* of a very small animal, such as a shrew, weighing 2·5g is 2·58ml/g/h, that is 22 times greater than that of a cow weighing 600kg which consumes 0·114ml/g/h. Warm-blooded animals, or homeotherms, consume more oxygen than cold-blooded animals, poikilotherms, even when they are at the same temperature. For example, a resting lizard, at 30°C (86°F) and weighing about 1kg (2·2lb), needs 0·07ml/g/h of oxygen whereas a bird of the same size consumes 0·79ml/g/h. Maximal levels of activity cause a five- to 12-fold increase above the resting levels in both animals, (lizard to 0·4ml/g/h and bird to 9·49ml/g/h). The maximal rates of oxygen consumption in cold-blooded animals are clearly very modest and would provide for equally modest levels of activity. It is not surprising, therefore, that these animals rely extensively on anaerobic energy production. They accumulate considerable oxygen debts during periods of activity and take several hours to recover afterwards. Recovery in warm-blooded animals, on the other hand, is much more rapid.

Except in circumstances in which anaerobiosis contributes significantly to energy production, increased metabolic activity of all types, particularly that associated with exercise, results in closely regulated changes in the depth and rate of breathing movements as well as in heart rate and the volume of blood pumped per beat. In the most advanced gas exchange systems these changes match the increased oxygen consumption in a precise fashion. The initiation of breathing movements and their control is an important function of groups of neurons situated in the central nervous system; in vertebrate animals, for example, these neurons are located in the medulla, the most posterior part of the brain. Information about the partial pressure levels for oxygen and carbon dioxide in the blood and about activity in the muscles is sent to the respiratory control center from sense organs in the blood and tissues. Neurons controlling heart output receive similar sensory information. Breathing air or water containing high levels of carbon dioxide or low levels of oxygen often stimulates greater ventilation volumes and changes in blood flow.   GS

Blood Circulation

The processes of life require substances to be moved from one part of the body to another. Oxygen must be brought to the tissues for use in respiration, and carbon dioxide and other waste products must be removed. The products of digestion must be carried from the gut to other parts of the body, where they are to be stored or used for growth or metabolism. If the distances are small enough, these movements can occur fast enough by diffusion: random molecular movements will make the substances diffuse away from parts of the body where they are being produced, and towards parts where they are being used up. Thus, flatworms are no more than 1mm (0.04in) thick, although they may be several centimeters long and wide. No part of the body is more than 0.5mm (0.02in) from the surface, and oxygen and carbon dioxide move between the tissues and the environment entirely by diffusion. The gut has branches reaching all parts of the body, so none of the tissues is more than a fraction of a millimeter from the nearest gut branch, and all of them receive adequate supplies of foodstuffs by diffusion. Flatworms need no special system for transporting substances around the body, and have not got one.

Most larger animals need to move substances over longer distances. Most of the tissues are too far from the body surface (or from the lungs or gills, in animals that possess them) to get enough oxygen by diffusion. Most tissues are too far from the gut to receive foodstuffs fast enough by diffusion. Such animals have evolved systems of blood vessels in which blood circulates, carrying oxygen, foodstuffs and waste products either in solution or (in the case of oxygen) combined with respiratory pigments (see box).

Blood is pumped through these systems by hearts. Most animals have just one heart but cephalopod mollusks (squids and so on) have three and annelid worms have many. The simplest kind of heart is a tube with muscular walls which squeeze blood along by peristaltic waves of contraction, just as food is moved along the intestine. Sea squirts have hearts like this and can pump the blood in either direction: they pump it in one direction for several minutes, and then reverse the flow. The hearts of other animals pump in one direction only, and have valves that prevent reverse flow. The hearts of mollusks and fish have two main chambers, a relatively thin-walled atrium (or auricle) and a more muscular ventricle. The atrium contracts first, squeezing blood into the ventricle which then contracts, driving the blood around the body. Amphibians and reptiles have two atria which discharge into a single ventricle, and birds and mammals have two atria and two ventricles.

There are three kinds of blood vessel: arteries, veins and capillaries. Arteries carry blood away from the heart and veins bring it back to the heart. Thus, arteries carry blood at high pressure and veins at relatively low pressure. Accordingly, arteries generally have relatively thick walls and veins have relatively thin ones. The larger arteries of vertebrates have elastin (a protein with rubber-like properties) in their walls. They swell at each heart beat, stretched by the pressure of the blood that is forced into them, and shrink again by elastic recoil between heart beats. This helps to smooth the flow of blood, keeping blood flowing through the smaller blood vessels throughout the heart beat cycle. The capillaries are the finest blood vessels, with diameters of only a few micrometers and walls just one cell thick.

The arteries and veins form branching systems, reaching all parts of the body. The capillaries (of animals which possess them) connect the finest branches of the arteries to the finest branches of the veins, completing the circuit back to the heart. Oxygen, foodstuffs and waste products diffuse into or out of the capillaries, through their thin walls. Oxygen diffuses into the blood in the capillaries of the gills or lungs, and out again from the capillaries of the tissues that use it. Foodstuffs diffuse into

BLOOD CIRCULATION

The Color of Gas Transport!

The capacities of different types of blood to carry the respiratory gases, oxygen and carbon dioxide, are enormously increased by the presence of blood pigments such as the hemoglobins of vertebrates and the hemocyanins found in some mollusks and crustaceans. The point can be illustrated by comparing mammalian whole blood which is made up of both plasma and red and white blood cells with plasma alone. The graph (1) shows the oxygen concentrations to be found in blood and in plasma over a range of partial pressures from 0 to 100mm of mercury. Clearly, at any particular oxygen partial pressure, much more oxygen is contained in whole blood than in plasma, and the difference is due entirely to the hemoglobin in the blood cells. The graph also shows that the amount of oxygen which is carried in blood does not increase in a linear fashion as the partial pressure rises, as it does in the plasma, for example, but follows an S-shaped curve. This relationship between oxygen concentration and partial pressure is often referred to as

consists of a complicated, folded chain of amino acids attached to an iron-containing group of atoms called heme. The heme groups are the parts of this very complicated structure that actually react with oxygen, each heme being capable of combining with one molecule of oxygen.

The S shape of the dissociation curve suggested to the early investigators that interactions occurred between heme groups. Deoxygenated hemoglobin appears to be reluctant to take up oxygen at first and the dissociation curve rises slowly. But then, as oxygen combines with one heme group in the hemoglobin molecule, the appetite for oxygen grows. The dissociation curve steepens and subsequent combinations are more easily achieved but the curve finally flattens out again as the hemoglobin molecules tend to be fully saturated with oxygen.

When the structure of the hemoglobin molecule was worked out, it was disturbing to find that none of the four heme groups that were supposed to be interacting with one another was actually in contact with

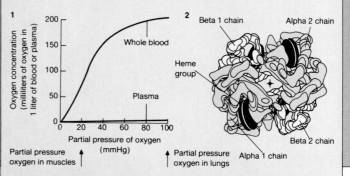

the oxygen dissociation curve of blood.

Studies of the three-dimensional structure of the hemoglobin molecule (2) using X-ray crystallography, have provided some exciting explanations of what happens when oxygen and other compounds combine with hemoglobin, and they help to explain the S-shaped oxygen dissociation curve. A complete molecule of hemoglobin is made up of four interlocking subunits, each of which

any other. It was then realized that the whole protein molecule must alter slightly in shape, the structural relationships of the four subunits must vary, as oxygen is taken up or released. The hemoglobin molecule is thought to change from a T (tense) structure when it is deoxygenated to an R (relaxed) structure when it is oxygenated. It is more difficult for oxygen to penetrate the hemoglobin and combine with the heme groups when the molecule is in the T state.

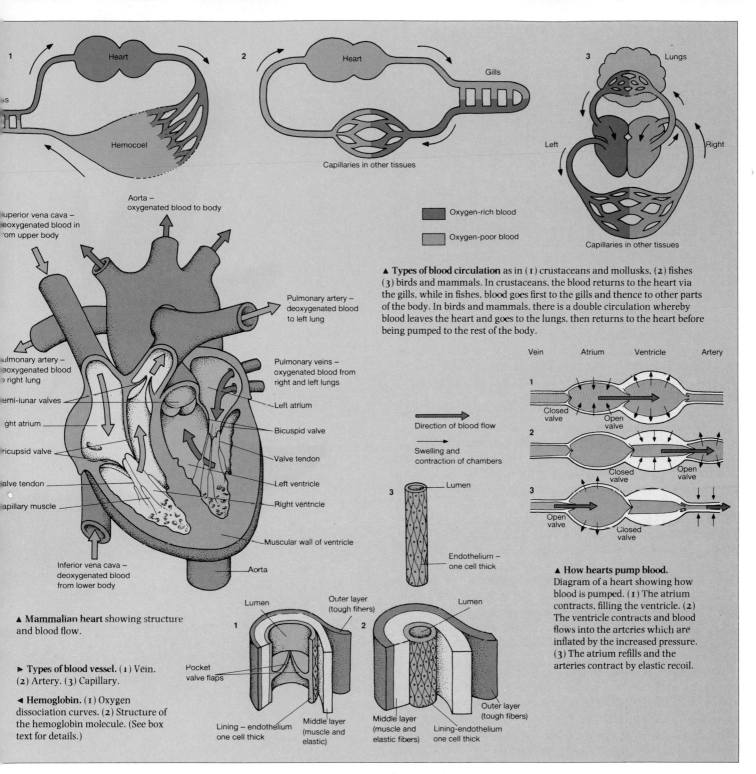

1 Heart

Hemocoel

2 Heart

Gills

Capillaries in other tissues

3 Lungs

Left

Right

Capillaries in other tissues

Oxygen-rich blood

Oxygen-poor blood

▲ **Types of blood circulation** as in (1) crustaceans and mollusks, (2) fishes (3) birds and mammals. In crustaceans, the blood returns to the heart via the gills, while in fishes, blood goes first to the gills and thence to other parts of the body. In birds and mammals, there is a double circulation whereby blood leaves the heart and goes to the lungs, then returns to the heart before being pumped to the rest of the body.

Superior vena cava – deoxygenated blood in from upper body

Aorta – oxygenated blood to body

Pulmonary artery – deoxygenated blood to left lung

Pulmonary artery – deoxygenated blood to right lung

Pulmonary veins – oxygenated blood from right and left lungs

Semi-lunar valves

Right atrium

Tricuspid valve

Valve tendon

Capillary muscle

Left atrium

Bicuspid valve

Valve tendon

Left ventricle

Right ventricle

Inferior vena cava – deoxygenated blood from lower body

Aorta

Muscular wall of ventricle

▲ **Mammalian heart** showing structure and blood flow.

► **Types of blood vessel.** (1) Vein. (2) Artery. (3) Capillary.

◄ **Hemoglobin.** (1) Oxygen dissociation curves. (2) Structure of the hemoglobin molecule. (See box text for details.)

Direction of blood flow

Swelling and contraction of chambers

3 Lumen

Endothelium – one cell thick

Vein   Atrium   Ventricle   Artery

1 Closed valve   Open valve

2 Closed valve   Open valve

3 Open valve   Closed valve

▲ **How hearts pump blood.** Diagram of a heart showing how blood is pumped. (1) The atrium contracts, filling the ventricle. (2) The ventricle contracts and blood flows into the arteries which are inflated by the increased pressure. (3) The atrium refills and the arteries contract by elastic recoil.

1 Lumen   Pocket valve flaps   Lining – endothelium one cell thick   Middle layer (muscle and elastic)

2 Lumen   Middle layer (muscle and elastic fibers)   Lining-endothelium one cell thick   Outer layer (tough fibers)

the capillaries of the gut wall, and out again from the capillaries of other tissues. The arteries of arthropods and of gastropod and bivalve mollusks do not end in capillaries, but open into blood-filled cavities called hemocoels, which are the main body cavities of these animals.

In insects the blood circulation simply passes through the heart to the hemocoel and back to the heart. Oxygen travels to the tissues along the air-filled tubes called tracheae (see box), and the blood is not involved in carrying it. Most other animals with blood systems have gills or lungs, and carry oxygen in the blood. In crustaceans and most mollusks the arteries send branches to all parts of the body, but open into hemocoels or spaces between cells. The blood returns from the hemocoel to the heart by way of the gills. In fish it goes to the gills and

then to other parts of the body, before returning to the heart.

Mammals and birds have a double circulation. Blood leaving the right ventricle goes to the lungs, where it takes up oxygen and releases carbon dioxide. It is brought back to the left atrium, passes through to the left ventricle and is driven out on a second journey, to all the tissues except the lungs. There it releases oxygen and takes up carbon dioxide. It is brought back to the right atrium, and the cycle begins again. A very similar double circulation occurs in reptiles, although their hearts are not completely divided into left and right halves. Blood from both atria passes through the single ventricle, but remarkably little mixing occurs. Most of the blood from the right atrium goes to the lungs, and most of the blood from the left atrium goes to the other tissues.   RMcNA

Living in Water but Breathing Air
Diving animals

Many air-breathing animals live in, and under, water and so have to modify their breathing behavior quite considerably. Small insects, such as mosquito larvae, can exchange gas at the water surface by means of a single spiracular tube, opening at the tip of the abdomen. Beetles, like *Dytiscus*, and bugs, such as the water boatman (*Notonecta*), attach air bubbles to some part of the body surface and take them down below the water surface as oxygen stores. Some insects, such as dragonfly larvae, develop gills as expansions on the ends of their tracheal tubes that are still filled with gas and which exchange oxygen and carbon dioxide with environmental water through the thin surface of gills.

All classes of air-breathing vertebrates have well-adapted diving animals among their members. Aquatic reptiles, such as crocodiles, turtles, marine iguanas, and sea snakes, birds such as penguins, divers, grebes, cormorants and ducks, and mammals such as whales, dolphins, otters, seals and walruses, are all able to survive long periods under water even though their gas exchange is ultimately dependent on breathing air at the surface.

During prolonged dives these very different animals show surprisingly similar responses. The heart slows down, a response called diving bradycardia, and its output of blood falls. In addition, blood vessels in most of the body's tissues, such as muscles and the alimentary canal, become smaller in diameter (vasoconstriction) and so reduce or cut off the local blood supply. The consequence of this reduced blood supply is that these tissues have to rely on anaerobiosis and so produce considerable quantities of lactic acid which remain in the tissues until the blood flow is restored after a dive. The vessels of the brain and heart are notable exceptions to the overall vasoconstrictor response. The reduced output from the heart is, therefore, preferentially conveyed to these two vital organs which are extremely vulnerable to oxygen shortage. In this way, the limited stores of oxygen contained in the lungs and blood are conserved for those regions which have the greatest need.

Recent work on birds and mammals suggests that most normal dives do not extend to the stage at which bradycardia is marked and high levels of lactic acid accumulate in the tissues, although all diving animals are capable of extending their dives without difficulty. Some of the performances are extremely impressive. Turtles can remain submerged for several hours and the Weddell seal is capable of dives lasting more than one hour. Some birds, such as penguins and ducks, have been reported to dive for periods up to 10 or 15 minutes. Well-trained men can manage about two minutes of breath-hold diving, although expert pearl divers, such as the female Ama of Korea and Japan, dive for about 45 seconds but with only a 60-second rest between dives. Clearly dive durations will depend enormously on the activity levels under water and these are very difficult to monitor in freely diving animals.

Humans have been able to increase their diving abilities very greatly by taking supplies of gas underwater. However, the continuous breathing of gas at the high pressures found at considerable depths creates problems of its own. High partial pressure of nitrogen causes nitrogen narcosis in which there is lack of concentration and dangerous overconfidence in the diver.

▲▶ **Survival in water**—a selection of animals that depend on air from the atmosphere for their oxygen, but which spend some or all of their lives below water. (1) King penguin (*Aptenodytes patagonicus*); this species often dives beyond 50m (165ft) and rarely as far as 240m (790ft). (2) The diving beetle *Dytiscus marginalis* carries bubbles of air from the surface below its wing cases, from which it can extract oxygen. (3) Mosquito larvae (*Culex* species) exchange gases at the water surface by means of a single spiracular tube which opens at the tip of the abdomen. (4) The larvae of damselflies (*Coenagrion* species) develop gills as expansions at the ends of their tracheal tubes. (5) Yellow-bellied sea snakes (*Pelamis platurus*) are fully air-breathing and must surface periodically. (6) Blue whale (*Balaenoptera musculus*) with throat grooves extended while feeding; whales have relatively small lungs and when they dive much of the air is pushed into the wind pipe and branches where the thick linings slow down gas exchange, which partly alleviates the problem of the "bends." (7) A human and aqualung.

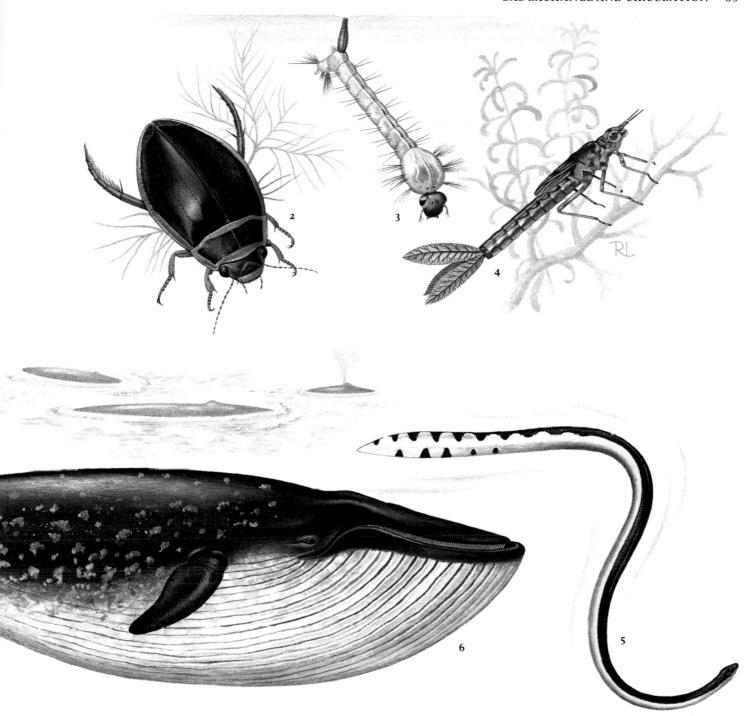

Substituting helium for nitrogen in the gas mixture being breathed can largely overcome this problem. Another difficulty is caused by the reduction in pressure as a diver comes to the surface. This results in gas coming out of solution in tissue fluids and blood, causing bubbles to form and giving rise to decompression sickness, of which the best-known symptom is the muscular pain called the bends. Decompression has to be slow to avoid this complication. A 30 minute dive at 140m (460ft), for example, would require a 10 hour decompression period. To overcome the disproportionate relationship between time spent diving and that spent returning to normal atmospheric pressure, a technique called saturation diving has been introduced. In this, men live at high pressures for several days, being accommodated in special chambers at high gas pressures between shifts spent working in the water. Only at the end of the prolonged period at high pressure are the men and the living chamber brought to the surface for slow decompression.

There has been a great deal of speculation as to why animals do not suffer from nitrogen narcosis and decompression sickness. Some animals dive to considerable depths and return to the surface quickly. For example, Sperm whales have been entangled in marine cables at depths between 800 and 1,100m (2,600–3,600ft) and the Weddell seal makes feeding dives to 600m (2,000ft). At least part of the explanation is that animals take a very limited quantity of gas under water with them and do not breathe continuously as human divers do. Other specializations, such as modifications to blood vessels, are probably involved but they are not well understood.   GS

The Internal Environment

ANIMALS successfully live in an amazing variety of environmental situations. They live in the oceans, in fresh waters, on the land and in the air. They live in polar regions and the tropics, in barren deserts and lush rain forests, high in mountain ranges or in the depths of the sea. They live in scorching heat and biting cold, in near complete dryness or immersed in water. Environmental conditions may change almost continuously and vary dramatically over wide ranges, or they may be nearly constant for many years.

In all of these different situations animals' cells must function properly to keep them alive. The chemical reactions in those cells must proceed reliably, at proper speeds. Evolution has armed animals with a variety of strategies for coping. Some of the most important of these strategies involve the internal environments which animals produce in their bodies for their own cells. Here are described important features of the regulatory patterns, mechanisms and controls occurring in the internal environments of multicellular, multilayered animals. It emphasizes water (the universal biological solvent), substances dissolved in water (solutes), and temperature.

◄ **Coating of sand.** A herd of Northern elephant seals (*Mirounga angustirostris*) protected from the sun's heat by a layer of sand thrown on to their backs.

Tolerance and adaptability of animals to environmental changes. . . Responding to the environment. . . Resistance to changes. . . Acclimation. . . Conforming to change. . . Regulating internal changes. . . Behavioral response to change. . . The body fluids and composition. . . Excretory organs and mechanisms. . . How marine animals cope with salt water. . . The problems of freshwater animals and those that live in estuaries. . . Animals that move from land to water—amphibians. . . How terrestrial animals keep their water. . . The special problems of parasites. . . Body temperature and its regulation. . . Heat from outside—ectotherms. . . Heat from inside—endotherms. . . Varying body temperatures—heterothermy. . . Antifreeze in animals. . .

FREE-LIVING single-celled animals tolerate and resist environmental conditions as varied as those of freezing polar seas and hot springs. It is also apparent, however, that the world contains many places, such as deserts and the atmosphere, in which single-celled animals cannot live but which are occupied by large numbers of multicellular animals, from small insects to mighty elephants. Thus, it seems that one of the important evolutionary advantages of being multicellular is that different cells in different parts of animals may be specialized for different structural purposes, or to carry out different functions. In turn, these specializations allow such animals to live under more varied sets of external conditions.

An important aspect of this greater adaptability is that, in multicellular animals with bodies made up of more than single layers of cells, the internal environments in which the enclosed cells, tissues and organs function are often less extreme or less variable than the outside world. As the structural and functional complexity of animal bodies increases through evolution, this ability to moderate and control important properties of the internal environment also increases.

Tolerance and Adaptability

It becomes obvious why regulation of the internal environment is important to so many kinds of animals if truly extreme external conditions are considered. Living cells cannot function in the complete absence of water or at very low or very high temperatures. Most known kinds of animals operate with their solid tissues containing 60 to 80 percent water, with a limited range of concentrations of substances dissolved in the fluids inside and outside the cells, and at temperatures of 0°C to 45°C (32°F to 113°F).

Animals may still survive, however, and function well in external conditions which are not optimal. Small but substantial minorities of many groups of multicellular animals exist normally and successfully under conditions far outside the apparently optimal ranges, such as burrowing worms in mud flats lacking all oxygen and aquatic insects in salt-saturated desert pools. But, if some specially adapted animals can survive in seemingly hostile conditions, why are the majority of kinds unable to do the same? The answer to this question is still unknown.

Responding to the Environment

Animals faced with variations in their external environments have several options available as responses. Each pattern of response has different effects on conditions in the animals' internal environments. Most groups use combinations of two to several options, depending upon the circumstances. There are basically two types of adaptations: non-genetic (or temporary) ones which occur over time spans much shorter than the life times of animals; and genetic (or permanent) ones which involve successive generations.

Resistance. Different species can tolerate environmental conditions over different ranges of values. More resistant forms tolerate wider ranges (salmon can live both in fresh water and the sea), while less resistant ones tolerate narrower ranges (pike live only in fresh water). Resistances of specific kinds of animals often vary at different stages of their life histories (growing baby birds need almost constant feeding; most adult birds can survive days without food). Different aspects of bodily functions often have different resistances (reproduction is usually much less tolerant of changes in environmental conditions like temperature, while adult survival may be very tolerant of similar changes). In the temperate zones and polar regions, but also sometimes in the tropics, seasonal variations often occur in the resistances of given life history stages; Arctic hares in winter tolerate low temperatures that would kill them if they occurred suddenly in the summer. Just how resistant particular animals are to particular sets of conditions also varies with the duration of exposure to those conditions. More extreme conditions can be tolerated for shorter periods, less extreme conditions for longer periods. Long-period exposures to moderate conditions often increase the resistances of individual animals to more extreme conditions.

Capacity. Animals exposed for long periods of time to particular sets of external conditions, such as high temperature, high

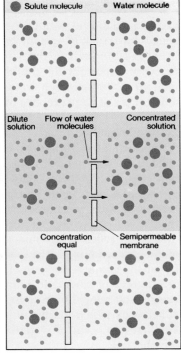

▲▼ **Resist or avoid.** Faced with harsh conditions in temperate and polar winters, animals have several options. They can tolerate the conditions, as with the Arctic hare (*Lepus timidus*) ABOVE, or simply move to warmer areas, as with these House martins (*Delichon urbica*) BELOW collecting on telegraph wires before migration.

▼ **Realities of life.** Animals have to cope with and control physical and chemical processes that do not necessarily act to the benefit of the animal. Such a process is osmosis, the basic principles of which are shown below. Water moves from areas of high solute concentration to those of low concentration until the concentrations are equal.

salinity, or low dissolved oxygen levels in water often improve in their abilities to function as times goes on. Such improvements frequently result from increases in the capacities of the animals to carry on essential processes. A term which is often used to describe the process of non-genetic adaptation of capacity is acclimation; for example a fish swims almost as fast in cool water in winter as it does in warm water in summer. Genetically based (ie inherited) capacity adaptations also occur; leopard frogs from cool northern areas jump more strongly at intermediate temperatures than leopard frogs from warmer southern temperatures.

Conformity. Within tolerance limits, some animals faced with external environmental changes permit parallel changes to occur in their internal environments (the body temperatures of most invertebrates). Animals which change passively in these ways are called conformers.

Regulation. Within tolerance limits, other animals faced with external environmental changes will control their internal environments to some degree, reducing the amounts of internal change occurring, as with blood salt concentrations in salmon migrating between fresh water and the sea. Animals which moderate or eliminate internal changes by physiological methods are called regulators.

Behavior. Most animals live in complex environments which provide a range of choices in external conditions. (Animals which either have limited mobility or are effectively unable to move their position at all are obvious exceptions to this.) Under such conditions, animals can regulate the intensities or durations of exposure to particular sets of external conditions simply by moving around. Many kinds of animals combine behavioral and physiological adaptations. Long-distance migration is an example of such adaptations.

The Body Fluids

As has been mentioned, the bodies of complex animals contain up to 80 percent water. Many chemicals (solutes) which may be mineral, (such as sodium chloride—salt) or organic (such as sugars, proteins, fats etc) are dissolved within this "fluid," either as constituents of individual cells or part of, eg, blood.

In all animals there is a continual exchange of water and solutes with their external environments through body surfaces and body openings. The direction of movement of water and solutes will vary as will the amounts, but there will always be exchanges. These exchanges are governed by the laws of physics and chemistry and must be controlled. One of the key "physico-chemical" processes that has to be controlled is osmosis. Whenever a situation exists where two fluid media containing different concentrations of solutes are separated from each other by a membrane, there is a tendency for water to pass from the solution containing the lower concentrations of solutes to the one containing the higher—in essence this is osmosis. The solution into which the water moves is said to have a higher osmotic concentration than the other.

Physical-Chemical Processes and Principles

Several different processes are used by animals in the course of carrying out movements and exchanges of water and solutes. Different animals will use some or all of these at different places and times, also in varying combinations and at varying rates. This diversity of possibilities is what permits animals to be sufficiently flexible that they can adapt to many different environmental conditions—both internally and externally. Movements and exchanges of water and solutes take place between animals and their external environments and between the many fluid-filled compartments making up their internal environments, such as circulating blood in mammals, tissue fluids between cells and fluids inside cells.

Bulk movements of water usually occur as the result of muscular movements in the walls of body cavities or chambers (examples include mouth and throat movements of animals drinking, blood circulation resulting from heart beats). Driving forces for these movements are pressure differences in space: water flows from higher pressure regions to lower pressure regions. Pressure differences may result from either compression or suction. Bulk movements into individual cells can occur as a result of pinocytosis at the cell membrane: microscopic droplets of fluid are enclosed in pockets of cell membrane which then close off from the outside and move into the cytoplasm.

Movements of water by diffusion or osmosis occur across membranes (skins, intestinal walls, cell membranes—any biological membranes) which are not completely impermeable to water. Water diffuses across such membranes from the lower solute concentration to the higher solute concentration side.

Movements of dissolved substances occur in connection with bulk water movements. Bulk flows of water necessarily carry along with them any substances dissolved in the water but the movement is not specific to individual substances. Movements of individual kinds of solutes (dissolved substances) may be either passive (not requiring much, if any, metabolic energy from the animal) or active (energy requiring processes).

Excretory Organs and Mechanisms

All animals must have some means for removing excess amounts of water and solutes from their bodies, as well as potentially toxic waste products. All animal groups do this using one or more types of excretory processes, structures or organs to do this work. In animals having more than one kind of excretory organ, each generally functions differently from the other. Kidneys, or organs that function as kidneys have a primary role in the elimination of metabolic wastes from animals' bodies, especially, but not only, nitrogen-containing wastes, such as urea and ammonia.

Single-celled organisms often have one or more contractile organelles within the cell which eject small volumes of fluid from their bodies. These are called contractile vacuoles. Multicellular organisms in the simplest groups, such as sea anemones, similarly carry on their excretory activities directly across membranes of individual cells into the outside world.

The more complex animals have either more complex specialized cells or organs of excretion. There is, unfortunately, no simple general evolutionary trend in structural patterns which can be easily described. Different phyla, sometimes even different groups within a single phylum, have excretory organs which are radically different in structure from one another.

The basic processes carried on by all of these organs are the same. A portion of the circulating body fluids of an animal either flows into the upper parts of the cavity of the organ or moves into it in response to differences in osmotic concentration. This fluid moves down the length of the cavity and is gradually converted into urine by the cells lining the cavity. The change is brought about by reabsorption of water, by adding waste solutes to the fluid, and by conserving other solutes by active absorption from the fluid.

The final urine composition, its relative volume and its absolute rate of production are all usually carefully controlled by an animal. Most animals also have some flexibility and adaptability with respect to each of these features so that changing metabolic needs and environmental conditions can be tolerated and adjusted to. Many animals in the more highly evolved groups have other ways of eliminating unwanted material from their bodies as well as via the kidneys, perhaps because the kidneys alone cannot cope adequately. Many different non-kidney (extrarenal) excretory mechanisms are used. Starfish and sea urchins, for example, have no kidneys at all and apparently excrete everything by means of motile cells which move through the body wall of the animal and disappear into the sea. Various insects and other arthropods move particularly hazardous substances into specialized tissues where they are accumulated. These tissues sometimes stay with the animal until it dies, or they may be eliminated during molting. Some tunicates accumulate wastes in special cells which are periodically eliminated from their bodies.

Among the vertebrates, many cartilaginous fish (sharks, skates, rays, chimeras) have special rectal glands near their cloacas which help eliminate excess amounts of certain salts, especially sodium chloride. Marine fish such as flatfish and sea bass excrete these salts from their gills, primarily through specialized cells called chloride cells. Freshwater fish take up such salts from their external environments by means of similar cells in their gills. Marine reptiles (sea turtles, sea snakes), some terrestrial reptiles, such as many kinds of lizards, and many non-perching birds, for example ostriches and shore birds, have salt-excreting glands at various locations in their heads. Some sea snakes have such glands under their tongues, while crocodiles living in estuaries have them in their tongues. Such salt glands are very important for the elimination of quantities of salt without losing as much water as would happen if the same amount of salt were excreted by the kidneys.

Marine Animals

Animals that live in aquatic environments have particularly difficult problems when it comes to controlling water and solute flow in and out of their bodies, because they live in an environment that is itself made up of water containing solutes. Since their body walls are more or less porous membranes they find themselves effectively part of an osmotic system, in which unless controlled, water and solutes will flow in or out of the animals depending on the type of watery habitat they live in. By far the greatest diversity of aquatic animals, both in terms of numbers of kinds and numbers of individuals, live in the oceans and related marine habitats. There are three primary patterns by which marine animals regulate their body fluids. The first two occur in water-breathing forms, the third in air breathers.

EXCRETORY ORGANS AND PROCESSES

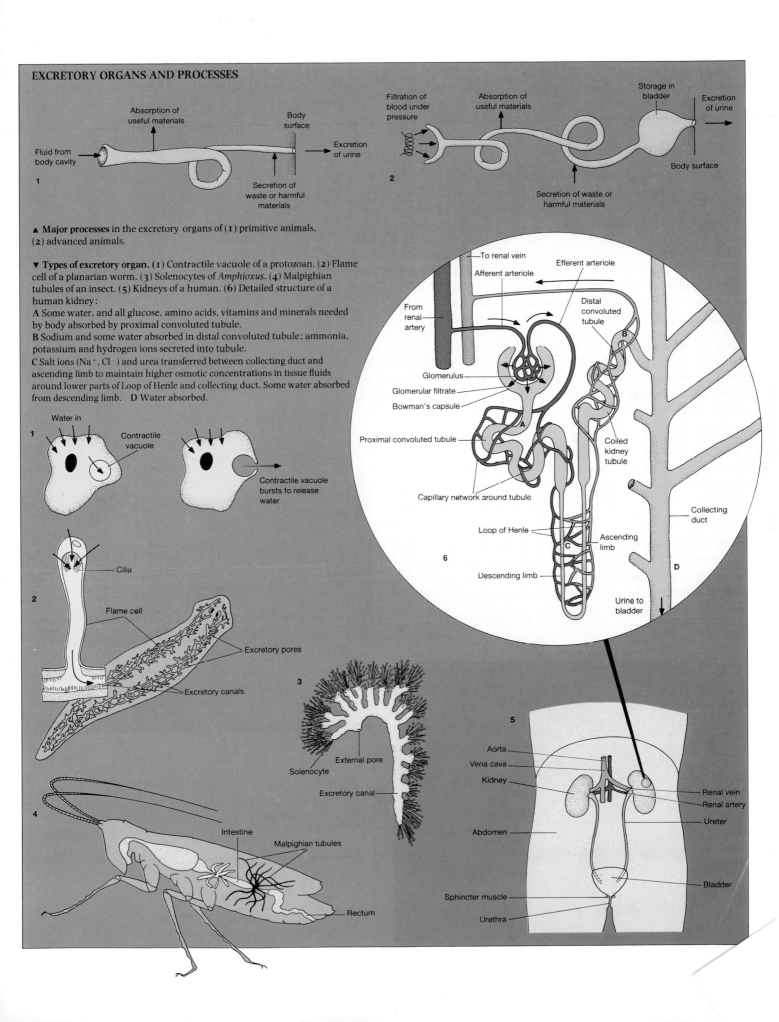

▲ **Major processes** in the excretory organs of (1) primitive animals, (2) advanced animals.

▼ **Types of excretory organ.** (1) Contractile vacuole of a protozoan. (2) Flame cell of a planarian worm. (3) Solenocytes of *Amphioxus*. (4) Malpighian tubules of an insect. (5) Kidneys of a human. (6) Detailed structure of a human kidney:
A Some water, and all glucose, amino acids, vitamins and minerals needed by body absorbed by proximal convoluted tubule.
B Sodium and some water absorbed in distal convoluted tubule; ammonia, potassium and hydrogen ions secreted into tubule.
C Salt ions (Na+, Cl−) and urea transferred between collecting duct and ascending limb to maintain higher osmotic concentrations in tissue fluids around lower parts of Loop of Henle and collecting duct. Some water absorbed from descending limb. D Water absorbed.

Pattern 1. Most kinds of invertebrates and some vertebrates (specifically hagfish, sharks, skates, rays and the coelacanth) have body fluids whose osmotic concentration is roughly equal or slightly greater than the sea water in which they live, meaning that there is a slight tendency for water to enter the animal. Most of these animals regulate their internal environments in parallel with any external changes within quite narrow ranges. Most maintain the chemical compositions of their body fluids which are quite different from that of sea water. Two widespread patterns of regulating the chemical compositions are: (a) over 90 percent of the osmotic concentration is due to inorganic salts, especially sodium chloride; (b) inorganic salts (still primarily sodium chloride) make up 50 to 70 percent of the osmotic concentration, the remainder deriving from dissolved organic components.

These animals have little difficulty in keeping steady the water levels in their bodies. Diffusion of water across their body surfaces occurs slowly, in the inward direction, or not at all. Some animals swallow sea water, either deliberately or by accident, with their food, and excess body water is eliminated as urine. These animals do have to expend considerable energy regulating the chemical composition of their body fluids, and there are four principal processes involved.

At least the gills (external respiratory organs) but also often other parts of their outer body surfaces, are more-or-less open to diffusion of different solutes. Thus, various solutes can move into or out of their bodies by diffusion, the directions of the movements depending upon whether concentrations of these solutes are higher outside than inside, in this example, or vice versa. Most animals have relatively little control over these properties of their own body surfaces.

The same parts of the body surfaces which are open to diffusion are also often the sites of a variety of active processes (ie needing energy to be expended) which more rapidly move larger amounts of solutes inward or outward, as is dictated by the physiological condition of the animal. These movements may be in the same direction as the diffusion occurring simultaneously or in the reverse direction. Animals can often

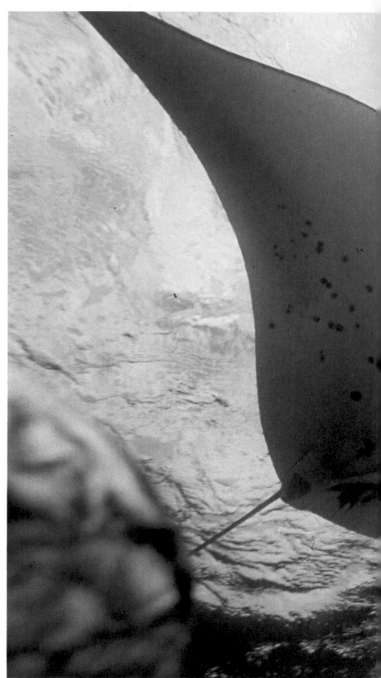

◄▲► **Dehydrate or burst**—the problems of water balance in marine animals. ABOVE In selachians such as Giant manta rays (*Manta alfredi*) there is a slight tendency for water to enter across their body surfaces from the sea and they partly alleviate this by using energy to excrete water from their kidneys. Bony fish, such as the remoras that have attached themselves to the underside of the manta ray and angel fish (*Pomacanthus paru*) LEFT, lose water through their body walls into the sea; this is partly compensated by drinking and by excreting concentrated urine. Other marine animals, such as the sea snake shown RIGHT, slowly dehydrate in the sea, and there are further losses when they surface to breath. Such animals get water mainly from their food rather than by drinking, because drinking results in excess salt in their bodies, which has to be excreted.

vary the rates of these processes as required to adjust to changing conditions. Active swallowing of sea water is included here as a process, although clearly it is non-specific with respect to individual solutes.

In addition to changes across the outer body surfaces, many solutes enter or leave animal bodies across the walls of the digestive tract. Both diffusion and active processes take place. Many organic solutes, which are important to osmotic regulation, are derived from food. Solutes either excreted by the gut walls into the gut lumen or not absorbed across them are eliminated with the feces.

As described earlier, multicellular animals, starting with the flatworms, all have specific excretory organs which are used to eliminate from their bodies excess water, various undesirable metabolic waste products and excess quantities of solutes which are important in the regulation of the body fluid chemistry.

When all four of these processes operate in an integrated fashion under the control of nervous and hormonal systems in animals, the final outcome is the regulation of the body fluid's osmotic concentration so that it is roughly equal to that of the environment. The chemical composition of the body fluids is kept different from the environment.

Pattern 2. The body fluids of some kinds of marine invertebrates (especially various crustaceans and other arthropods) as well as most marine vertebrates (all fish except those listed previously, and reptiles, birds and mammals) have osmotic concentrations which are much lower than the sea water in which they live, that is water tends to be lost. Most of these animals can only tolerate relatively narrow ranges of salinity but they are able to maintain the osmotic concentrations of their body fluids as well as the relative abundances of dissolved salts. The chemical compositions of their body fluids, in terms of relative abundances of different solutes and their absolute concentrations, are very different from that of sea water. Once again, however, sodium chloride is the major solute, generally making up 70 to 80 percent of the total osmotic concentration in their bodies.

Animals that have lower osmotic concentrations than their surroundings must contend with continuous water loss, so free water must be obtained from somewhere. There are only three sources possible: water contained in their food; water released from their food as a result of biochemical processes taking place within their bodies; and sea water swallowed either deliberately or by accident when they swallow food items. The first two sources may be significant for plant-eating forms (surgeon fish, manatees) and for those which graze heavily on plankton (baleen whales). For most carnivores, feeding on relatively larger animals, meals are likely to occur less often and more irregularly so that food-related water supply can only be sporadic. Thus, for this last category (from sea basses to porpoises), which probably includes most marine animals of this group, drinking sea water is the only option available.

Sea water contains two to three times more solutes than their body fluids, so that these forms must do something with the water they swallow to eliminate the large amount of salt it brings. Most of the salt absorbed is sodium chloride. The salts which are absorbed are excreted promptly, with relatively little

water loss. Substances such as sodium chloride are usually eliminated by one or other of the specialized organs which are different from the regular excretory organs. Others are excreted with the urine, which is as concentrated as the animals' kidneys can make it, and as small in volume as possible. The rest of the salt, primarily made up of substances such as calcium, magnesium, sulfate and phosphate salts, is excluded from the body in the feces. As water is absorbed from the gut, the concentrations of the substances increase until they start to precipitate out of solution. Precipitated salts, such as calcium and magnesium sulfates, make up a sizeable fraction of the feces

The large amount of salt taken in by these marine animals is aggravated to some extent by salt also taken in with food and by diffusion inward of salts from the sea water outside, across the permeable parts of their body surfaces, such as gills. Usually only relatively small areas of the body wall are permeable.

Pattern 3. Air-breathing marine vertebrates, including marine reptiles (turtles, snakes), birds (shearwaters, most plovers) and mammals (seals, dolphins), also have their osmotic concentra-

tions lower than that of sea water. They are also efficient regulators of their osmotic concentrations as well as the relative abundances of dissolved substances. Since they lack gills, however, and generally have body surfaces that do not allow much movement of water by osmosis, they are only slowly dehydrated. Thus, their water balance problems are less severe than those of most pattern 2 animals.

They still have the same about equally serious basic problems, however, because they continuously lose water to the air by evaporation as they breathe. The high metabolic rates of birds and mammals make the problems more severe for these groups. They compensate for these evaporative water losses in the same way as pattern 2 animals, although, in most cases, food-related water intake seems to be more important than actual drinking.

Excess salt derives primarily from eating marine animals or algae and is generally eliminated by the kidneys and guts in the mammals and in the few marine perching birds. The kidneys of these produce urines that are much higher in concentration than those produced by the other marine animals.

◄ **Living on the tideline,** means that animals, such as the soldier crabs *Mictyris longicarpus* on the East Australian coast, face drying out on land for part of the day, but excess water intake when submerged.

The kidneys of marine reptiles and all marine birds, except the few just described, are unable to produce urine that is much more concentrated than the animal's own blood. Thus excess salt in these groups is eliminated primarily by restricting absorption through the intestinal wall, and by the specialized salt excretion organs described earlier.

Freshwater Animals

Water-breathing aquatic animals living in fresh water (flatworms, crayfish, fish) all have internal osmotic concentrations which are much higher than the osmotic concentrations of the waters in which they live. Accordingly, they are continuously flooded with water, which they must eliminate to avoid swelling up and bursting. The details vary greatly between groups, but the basic pattern is that these animals have somewhat lower body fluid osmotic concentrations than pattern 2 marine animals do, thus reducing the driving force for flooding with water by osmosis. Their kidneys or equivalent excretory organs produce as large volumes as possible of urines which are as dilute as possible. Thus, they eliminate their continuing water loads while minimizing their losses of essential solutes (once again primarily sodium chloride in most forms).

Minimizing solute losses, however, does not mean that they suffer no losses—urines are not distilled water. Therefore, freshwater animals must also take in the required solutes to replace those lost in urine, plus small amounts lost by diffusion across permeable parts of body surfaces. They obtain these solutes partly from their food and partly by active uptake mechanisms in various parts of their body surfaces, especially the gills.

Estuarine Animals

The last category of aquatic animals considered here is the small, diverse group of forms which can tolerate a wide range of salinity. These include representatives of several phyla: mollusks (mud snails), annelids (blood worms), arthropods (blue crabs) and vertebrates (killifishes) are major groups. These are mostly animals that live in the very variable conditions of estuaries. It is hard to generalize about water and solute regulation in these animals, because they often differ greatly from one another. They are alike in that they can tolerate external osmotic concentrations ranging from fresh or nearly fresh water, to full sea water, or nearly that. Many of the invertebrates change their body fluid concentrations in parallel with external changes. They do this by taking up or eliminating both water and solutes, as dictated by external conditions. Some of the invertebrates, especially many arthropods (fiddler crabs), and most of the vertebrates (salmon), are very good at regulating their internal osmotic concentrations. Some hardly change their body fluid concentrations in moving from fresh water to the sea or vice versa. Thus, these animals are pattern 2 marine animals in concentrated media, freshwater animals in dilute media.

Amphibious Animals

Amphibious animals spend most of their lives near the edge of the water, sometimes in the water and sometimes on the land. Most amphibious invertebrates (intertidal snails, crabs) are marine; most amphibious vertebrates (frogs, toads) live around fresh waters. The amphibious life style has associated with it an array of different physiological challenges. When they are in the water, amphibious animals must function as aquatic organisms. Marine invertebrates and the few kinds of marine vertebrates are either pattern 1 or pattern 2 forms. The freshwater forms are like other freshwater residents of their groups. When on land, amphibious animals must function as terrestrial organisms, although most of them stay close enough to the edge of the water so that they can readily return to it if conditions become too severe. One of the most important stresses they face on land, drying out (desiccation), results from evaporative water loss.

Compared with fully terrestrial representatives of their own groups, amphibious animals tend to lose water by evaporation from their surfaces at relatively high rates. Thus, many show tolerance of evaporative water losses. Tolerance to desiccation is usually associated with some degree of flexibility in the mechanisms for water conservation. There seems to be relatively little that most animals can do to reduce rates of evaporation across their body surfaces but most are able to decrease rates of urine production, increase urine concentrations and decrease fecal water losses. Urine concentration also often changes, reflecting changes in the nature of excretion mechanisms for waste nitrogen that further contribute to water conservation.

Terrestrial Animals

The importance for terrestrial animals of evaporative water losses has already been mentioned. However, unlike the amphibious forms, most terrestrial forms have general body surfaces which are relatively impermeable to water; therefore, they do not lose very much water by that route. The main route for most water losses is usually the external respiratory organs, where evaporative water loss is inseparable from breathing. Water is also lost from terrestrial animals through their urine and their feces. All these water losses must be compensated for by some combination of water drunk as liquid, taken in with the food as preformed water or derived from the food as metabolic water. Some arthropod groups, including a number of kinds of desert insects, are also able to take up water through their outer surfaces directly from water vapor in the air.

The local environments of different terrestrial animals are often crucial in determining just how rapidly water is lost by evaporation. Large animals which cannot easily find shelter and which live in hot, dry environments must confront this problem directly. Some, such as desert goats and donkeys, simply evaporate a lot of water, most often as part of their efforts at regulating their body temperatures, and drink frequently. These animals usually cannot tolerate very much body weight loss caused by evaporation (dehydration).

Other large animals have evolved different strategies. Some of the most successful (Dromedary camels and the oryxes) have developed much greater tolerances for dehydration—under some conditions camels can tolerate losing over one-third of their body mass as water. They also have the ability to survive wide daily changes in body temperature—sometimes more than 10°C (18°F) between mid-afternoon highs and late-night lows. Since they are large animals, weighing hundreds of kilograms, these temperature changes result in large reductions of evaporative water loss, to levels far below those which would occur if they regulated their body temperatures as precisely as do most other mammals their size. Camels and oryxes also have several other, less dramatic, adaptations for water conservation, including their feeding and drinking habits (oryxes almost never drink and eat mostly at night, when food plants have higher water contents), their kidney function and their respiratory systems.

Smaller animals living in hot, dry-desert or near-desert environments (scorpions, gerbils) have a wider variety of adjustment possibilities. Simply as a result of being smaller, these animals have available to them a far larger range of microhabitats than do large animals. Thus, small animals, whether vertebrates or invertebrates, can more easily avoid direct confrontation with the harshest external conditions of their habitats. They do this to some extent physiologically but primarily by suitably varying their behavior. By picking the times and places where they rest or are active, they never have to deal with very high temperatures or desiccating conditions.

In cooler, moister (mesic) environments, terrestrial animals are more easily able to maintain normal levels of body fluid concentrations. Most terrestrial animals regulate body fluid osmotic concentrations at levels equivalent to one-quarter to one-third of sea water concentration; sodium chloride contributes 70 to 80 percent of this concentration. Since terrestrial animals are, by one means or another, air breathers, they are physiologically similar to the pattern 3 marine animals.

Most terrestrial animals in moist environments obtain most of their water by drinking. Preformed water in food is, however, enough to supply all the water needed by some forms (for example, African Mountain gorillas which feed mainly on very succulent plants, and mosquitoes and other blood-sucking insects and leeches which feed directly on the body fluids of other animals). The salts and other solutes needed by terrestrial animals in moist environments are usually obtained from the food. Some groups, especially mammals like cattle, buffalo and deer, supplement their salt supplies by licking salt-rich mineral deposits at locations called salt licks. Water, salt and other solutes in these animals are balanced primarily by means of regulation of rates of urine production by the kidneys and variations in urine composition. Changes in evaporative water loss through respiration and in the water contents and chemical compositions of the feces are generally much less important than renal adjustments.

Parasites

Some very special sets of environmental conditions which, in turn, have led to the evolutionary development of some equally special sets of physiological adaptations, are encountered by the variety of animals which operate as parasites on other animals. Internal parasites, such as intestinal roundworms, tapeworms, or blood flukes, are essentially specialized aquatic animals living in environments of which the volumes and compositions are already suitably regulated by the organ systems of their hosts. The principal unusual metabolic condition faced by some internal parasites, primarily intestinal parasites, is that they live in environments which are completely lacking in oxygen. The lack of oxygen does not necessarily seriously change the nature of their water and solute regulatory activities, to the extent they carry on such activities, but it has led to many changes in the biochemical mechanisms which provide energy for these activities.

External parasites (ectoparasites) are very varied. Such animals living on the bodies of aquatic animals have some combinations of the water and solute adaptations of normal, free-living animals in their environments and of internal parasites in the same hosts. Ectoparasites on terrestrial animals may be like other terrestrial fluid feeders, or they may be highly specialized for their own particular situations. Water and solute physiology has never been studied in many of these animals, so that little or nothing is known about these aspects.

Body Temperature and its Regulation

Exchanges of heat energy occur universally and continuously between all animals and their environments. No living system is so well insulated or isolated from its surroundings that it can

◄► **Deadly dehydration.** Most land animals lose water continuously through breathing and from their surfaces. This is exacerbated for animals living in dry climates where water is difficult to find and temperatures high. For example, on the African savannas, daily treks to water holes to drink are a necessity for most large mammals such as this large Brindled gnu (*Connochaetes taurinus*) RIGHT. In the desert there is no free water available and beetles, such as *Onymacris unguicularis* shown LEFT collect moisture in condensation on their bodies during the early morning mists.

prevent or avoid such exchanges. All processes occurring within animals take place at the temperature of the animal. As a result, temperature is one of the most important variables affecting all aspects of animal function.

The rates at which heat exchanges occur between animals and their environments, and the net directions of those exchanges, are determined primarily by: the amounts and directions of temperature differences which exist between internal and external environments; the areas of surface available for exchanges; and the thermal conductivity of the available surface areas. There are other factors that can modify these rates, including the degree to which body surfaces come into physical contact with other surfaces (conductive exchanges); how much radiant energy may be coming in or leaving (radiative exchanges); and how fast the fluids on either side of the body surfaces are mixing with more distant fluids (convective exchanges). Air-breathing animals, especially terrestrial animals, also lose considerable heat associated with water losses by evaporation (evaporative exchanges) from the various surfaces of their bodies.

Heat from Outside—Ectotherms

The vast majority of living animals depend largely on heat energy from the environment to regulate body temperature, that is, they are ectotherms. Most ectotherms, which are at least moderately mobile and which live in a reasonably complex external environment, make some effort to regulate their body temperatures behaviorally in the face of external variations. They have some fairly narrow, specific range of preferred body temperatures. Some kinds (scarab beetles, horned lizards) are extremely good at maintaining these preferred temperatures over periods of time as long as large parts of a day. Even those animals which are most efficient at behavioral regulation of body temperature eventually encounter conditions beyond their capacities for adjustment, however, and they must tolerate substantial changes in their body temperature. Thus, a basic condition of life for most ectotherms is the tolerance of some (often a considerable amount) change in body temperature. Animals living in the depths of the seas are notable exceptions to this as the sea water has a constant temperature.

Those ectotherms which can tolerate more variation in body temperature can occupy more different environments than those that can cope with less variation; as a result they often have wider geographic ranges, such as swordfish, Old World green toads. It may be surprising to find that widely distributed ectotherms can be uniformly fast in their movements and equally active in all parts of their ranges, even though the cooler parts of these ranges may have much lower temperatures than the warmer parts. The basis for this metabolic independence to temperature is usually the occurrence of a complex set of physiological adjustments which are collectively called acclimation.

Some ectotherms live in environments in which the temperatures may sometimes be above or below the animals' tolerance limits, even taking acclimation into account. This is the case, for example, for temperate-zone insects in winter and desert lizards in summer. There are several options open to such

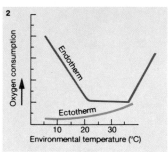

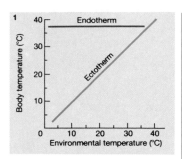

▲ **The advantages and disadvantages** of being "warm" or "cold blooded." Relation of (**1**) body temperatures and (**2**) oxygen consumption to environmental temperature in endotherms and ectotherms.

▲ **Keeping cool.** A Perentie monitor (*Varanus giganteus*) shelters from the midday sun to avoid heating up too much. In the morning, it would have had to bask to gain heat before becoming fully active.

▼ **Heat exchanges in a mammal**— summary of the thermal energy changes that occur in a terrestrial endothermic animal.

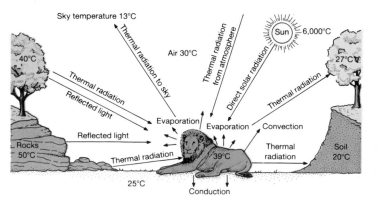

animals. But, if the timing of these conditions is unpredictable, such as unseasonal cold snaps or heat waves, the populations may simply be killed.

The species involved, such as intertidal mussels and butterflies, must then reinvade the affected areas after conditions return to tolerable levels. If these conditions are more predictable, such as seasonal changes in temperature in temperate habitats, the animals may respond in a variety of ways. They may avoid the bad periods altogether by migrating to another region at the appropriate time, returning after conditions have improved. They may avoid direct confrontation with bad conditions by seeking out more moderate microhabitats, such as burrows in the mud of lake bottoms or crevices in large rock masses, in which they can survive, usually by becoming inactive (torpid) for some time. Some animals, such as freshwater fairy shrimps and temperate zone moths, tolerate the bad conditions directly by entering or producing a different life history stage which can withstand the adversity. Many ectotherms survive cold winters, for example, as eggs or pupae that are resistant to low temperatures. Finally, they may tolerate the bad conditions directly without either producing a new generation or metamorphosis, but by changing their physiology in non-

acclimatory ways that make them resistant to the situation.

Heat from Within—Endotherms

Animals which can regulate body temperature using mostly heat generated within themselves (endotherms) are rarer than ectotherms. A good case can be made that there are no animals that are true endotherms, if a condition for being a true endotherm is perfect, physiologically based constant temperature in all parts of the body over some reasonable range of external temperatures. Here, however, most mammals and birds, as well as selected insects, will be considered to be endotherms.

Endotherms vary greatly in the degree to which they can tolerate ranges of environmental temperature, and in the precision of their capacities to regulate body temperature. Some endotherms regularly tolerate core body temperature changes larger than 10°C (18°F). Others expend large amounts of energy maintaining core temperatures within a range no larger than plus or minus 1°C (1.8°F). Therefore, once again, if some forms can function well with variable body temperatures, why can not they all? What is special about body temperatures of 37°C (98.6°F), which is common in many mammals, and 39°C (102.2°F), which is typical of many birds, compared, say, with

35°C (95°F), or any other temperature high enough to permit rapid biochemical reactions but low enough to avoid altering the state of the proteins that make up the body? At the moment there are no good answers to such questions.

To be an endotherm, the animal must create enough heat by its own metabolism so that by physiological means it can regulate its body temperature at levels different from the external temperature. This means that the animals adjust either their rates of heat production or their rates of heat loss, or both, to maintain the desired internal temperature. Much of the time, most endotherms live in environments which are substantially cooler than they are. Thus, control of heat losses is usually of most concern.

Several strategies have come into existence in the course of evolution to accomplish this control. Some animals have developed insulating layers which cover most of their body surfaces. Most mammals have fur. Bare-skinned mammals, such as whales and pigs, have layers of fat beneath their skins; humans use clothing—a cultural response to this need. Birds have feathers. Endothermic insects usually heat up their bodies during periods of activity. Some of these, particularly many moths and bumblebees, have modified scales on their bodies which resemble fur.

Animals living in environments which produce almost continuous cold stresses often have special modifications of their circulatory systems that permit them to keep their extremities alive and healthy, but operating at temperatures well below core temperatures. These extremities would otherwise lose a lot of heat rapidly because of large surface-to-volume ratios. Such animals are called regional heterotherms.

Animals living in environments which, predictably and usually seasonally, produce very severe cold stresses may avoid those stresses by finding more moderate microenvironments, such as burrows, and become torpid in these environments until the bad period is over, as in hedgehogs and some bats. These animals are mostly hibernators. Highly mobile animals, especially some insects and many birds, migrate to more moderate regions during periods of excessive cold.

Even in very cold conditions, however, circumstances may arise when the animals will have to get rid of a lot of excess heat, usually at short notice. For example, a reindeer living on the arctic tundra in winter may be attacked by a pack of wolves and have to run for its life. Running is heavy work that generates a great deal of heat. The animal that one moment was doing everything possible to conserve heat, so as to not to have to do any more work than necessary in gathering food, the next moment must lose excess heat very rapidly so as not to raise its body temperature above tolerable limits and collapse from heat prostration. The reindeer accomplishes this mainly by evaporating more water in association with its harder breathing while running. It also will increase the amounts of blood flow to its limbs, raising their surface temperatures and thus increasing the rates of heat loss.

Endotherms in hot environments must work hard to keep their body temperatures from rising excessively. They accomplish this mainly by increasing rates of heat loss in various ways. They may increase the rates of evaporative water loss, either from their respiratory tracts (often by panting) or by

▶ **Small comfort** for a family of cheetahs (*Acinonyx jubatus*) resting under a very small tree. Mammals avoid over-heating by evaporation of sweat from their skins and by panting, as well as by seeking shade.

▶ **Panting to keep cool** BELOW RIGHT, is the only option for birds that cannot avoid direct sun, such as this nesting Little ringed plover (*Charadrius dubius*). Birds do not have sweat glands in their skin so can only cool down by gaping and allowing moisture to evaporate from their mouths.

▼ **Moth fur.** Some moths, such as this dalcerid *Acraga moorei*, have enough heat insulation for the heat generated within their bodies to warm them above the temperature of the environment; they are thus said to be endothermic. It is unusual for animals, apart from mammals and birds, to be endothermic.

sweating (relatively few mammals have sweat glands, however, and birds and insects have none). Some animals moisten the body surface with saliva (many mammals) or urine (some long-legged birds urinate on their legs) thus increasing evaporative cooling. Some animals may change behavior and become nocturnal, thus avoiding direct contact with the heat of the day, as with some rodents. Some animals migrate to cooler areas, such as higher elevations in mountains, during hot periods, as in desert bighorn sheep. Finally, they may find milder microenvironments, such as burrows, and become torpid during hot periods. These animals are aestivators (estivators), as with Round-tailed ground squirrels.

It is apparent that endotherms, far more than any other animals and especially those living in warm or hot conditions, must use large amounts of water in their efforts to regulate their body temperatures. Their generally higher body temperatures are associated with higher metabolic rates which, in turn, produce the heat needed to permit physiologically based regulation of body temperature. Higher metabolic rates mean higher respiratory rates, which mean higher rates of evaporative water loss.

Varying Body Temperatures—Heterothermy

A wide variety of animals demonstrate substantial variations in body temperature between different parts of their bodies—these are called regional heterotherms. Several of the more striking examples of these are some kinds of insects, some fish, most kinds of water birds, sloths, seals, porpoises and whales. Certain groups of people, most notably Australian aborigines, can also function in this way.

The primary evolutionary stimulus for the development of regional heterothermy appears to have been the need for conservation of food energy by animals living in situations involving continuing high rates of loss of body heat. For example, various larger beetles, members of two moth families and bumblebees are small in size, and hence have large surface to volume ratios. Their flight muscles operate properly only at temperatures of 30°–40°C (86–104°F). Therefore these animals have evolved mechanisms for conserving in their thoraxes much of the heat the muscles produce as they go through their very rapid contraction cycles, with the result that the thoraxes are much warmer than the rest of their bodies. The problem for the insect is that much of this heat may be lost through diffusion and convection to its colder surroundings.

The insects partially counter these high heat losses with effective layers of insulation (modified cuticular scales which look like fur) on their outer thoracic surfaces; and by controlling the pattern of blood flow in their bodies so as to restrict heat transfer from the thorax to other body parts.

Regionally heterothermic vertebrates all work to counter high rates of peripheral heat loss by development of what are called "cold shells." They maintain core temperatures at normal levels, usually somewhere between 30° and 42°C (86 and 108°F), while permitting their extremities to cool to near external temperatures (to near 0°C (32°F) in high latitude environments or temperate environments in winter). They do this at the same time as they maintain normal rates of blood

circulation to their limbs, thus keeping the tissues in their limbs alive and functional.

The basis for this ability is most often some type of counter-current heat exchanger in the blood supplies to the limbs. There are many variations in the structure of these heat exchangers but the underlying principle in all cases is close contact between small blood vessels carrying blood to and from the limbs. Physically closely packed arterioles and venules in heat exchangers usually located near the base of the limbs permit rapid and efficient heat exchanges across the walls. As a result heat in the arterial blood entering the limb is transferred to the venous blood passing out of the limb, so that the initially cool venous blood leaves the exchanger at a temperature very close to the core value. The heat that otherwise would have been lost to the outside world across the limb surfaces has almost completely been recycled back into the core.

Heterothermic fish (some tuna fish and some sharks) use a variation of this mechanism to keep the muscles used in movement warm in cold water. Australian aborigines have more effective mechanisms than most other people for controlling patterns of blood flow in their limbs so as to reduce heat losses across their skin.

Regional heterotherms provide some of the most striking illustrations known of the variety and complexity of thermal adaptive processes. Consider, for example, the nerve cells in the outer parts of the bare legs and in the feet of water birds swimming in ice-cold water or standing on the ice next to partially frozen ponds or coastal bays. These birds are all regional heterotherms, most having countercurrent heat exchangers in their circulatory systems near the bases of their legs. Thus, they have warm body cores, which they regulate carefully at a temperature of 39°C (102.2°F), and cold extremities, which they also regulate fairly carefully at temperatures only a few degrees above freezing. The nerve cells carrying motor impulses from the spinal cords of these birds to their legs and feet, and those carrying sensory impulses into the spinal cord, have nerve fibers which are in part at 39°C (102.2°F) and in part at, say, 2°C (35.6°F). Both segments of these axons successfully transmit their electrical impulses, with little differences in either speeds of conduction or properties of the impulses. Thus, different parts of single cells can function normally at dramatically different temperatures in these animals. By contrast, experiments with impulse transmission in the nerves of more ordinary endotherms usually show that detectable failures in

Cold feet—a flock of Gentoo penguins (*Pygoscelis papua*) endure a snow storm in Antarctica ABOVE. They employ a counter-current heat exchanger system to maintain normal body temperatures (see BELOW) while allowing their extremities to cool near to external temperatures.

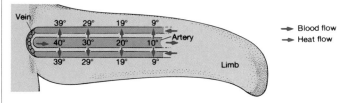

The condensation on this hibernating Peacock butterfly (*Inachis io*) indicates that its body temperature is as low as that of the outside temperature.

Antifreeze in Animals

A variety of adaptations for survival at very low temperatures also exist. Many animals are severely damaged if some of their tissues freeze during cold conditions (frostbite is a serious injury). However, vast numbers of terrestrial animals from the temperate zone to arctic or antarctic zones routinely survive winter conditions in which their temperatures fall as low as −30°C to −40°C (−22°F to −40°F).

Many insects which must over-winter in exposed situations, such as the pupae of most moths and butterflies, as well as many inhabitants of the bark and trunks of trees, avoid physically freezing by gradually accumulating in their bodies extremely high concentrations of an organic chemical, glycerol, which acts as an antifreeze. The presence of the glycerol lowers the freezing temperature of the body fluids far enough so that, except for very rare, excessively harsh conditions, which may kill large numbers of animals, little or no actual internal ice forms.

At the same time, whatever ice does form is restricted to locations in tissue spaces outside cells.

Other insects, and especially a variety of spiders that survive as adults over the winter, develop in their body fluids low concentrations of more complex, glycoprotein compounds (compounds that are part protein, part sugar), which have an unusual ability to inhibit the initiation of freezing in solutions, even when the solutions are colder than their expected freezing temperatures, that is when they are supercooled. If these animals do begin to freeze the glycoproteins in their body fluids also work to slow the rate of freezing.

Glycoprotein supercooling stabilizers are also essential features of the biochemistry of most bony fish living in the Arctic and Antarctic Oceans. The expected freezing temperatures of these fish are all above the normal temperatures of their marine environments under the sea ice.

performances of the nerve fibers start appearing when they are cooled below 25°C (77°F) or so, and complete blockage of transmission occurs at temperatures of 10 to 15°C (50 to 59°F).

Other animals, known as temporal heterotherms, vary their body temperatures on a regular basis at different periods of time. This group includes hummingbirds, many bats, and most of the mammals which either hibernate (get torpid during cold seasons) or aestivate (get torpid during hot and/or dry seasons). All of these animals have the ability to make use of the energy-conserving process of adaptive hypothermia at times in their lives when energy conservation is particularly important. Adaptive hypothermia is defined as a normal, physiologically regulated, temporary period of inactivity in which body temper-

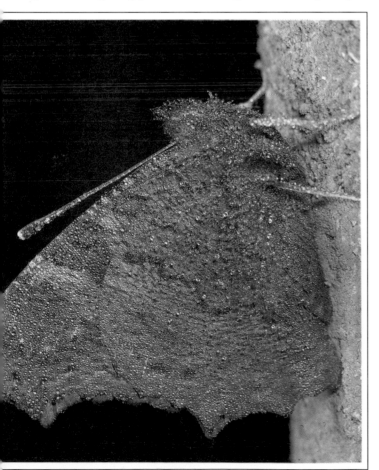

ature is not maintained and the body temperatures fall to levels equal to or somewhat above those of the external environment.

There are many patterns of adaptive hypothermia used by different animals. Regulated shallow hypothermia occurs where animals become more or less lethargic, but are capable of coordinated movements and responses, and in which body temperatures are reduced to no more than about 10°C (18°F) below the normal, active levels. Torpor or profound hypothermia is where animals become dormant in a way much more profound than deep sleep, and body temperatures fall to within 1°C (1.8°F) of external temperature. Other features of torpor include greatly reduced metabolic rates, long periods of no breathing (apnea), low heart rates, and the retention of the ability to rouse spontaneously and to return to normal body temperatures and activity levels. Torpor can occur either on a daily basis (each night for hummingbirds, each day for many bats) or seasonally, when the term hibernation is used.

Hibernators, especially many smaller mammals, are temporal heterotherms which routinely survive long periods of torpor at body temperatures as low as 2 to 5°C (35.6 to 41°F). At low body temperatures, these animals greatly reduce both the frequency and the strengths of their heart beats, but the heart continues to beat. They also return to near-normal frequencies and strengths of heart beating during arousal from hibernation, well before "normal" body temperatures of about 37°C (98.6°F) have been reestablished. By contrast, the hearts of most non-hibernating endotherms are irreversibly stopped by temperatures in the range 7 to 15°C (44.6 to 59°F). The most temperature-sensitive parts of such hearts seem to be the pacemakers, which initiate the heartbeat.

Whatever pattern of adaptive hypothermia is used, its overall result is to reduce the animal's need for food sufficiently to enable it to survive time periods when food gathering would be either difficult or impossible. There are many other examples of dramatic physiological differences between heterotherms and other animals. The point is clear that the phenomenon of heterothermy and the physiological capacities of heterotherms are striking demonstrations of the variety, subtlety and flexibility of evolutionary responses to pervasive, continual environmental challenges. They permit highly active, energy-requiring animals successfully to occupy many habitats which can only be tolerated by these animals for parts of each year, in terms of both physical conditions for life and food availability. MSG

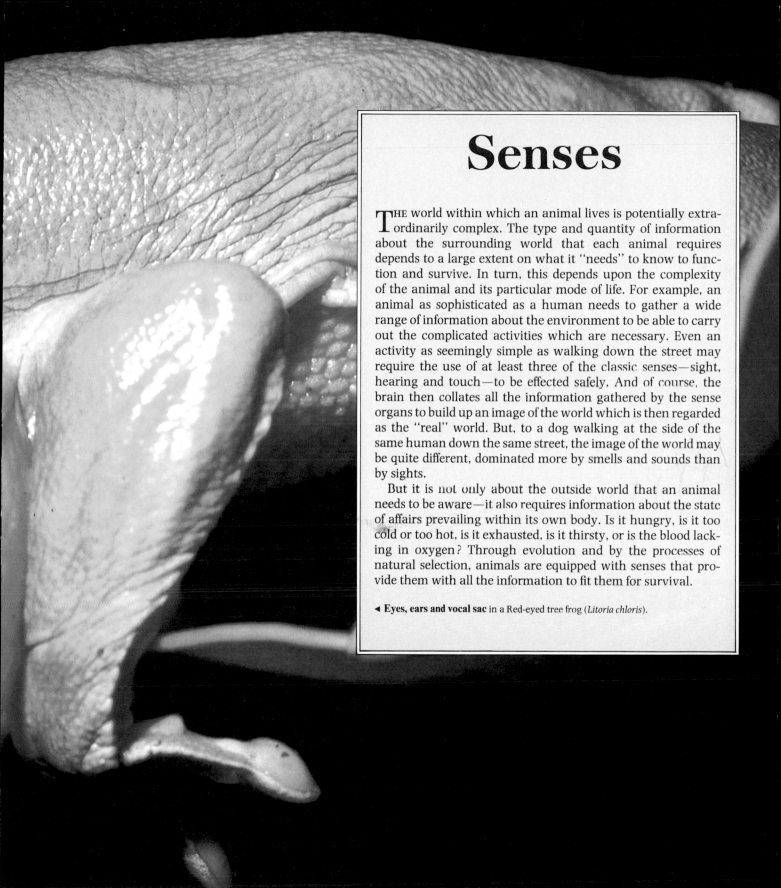

Senses

THE world within which an animal lives is potentially extra-ordinarily complex. The type and quantity of information about the surrounding world that each animal requires depends to a large extent on what it "needs" to know to function and survive. In turn, this depends upon the complexity of the animal and its particular mode of life. For example, an animal as sophisticated as a human needs to gather a wide range of information about the environment to be able to carry out the complicated activities which are necessary. Even an activity as seemingly simple as walking down the street may require the use of at least three of the classic senses—sight, hearing and touch—to be effected safely. And of course, the brain then collates all the information gathered by the sense organs to build up an image of the world which is then regarded as the "real" world. But, to a dog walking at the side of the same human down the same street, the image of the world may be quite different, dominated more by smells and sounds than by sights.

But it is not only about the outside world that an animal needs to be aware—it also requires information about the state of affairs prevailing within its own body. Is it hungry, is it too cold or too hot, is it exhausted, is it thirsty, or is the blood lacking in oxygen? Through evolution and by the processes of natural selection, animals are equipped with senses that provide them with all the information to fit them for survival.

◄ **Eyes, ears and vocal sac** in a Red-eyed tree frog (*Litoria chloris*).

Receptors sensitive to the external and internal worlds. . . Echolocation by bats. . . How messages reach the brain. . . Filtering out the signals. . . Looking for stimuli. . . Vision. . . Seeing in color. . . Types of eye. . . The nature of light and its effects. . . How sight is used. . . Touch. . . Lateral line organs of fish. . . Keeping balance. . . Hearing. . . The nature of sound and its effects. . . Electrical senses in fish. . . The chemical senses—taste and smell. . . Moths that "smell" with their antennae. . .

ANIMALS need information of three basic types to function and behave. They need to be informed of the nature of the world around them; in humans, for example, there are the classic five senses of sight, hearing, touch, taste and smell. They also need to be kept informed about the state of affairs within their bodies. Humans have receptors that measure, for example, the concentrations of oxygen and carbon dioxide in the blood, and the information they supply affects the rate and depth of breathing. There is an elaborate system of sensors within the gut that manages the complex process of digestion. These receptors—the enteroceptors, as opposed to the exteroceptors with which we explore the world around—rarely lead to conscious sensation, although hunger pangs and muscle fatigue are cases where they do. Nonetheless, they are of vital importance in the proper regulation of an animal's physiology.

There is a third class of receptors, the proprioceptors, which is intermediate between the other two. These receptors inform an animal of the relations of parts of the body to one another, and of the body in relation to outside space. Sensors in the muscles and joints measure limb positions and the tensions in muscles. Much of the inner ear of mammals is devoted to providing the information that keeps them upright, and measures, rather like a gyrocompass, their movements in space.

These three categories are not quite mutually exclusive. When you use your eye to guide your finger, you are using a classic exteroceptor to do a proprioceptive job, and when "weighing" a brick in your hand the proprioceptors of the joints become exteroceptors. Nevertheless, these distinctions are useful in trying to work out the roles of the various receptors in the life of an animal.

How Messages Reach the Brain

The first step in the reception of any kind of sensory information is referred to as transduction. This is the process by which some form of physical energy or chemical structure acts on a sense cell to produce an electrical change which can be transmitted to the central nervous system in the form of nerve action potentials. The process of transduction differs according to the kind of sense (or modality—the word used to indicate the type of energy involved). Thus, when a photon of light hits a receptor in a vertebrate eye, its energy is absorbed by a special molecule, rhodopsin, which is "tuned" to change its state only when it captures a photon of the right wavelength.

This change of state sets in motion a train of events which leads to a change—actually a decrease—in the flow of charged sodium particles or ions through the receptor's membrane, and this in turn alters the voltage between the inside of the receptor and the medium around it. This electrical change starts the process that leads to a pattern of nerve impulses that travel

to the brain. In other modalities most of the events in transduction are the same, except for the first one. In mechanical senses, such as touch or hearing, it is the deformation of the receptor membrane that changes the flow of charged ions, and in the chemical senses it is the capture of a particular kind of molecule by the membrane.

Filtering out the Signals

To be of any use to an animal, receptors must be selective—a cell that responded to both touch and temperature change, for example, would not be of much value. A major theme of this article will be the way this selectivity, or "filtering" out of the different kinds of signal the world provides, is achieved. Some of the selectivity is produced by the receptors themselves—photoreceptors can only respond to light, chemoreceptors to particular molecular structures and so on. This is only a small part of the story, however. In the mechanical senses, the same type of cell, the so-called hair cell, is used throughout the vertebrates (fish, reptiles, amphibians, birds and mammals) to signal water movements, the direction of gravity, rotation of the head and sounds of different frequencies. It is not the receptors themselves that make possible the separate detection of these different kinds of mechanical action, it is the way the receptors are organized in the sense organ as a whole. Hearing, for example, requires the receptors to be attached to a tuned vibrating membrane. In a similar way, light from different directions can only be separately detected if eyes have image-forming systems that split the light reaching them according to the direction of its external origin. The precision with which animal senses sample the information the world has to offer owes a

great deal to what can only be described as the brilliant engineering that has gone into sense organ structure over the course of evolution.

Looking for Stimuli

There are certain aspects of animal senses which relate to all of them. It is somewhat misleading to refer to sensory "stimuli"—the patterns of light, sound, odor and so on—that activate the sense and ultimately affect behavior because this implies that sense organs are passive devices that wait for stimuli to present themselves. This is usually far from reality. Human eyes are in almost continuous motion "looking" for things to see. A bat, hunting at night using its echolocating sonar, emits high-frequency clicks continuously, and waggles its ears to detect the direction of the echo of an insect prey. Similarly, when a male moth encounters a molecule of sex attractant emitted by a female, he will turn into the wind and search through the plume of odor with his antennae, heading up the gradient of scent to find its source. The point of these examples is that the senses, far from being passive recorders of events, are generally inquisitive, actively exploring the environment for useful information.

Related to this "active" way in which the senses are used is a subtle, but very important, idea that must color any consideration of how the nervous system interprets the information from the senses. Thus, every movement, even a small eye movement, radically alters the position of the image on the retina, and yet nothing has changed in the outside world. In other words, many of the changes in pattern that the eye sees—and this applies to all modalities—are of the animal's own

◄ **Warship of the air.** Bats emit high-pitched cries; they can determine the direction and distance of any object producing an echo of these—just as warships use SONAR to hunt submarines in the dark depths of oceans. The wavelength of the signal has to be small if it is to be reflected from small objects, such as the insects they eat, so bats operate at frequencies from 40 to 100kHz (wavelength 0.85 to 0.34cm). The cries are not only used to detect prey, but also to map out the obstacles (trees and so on) in the bat's flight path. Shown here is a Common bentwing bat (*Miniopterus schreibersii*) from Australia.

making, and are not due to changes in the environment. Sensory physiologists have called this self-generated stimulation reafferent, as opposed to the exafferent, stimulation that arises from external events.

Clearly, to make sense of the changing patterns of sensory stimulation, an animal's brain must distinguish reafferent and exafferent activity. In the case of human eye movements, which the brain knows about in advance because it generates them, there seems to be a kind of cancellation mechanism which removes the reafferent image movement, so that the world is seen as a seamless picture, and not as a series of jerky stills from an old movie, which is how it appears on the retina. Reafferent information, however, can be useful. The way the visual world flows past our eyes when we walk, run or drive an automobile tells us a great deal about the distances of different objects, and how we should plan our future movements. The brain does not suppress this information and, indeed, it is its use that enables people with only one eye to be almost as mobile as those with full binocular vision.

Most animals have sensory equipment that is quite similar to that of humans, and the three broad categories of vision, mechanoreception (which includes the various kinds of hearing) and the chemical senses of taste and smell, probably encompass most of the ways that animals find out about their world. There are two important senses, however, that humans do not possess, and their discoveries were major events in the history of the physiology of sense organs. These senses are the echolocating ability of bats and some marine mammals and

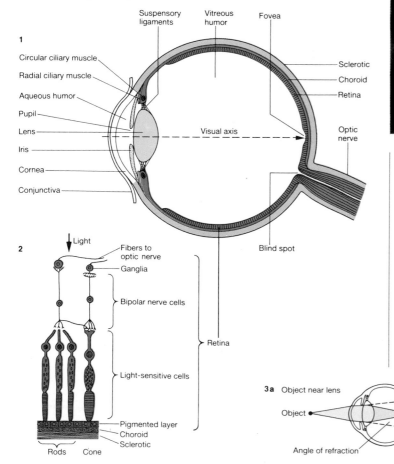

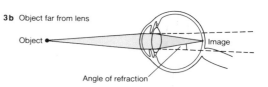

▲ **Equipped for night vision,** the eyes of owls, such as this Long-eared owl (*Asio otus*), have very wide pupils to allow maximum light to enter the eye.

◄▼ **The mammalian eye** and its operation. (**1**) Structure of the human eye with (**2**) detail of the light-sensitive layers; note that the light passes through a layer of nerves before reaching the light-sensitive cells. (**3**) Focusing (accommodation) for (**a**) a near object and (**b**) a distant object. Note that the lens does the fine focusing, while the cornea causes the main diffraction of the light rays.

► **A powerful lens** is necessary in the eyes of aquatic animals, such as this Atlantic cuttlefish (*Sepiola atlantica*) because, with water either side of it, light is not focused by the cornea.

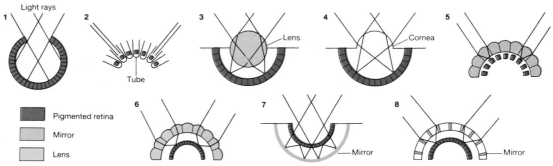

▲ **How different animals see**—
diagrammatic representations of the
eight different ways of producing an
image in "eyes." (1) Pigmented cup
of flatworms. (2) Compound
pigment cups of tube worms.
(3) Lens eye of fish and cephalopods.
(4) Corneal refraction eye of
mammals etc. (5) Apposition
compound eye of day-active insects
and crustaceans. (6) Superposition
compound eye of nocturnal
insects. (7) Simple mirror eye of
scallops. (8) Superposition mirror
eye of shrimps and lobsters.

the use of weak electric pulses by certain fish in navigation and communication.

Vision

Of all the senses, vision is the most valuable for determining the identity and layout of objects in the surroundings. Light travels in straight lines and, provided that an animal has an eye with an imaging system, this means that its retina receives a picture that is an accurate two-dimensional projection of the world around. With two separated eyes that give slightly different views of a scene, or with one eye that moves relative to the world (roughly the situation in insects), the brain can build up a full three-dimensional representation of at least the near world. Humans have such faith in the reconstruction that the brain makes from visual images that it is taken for the "real" world. Without the huge computing power of the brain, however, there would be nothing. The optical image in the eye is, on its own, as uninformative as an undeveloped photograph.

Nevertheless, that image is the vital first step in the visual process because, without it, only the average light intensity of a scene devoid of any detail would be seen. In the course of evolution, about eight different ways of producing images have been tried out. In the simplest animals, such as flatworms and annelid worms, occur the simplest optical systems consisting just of a retina lining a cup of black pigment. The pigment cup shields some receptors from light from one direction, and others from other directions, so that a crude image is formed simply by shadowing, as in a pinhole camera. A variation of this pattern, which is probably the way compound eyes originated, is for each receptor to be placed at the bottom of its own pigmented tube, so that each views a slightly different direction of space; such "prototype" compound eyes like this can still be found in some fanworms. Systems that rely just on shadowing for their optics waste light, however; what the receptors do not see is absorbed by black pigment. Almost any optical collector—a lens or mirror system, will improve upon this.

Eyes with lenses have evolved many times and, like life itself, always in the sea. Human eyes are a modification of the eyes of marine ancestors. It is important to know this, because an important image-forming mechanism—the curved cornea that separates air of low refractive index from water of high refractive index—was not available to marine animals. With water inside and outside, all the optical work had to be done by the lens itself (in humans the lens only does about a third of the focusing while the corneal surface does the rest. The real function of the lens is to adjust the focus.)

Powerful spherical lenses, in single-chambered eyes, evolved independently in fish, in the cephalopod mollusks (octopus and squid), probably twice more in the gastropod mollusks (for example, conch shells) and, interestingly, once only in the annelid worms in a group of marine carnivores (the alciopids). This is clearly a very effective design for an eye. Eyes (such as those of humans) which use corneal refraction are limited to the land vertebrates, the spiders (some of which, the jumping spiders, have visual acuity not much lower than that of primates) and the larvae of some insects (tiger beetles, for example). These single-chambered insect light receptors, however, are always replaced in the adult by compound eyes, for reasons that are quite obscure. An alternative to a refracting system for producing an image would be to use a curved mirror at the back of the eye, behind the retina, in a manner similar to a reflecting astronomical telescope. Only one example of this

is known, in the little eyes that surround the mantle edge of scallops, which cause the animal to shut its shells when a predator approaches.

Compound eyes, where many optical systems serve the retina, rather than a single one as in the human eye, are found mainly but not exclusively in the insects and crustaceans, and they represent the other great family of eye designs. In the most straightforward form, the apposition eyes of day-active insects, such as bees, each small group of receptors has its own private lens and views a very small region of the surroundings only a degree or so across. A bee's eye has about 5,000 of these optical units (or ommatidia) covering most of the 360 degrees of field of view surrounding the animal. In nocturnal insects and crustaceans which live in deeper water where the light is also dim, another kind of compound eye, the superposition

Seeing in Color

To resolve color, an animal must have receptors that are sensitive to different wavelengths of light. The visible spectrum for humans, is the wavelength range between 0.0004mm and 0.0008mm. Humans are trichromatic, that is, we have three kinds of visual pigment (rhodopsin) in different receptors (the cones), and these receptors are most sensitive to blue (420nm), green (534nm) and yellow (564nm). The colors that we see subjectively result from the balance of the stimulation the three types of receptors receive. In the dark we use only one type of receptor (the rods, most sensitive in the blue-green at 498nm), and we then of course cannot determine color, that is we are color-blind.

In insects the spectrum is slightly different. It extends down into the ultraviolet (wavelengths shorter than 400nm) but, except in the case of some butterflies, not so far into the red. Like humans, bees are trichromatic, but their receptors are most sensitive to ultraviolet (340nm), blue (450nm) and green (540nm), respectively (see ABOVE RIGHT). The flowering plants evolved in parallel with insects, and both groups exploit each other (for pollination on the one hand and nectar on the other). Thus, it is not too surprising that many flowers have ultraviolet markings that are invisible to humans, but which serve to guide insects to nectar sources. Similarly, many butterflies have ultraviolet markings used in sex

and species recognition.

At the other end of the visible spectrum are the infrared wavelengths. This range is exploited by some snakes, notably rattlesnakes and pit vipers (BELOW), to detect homiothermic ("warm-blooded") prey. Warm objects emit infrared radiation, and snakes detect this radiation with a pair of pit-like organs resembling pin-hole cameras, situated between the eyes and the nostrils. This seemingly useful way of finding prey can only be used by poikilothermic ("cold-blooded") predators: mammals emit too much background radiation.

▲ **An interpretation** of the visual acuity of an insect eye showing the colors of a yellow flower that humans might see if they had the photoreceptors of a bee. In reality, an insect would not perceive an image made up of the individual circles shown here.

▼ **Pit viper** (*Trimeresurus popeorum*) showing the heat-sensitive pit in front of the eye.

▲ ▼ **Compounding the image.** The "eyes" of insects, such as this horsefly ABOVE are actually composed BELOW of a mass of individual elements called ommatidia (1). Each ommatidium (2) consists of a cornea, a lens and a light-sensitive rhabdom surrounded by retina cells, which transmit the stimulus.

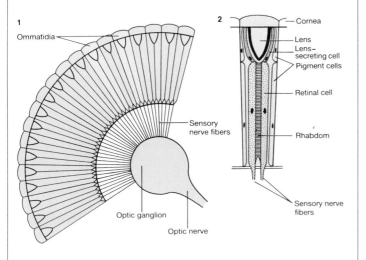

eye, has evolved. In these eyes the individual lenses (or, in the shrimps and lobsters, mirrors) do not form separate images, but contribute to a single deep-lying image which is very much brighter than the multiple images of apposition eyes. In neither type of compound eye is resolution particularly good, because the individual lenses are so small. The smallest angle that can be resolved in the bee is 1°, which is 60 times worse than our own 1 minute resolution but, for small fast-moving animals, this seems not to matter. Certainly, in terms of sheer numbers, compound eyes are every bit as successful as the single-chambered "camera"-type eyes of vertebrates.

The tendency of light to travel in straight lines, along "rays," is the property that makes image formation possible. Two other aspects of the nature of light are also important in the way eyes are built. Light is a wave form, with a wavelength in green light of 0.0005mm, and it also comes as discrete packets, or photons, which cannot be subdivided. A consequence of the wave form of light is well known to astronomers: the bigger the lens (relative to the wavelength of light) the better the resolution of the image. To resolve two stars, separated by an angle A (in radians: 1 radian = 57.3 degrees of arc) requires a lens with a diameter of $\frac{1.22\,\lambda}{A}$ (λ is the wavelength of the light). To resolve a small angle requires a large lens and if the figures for the human eye (pupil diameter 2.5mm in daylight) and for the bee (lens diameter 0.025mm) are put into the equation, they give angles of about 1 minute and 1 degree respectively, which are the actual limits of resolution in the two species. Thus, small as the wavelength of light is, it imposes a fundamental limit on how well humans, and other animals, see.

The fact that light arrives as single photons imposes limits to vision when the light is dim. At night, or in the deep sea, there are very few photons available to be received (it has been estimated that at the absolute limit of human vision, single receptors receive about one photon every 45 minutes!) The problem in dim light is basically a statistical one; the fewer photons there are to be counted, the less can be said about the relative brightnesses of the objects from which they originated, and this is the main reason why human and other animal vision becomes poor, and finally fails as the light dims. Interestingly, the cure for poor resolution in bright light and poor sensitivity in dim light is the same—make the lens bigger. It is no coincidence that Giant squid, which need good resolution to catch prey in dim light, have the largest eyes of all, up to 400mm (16in) in diameter.

Light has two further properties, color (see box) and polarization, which animals use. Humans are unable to detect the way light is polarized but a great many invertebrates can. Briefly, the waves that make up a single photon vibrate in only one plane, the plane of polarization. Different photons, however, have different planes of vibration, and light from the sun contains all possible vibration planes. When sunlight passes through the upper atmosphere, however, scattering particles separate out photons with different planes of vibration so that blue sky, as seen from the earth, is polarized to a greater or lesser extent, depending on the position of the sun. Thus, the pattern of polarization in the sky can indicate the sun's position to an animal even when the sun itself is not visible. In the 1940s, the great Austrian biologist, Karl von Frisch showed that bees make use of this pattern as a navigation aid: it substitutes for the sun as a compass in partially overcast weather. Terrestrial objects polarize light, too; water surfaces, in particular, polarize light completely at certain angles, as do various other shiny surfaces (some leaves and butterfly wings, for example). Thus, polarization provides further clues, in addition to color and brightness, for detecting the nature of objects. Insects are able to detect these differences because their rhodopsin molecules are aligned; those of humans are not appropriately aligned but it is possible artificially to appreciate what a bee might see by rotating the polarizing lens from a pair of dark glasses in front of the eyes—shiny surfaces become alternately light or dark.

Animals make use of their sense of sight in a myriad of ways. Even the simplest eye can help an animal select the right habitat, dark or light. Given a reasonable optical system, however, there is no reason why an eye should not provide the animal that bears it with as much information as is available to humans, or even more. What an animal does with the information then depends entirely on the capacity of its brain. It is hard to believe, for example, that insects see the world as humans do but, if an attempt is made to categorize the various uses of vision in humans—guidance over short distances, navigation over longer distances, object recognition, communication and so on—all are represented to some degree in the repertoire of insect behavior. At the other extreme, scallops (with mirror eyes) and fanworms (with small compound eyes) both use them for one purpose only: to detect predators. Not all animals exploit the potentialities of vision to the same degree.

The Mechanical Senses

All animals respond to mechanical disturbance. Even the protozoan *Paramecium* has a sophisticated mechanism for reversing direction when it touches an obstacle. Contact with one end causes a flow of charged particles which changes the internal voltage and, in turn, this causes the cilia to reverse their direction of beating, which reverses the animal's direction of movement. Contact with the opposite end has the opposite effect, again causing the animal to reverse direction.

Touch. A great many different tasks can be accomplished in higher animals by receptors that are sensitive to deformation. Receptors that indicate contact with the body surface (touch) are found in all animals. In insects they take the form of bendable hairs, each of which has one or more sense cells making contact with the base.

In humans, touch and, incidentally, the texture of surfaces that we scan with our fingers, are received by modified nerve endings in the skin, each of which has an elastic capsule around it (Pacinian corpuscle). The capsule has the effect of transmitting fast events—sudden taps—to the nerve, but the capsule bulges out when constant pressure is applied, and this is not transmitted. Deformation sensors also measure the stresses (tensions) and strains (length changes) produced by the action of an animal's muscles. These proprioceptive measurements are necessary for the proper coordination of locomotion. Muscle length is almost always measured by receptors incorporated

Electrical Senses in Fish

The electrical sense of certain fish, the mormyrids of Africa and the knifefish (gymnotids) of South America, was the last of the major animal senses to be discovered. In 1951, the Cambridge zoologist, Hans Lissmann, found that the mormyrid, *Gymnarchus*, emitted a continuous train of electrical pulses from its tail, that it could avoid obstacles successfully in the dark and that it would vigorously attack an electrode which "played back" its own discharge into the water. This suggested that the electrical pulses were used in navigation and possibly in communication.

The pulses produced by modified muscles in the tails of electric fish cause an electric field around the fish which is picked up by special receptors (2), derived from the lateral line system, in the head region. This field (1) is constant so long as the fish swims in open water. If there are obstacles in the water, however, the field becomes distorted: conducting objects intensify the field locally and non-conducting objects spread it out. The result is that the fish can detect the presence of plant stems, river banks and other fish up to a range of about 1m (39in). The system is extraordinarily sensitive: the minimum detectable voltage difference is approximately 1 volt in 100km (62mi). The mormyrids and gymnotids live in the murky waters of tropical rivers, and this extra sense substitutes to a large extent for sight, which is denied them in these conditions.

Other fish, notably the sharks and rays, have electrical receptors, but do not produce electrical discharges themselves. This ability to detect weak currents is used to locate the small potentials given off by living animals buried in the sand, notably by flatfish, on which they feed. Yet other fish (see RIGHT) —the electric eels and rays—have massive electric organs that are used to stun prey.

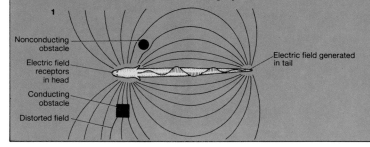

1
Nonconducting obstacle
Electric field receptors in head
Conducting obstacle
Distorted field
Electric field generated in tail

into elastic strands, or sometimes special muscle fibers, that run in parallel with the main muscles themselves; as the muscle lengthens, the strands stretch and the receptors are activated. In vertebrates, these muscle spindles and their equivalents in crustaceans, have their own muscle fibers associated with them, so that their "working range" can be independently adjusted. The arrangements for muscle tension measurement depend on the way an animal's skeleton is arranged. Insects, with external skeletons (cuticle) usually monitor deformations of the cuticle itself whereas, in mammals with an internal bony skeleton, tension is measured in the tendons that join the muscles to the bones.

Lateral line organs. One of the most interesting series of sense organs, all based on a single type of receptor, is the so-called acoustico-lateralis system of vertebrates. Its origins are found in fish, which have a series of shallow canals running over the body surface, which contain, at intervals, small clumps of hair cells, with tips that are usually embedded in a gelatinous cap, or cupula. The function of these organs, the lateral lines, is to monitor water currents around the body surface, providing the

fish with a type of "touch-at-a-distance" sense. The hair cells themselves have two kinds of projections, a single kinocilium, with its characteristic arrangement of internal filaments, and, to one side of this, an array of stereocilia which are similar structures but lack the internal filaments. When the whole bundle is bent in the direction of the kinocilium, the cell becomes more active, and bending in the opposite direction makes it less active. Thus, it can not only signal the strength of the stimulus that caused the bending, but its direction as well.

Keeping the balance. The same kind of cell turns up in the inner ear of vertebrates, performing three quite different functions. In one region (the utriculus) the hair cells have their tips in a jelly that contains small, heavy, stone-like otoliths. These tend to pull the cilia down in the direction of gravity and, if an animal changes the inclination of its head with respect to gravity, this change will be signaled by the hair cells. Thus, this is an organ of balance. Joined to the utriculus are the semicircular canals. These three canals, oriented at right-angles to one another, each contains a small bulge, and in this bulge is a group of hair cells with a cupula that almost fills the cavity. When the animal rotates its head, the fluid in the canals tends to remain still and, as the canal rotates around the fluid, the cupula is pushed one way or another. The result of this is that the hair cells signal head rotation in one of three planes depending on the particular canal. (If rotation is prolonged, the fluid and cupula tend to catch up with the head. When rotation stops the fluid carries on, and misleading signals, felt as dizziness, are the result.)

Hearing. The most impressive development of the hair cell system occurs in the cochlea, the organ of hearing in the inner ear. In mammals, sound waves are collected by the pinna, the visible external ear, and vibrate the eardrum. These vibrations are transmitted through the middle ear cavity by three small bones (ossicles) to another membrane which is the entrance to the inner ear, and to the cochlea itself. The cochlea is essentially a long coiled tube, containing a stretched, tuned fibrous sheet, the basilar membrane; the hair cells themselves, which ultimately detect the movements caused by sound, are in contact with this membrane along its entire length. The crucial component of the cochlea, which enables mammals to resolve the pitch (or frequency) of different sounds so well is the basilar membrane. At the end nearest the middle ear it is narrow, and this end vibrates strongly to high frequencies; it widens towards the tip of the cochlea, and vibrates to low frequencies. The best analogy is with a piano or a harp, where the length of the strings reflects their pitch. The actual arrangement of

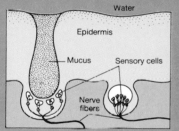

▲ **Electric ray** (*Hypnos monopterygium*), a species that produces an electric shock which is used to stun prey.

◀ **Electric field** produced (1) by the mormyrid *Gymnarchus* with (2) detail of two types of electroreceptors in its skin.

▼ **Lateral line organs of fish.** (1) Longitudinal section through the lateral line organ showing connections of the canal to the outside and position of the pressure receptors. (2) Detail of a single pressure receptor which comprises a cluster of sensory cells and their hairs, the latter enclosed in a gelatinous cupula. When water pressure moves the cupula, the hairs also bend, thus stimulating the sensory cells. RIGHT A bleak (*Alburnus alburnus*) showing the position of the lateral line system—the thin pale line along its length.

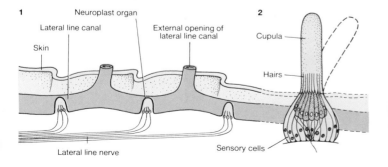

hair cells is quite complicated but, essentially, they have their bases on the basilar membrane and their cilia, as usual, in a gelatinous sheet that remains stationary. When sound of a pitch that corresponds to the appropriate position along the membrane occurs, the cells at that location vibrate, and the cilia are bent—the base waggling the fixed tip. Except at low frequencies, the hair cell activity represents the overall movement of the basilar membrane at each point, not the individual sound waves which are too rapid for the cells to follow. Thus, the pitch of a sound is coded primarily by the location of the active hair cells along the length of the cochlea.

In humans the range of audible frequencies is from about 20Hz (cycles per second) to 20,000Hz. This upper figure decreases remorselessly with age as the basilar membrane loses its elasticity. In bats, which use their ears for navigation and hunting, the upper limit is 100,000Hz or even higher. In reptiles, amphibians and fish, however, the ears are simpler; if the cochlea is present it is shorter, high frequencies are not detected and pitch discrimination is poorer. Sound is still used, however, as a means of communication; many fish make sounds, and everyone is familiar with the chorus of frogs. Unlike primate sounds or the songs of many birds, these vocalizations are very stereotyped and restricted in pitch. Therefore, frogs' ears, for example, are designed to hear frog calls but not much else.

The only other really noisy group of animals, with a sense of hearing to match, is the insects. As in the lower vertebrates, their songs tend to be stereotyped—strings of pulses with little or no frequency variation, usually made by scraping serrated parts of the body surface against each other. The ears, which may be located on the thorax, abdomen or even on the legs in some grasshoppers, consist of a drum to which a small number of receptors is attached directly. Most do not discriminate frequency: the information content of an insect song is contained in the arrangement of its pulses into syllables, rather than variations in pitch. Hearing in moths is rather special. Their ears respond to high frequencies (up to 40,000Hz) and they are not for communicating with one another, but for detecting the cries of hunting bats, the moths' main predators in the night world.

Sound waves travel in three-dimensional media such as air

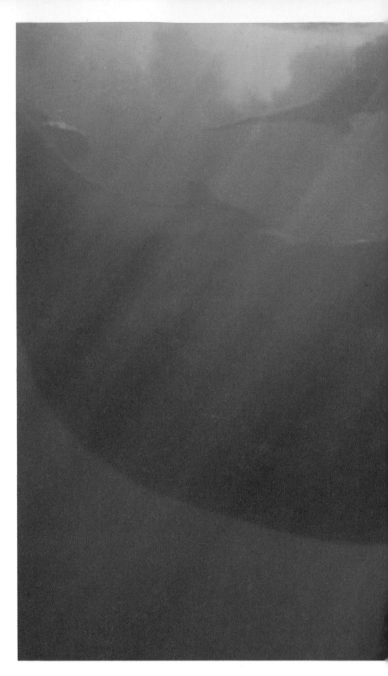

▲ **Underwater communication.** Soundwaves produced by whales can be heard over hundreds of kilometers—shown here are a humpback whale (*Megaptera novaeangliae*) and calf.

◄ **Ears bigger than eyes.** Frogs and toads do not have an outer ear but the middle ear is well developed with a superficially placed eardrum, clearly visible in this American bullfrog (*Rana catesbeina*).

► **Sound and balance**—structure of the human ear with detailed insets of the main sensory systems. Balance is controlled by the utriculus (**1**) and by semicircular canals and their ampullae (**2**). The utriculus contains chalky granules (otoliths) which lie above a sensory lining. When the head tilts, fibers from the lining pull on the otoliths and cause sensory stimulation. The ampullae respond to movements of the fluid in the semicircular canals caused by rotation of the head, which causes the cupula to be displaced and the sensory hairs to be stimulated. (**3**) Section of the organ of Corti which is found in the cochlea. When the liquid in the cochlea is made to vibrate through transmission of sound waves from the middle ear, the nerve endings in the organ of Corti are stimulated and send nerve messages to the brain.

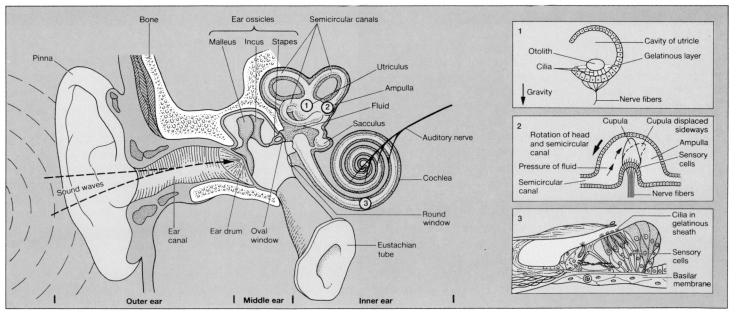

Bone

Ear ossicles

Malleus   Incus   Stapes

Semicircular canals

Pinna

Utriculus

Ampulla

Fluid

Sacculus

Auditory nerve

Sound waves

Cochlea

Ear
canal

Ear drum

Oval
window

Round
window

Eustachian
tube

Outer ear   **Middle ear**   **Inner ear**

1

Otolith

Cilia

Gravity

Cavity of utricle

Gelatinous layer

Nerve fibers

2

Rotation of head
and semicircular
canal

Pressure of fluid

Semicircular
canal

Cupula

Cupula displaced
sideways

Ampulla

Sensory
cells

Nerve fibers

3

Cilia in
gelatinous
sheath

Sensory
cells

Basilar
membrane

and water. A few animals make use instead of the vibrations in surfaces to communicate or to find food. Wolf spiders drum on the ground during courtship, and fiddler crabs bang the sand with their enlarged claws. The aquatic bugs, *Gerris* and *Notonecta*, detect the ripples on the water surface produced by struggling insects and, using receptors on their feet, they can establish the direction of the prey before pouncing. Similarly, many spiders use vibrations in their webs to locate prey and, from the frequency of the vibrations, distinguish between prey and potential mates.

Surface vibrations, however, do not travel far and are rapidly distorted; as a means of communication between animals, air- or water-borne sound is the most versatile. Acoustic signals can be detected over much longer ranges than chemicals, or visual displays (it has been estimated that the songs of whales can be heard over hundreds of kilometers in the sea) and the types of message that can be conveyed by sound are potentially limitless.

The Chemical Senses

In humans the chemical senses are usually divided into taste and smell. Taste is concerned with the palatability of substances dissolved in water already in the mouth, and smell much more with the detection of air-borne chemicals originating from a distance and captured by the membranes of the nose.

Smell can have a number of uses. Many animals use chemicals (pheromones) for communication; examples are the sex-attractant molecules of moths, the trail and alarm pheromones of ants and the territory-marking substances that many mammals produce. The detection of food, and of noxious substances resulting from decay are other functions of smell (olfaction) and, in some cases, smell may be used to establish the identity of particular places, such as the home streams where salmon return to spawn.

The distinction between taste and smell is not as clear in much of the animal kingdom. In aquatic animals, all chemicals are water borne (although fish still have distinct nostrils and

▲ **Chemical collectors** (antennae) of an African moon moth (*Argema mimosae*). Male silk moths respond to a chemical (bombykol) produced by virgin females, which they can detect hundreds of meters away. It has been shown that the antennae contain 17,000 odor receptors, and that 300 of these must be stimulated before the male moth will respond.

▶ **Pasting a grass stalk** with secretions ABOVE from its scent glands, a Brown hyena (*Hyaena brunnea*) leaves a record of its passage.

◄ **Howling in defiance,** OPPOSITE a Red howler monkey (*Alouatta seniculus*) uses sound as a means of contact in tropical jungles where vision is difficult.

◄ **Sound resonator** in a long-horned grasshopper. The left forewing has a special transparent resonator activated by the two wings scraping together.

▼ **Tasting.** (1) Taste areas of the tongue. (2) Section of tongue showing position of taste buds. (3) Detail of a taste bud.

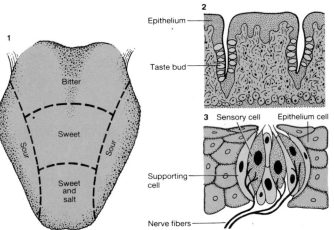

regions of skin in the mouth containing "taste buds") and, in the insects, it is often unclear whether a particular hair "smells" or "tastes" a chemical. Humans are rather insensitive to odors; we have fewer receptor cells in the nose than most mammals—although there are still about 15 million—and our sensitivity to a range of substances is as much as a million times lower than, for example, a dog.

It is generally recognized that there are four different components to taste: sweet, acid, salty and bitter. These can be shown to originate from taste buds in different regions of the tongue. Unfortunately, in spite of many attempts, there is no equivalent catalogue of odors. Recordings from mammalian smell receptors indicate that each is sensitive to a variety of odors, and it may be that a smell is reconstructed from the whole barrage of nerve activity that reaches the brain—a sort of "odor image"—rather than from the selective stimulation of special classes of receptor. This contrasts with the situation in insects, where particular types of receptor do seem to respond to restricted kinds of chemical. In the case of some pheromone receptors—such as that for the moth pheromone, bombykol—the receptors may be tuned to that molecule and nothing else. Bombykol is produced by virgin female silk moths from glands on the abdomen and this is picked up by the large feathery antennas of male moths. The response of males to bombykol is very specific. The chemical has been synthesized, and even the shifting of the positions of single hydrogen atoms in the central part of the chain results in a 100–1,000-fold decrease in effectiveness. Different moth genera use different attractants but, within a genus, the attractant is usually the same.

Almost nothing is known of the way odors are transduced, but it is a safe assumption that there is some kind of lock-and-key arrangement between molecular structures in the receptor membrane and odor molecules that results in the opening of ion channels when the appropriate type of molecule is captured.   MFL

Movement of Animals

ONE of the characteristics of animals which, for most non-scientists, differentiate them from inanimate objects is their ability to move organs, limbs, or even the whole body either by conscious action or involuntarily. Most animals are capable of some kind of observable movement whether it be the simple waving of the tentacles of a sedentary coral polyp, the swimming of fish, or the fast, coordinated dash of a cheetah in pursuit of prey.

Most animals possess the power of locomotion, that is, the ability to move from place to place. Locomotion in animals has many different functions, including finding food, escaping from predators, finding partners for sexual reproduction and so on. Single-celled animals (protozoans) move by the action of hair-like cilia or flagella, by amoeboid crawling and by several other techniques. Multicelled animals, however, move from place to place by a wide variety of methods. Earthworms or snails crawl, mammals may walk, run, swim or fly, while birds are considered to be the masters of the air and fish are wonderfully suited to propelling themselves through water. And, to achieve the various kinds of locomotion, muscles and skeletons work in harmony to provide the power. There remains much to be learnt about the techniques of locomotion.

◄ **Taking to the air,** a flock of Greater flamingos (*Phoenicopterus ruber*) first have to run across the water surface to gain speed.

Muscles and muscle types. . . How muscles work. . . Skeletons. . . Antagonistic action of muscles. . . Jointed skeletons. . . Hydrostatic skeletons. . . Crawling in earthworms, snakes and snails. . . Walking and running in humans and other mammals. . . The action of tendons. . . Swimming in water beetles, fish, cuttlefish. . . Swimming in dolphins. . . Oars and propellers. . . Buoyancy in fish. . . Gliding in flying fish and birds. . . Soaring in vultures and albatrosses. . . Principles of powered flight. . . Hovering in hummingbirds. . . Insect flight. . . Speeds on land. . .

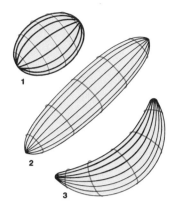

◄► **Muscle actions.** Three positions of an imaginary sausage-shaped animal which has circular muscles. In (1) the longitudinal muscles are contracted and the circular muscles relaxed. This is reversed in (2) and in (3) the longitudinal muscles on one side only are contracted. Nematode worms RIGHT move by means of alternate contractions of dorsal and ventral muscles.

THE forces required for most movement of multicelled animals are provided by the contraction of muscles. There are two main types of muscle: smooth and striated. Smooth muscles are concerned with the movements of certain internal organs, such as the rhythmic contractions of the gut. These are involuntary movements and the individual neither has conscious control over them nor is normally aware of the movements. Striated muscles are so-named because of the banded appearance of their fibers when viewed under the light microscope. They are responsible for most externally visible movements, such as the movements of limbs and other appendages. Contractions of most striated muscles are under conscious control and the individual is aware of the resulting movement or other action.

Fish, reptiles, amphibians, birds and mammals (vertebrates) have three main types of striated muscle: red and white skeletal muscle, and heart muscle. Red muscles have a good blood supply and obtain their energy by oxidizing foodstuffs to carbon dioxide and water. They have plenty of mitochondria, the subcellular sites of this process of oxidation. White muscles have a sparser blood supply, their cells have fewer mitochondria and they obtain energy by converting the carbohydrate glycogen to lactic acid. This process does not require an immediate oxygen supply although an oxygen debt is built up which has to be repaid later (see Gas Exchange and Circulation). The different uses of the types of striated muscle have been demonstrated in experiments with dogfish. These fish can swim slowly for hours on end, using only a narrow strip of red muscle sited along the sides of the body. They can swim very much faster for short periods, however, by using the larger quantity of white muscle in the tail, building up an oxygen debt as they do so.

► **Skeletal materials.** Much of the strength of skeletal materials, such as bone and shells, is due to the arrangement of their components. Just as fiberglass can be matched to a particular function by arranging the glass fibers in a particular direction, so too are the fibers and layers of natural skeletal material adapted to function. These three scanning electron micrographs show just three types of skeletal material. TOP One type of mollusk shell is constructed of a series of layers in each of which the crystals lie at different angles. BOTTOM The ossicles that form the internal skeletons of echinoderms (starfish etc) consist of a network of calcareous struts with spaces filled with living connective tissue. Greatly magnified, it looks rather like foam rubber. FAR RIGHT A common type of bone is constructed of a series of channels (Haversian canals) surrounded by concentric rings of bone, each ring with its constituent fibers lying in different directions.

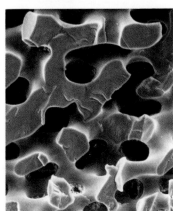

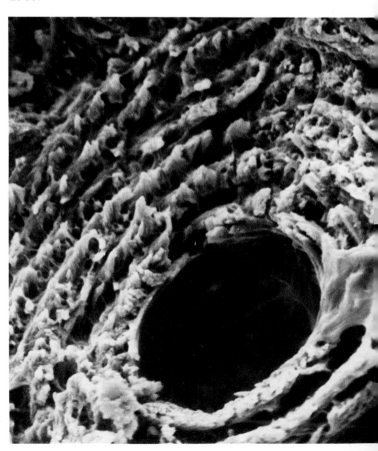

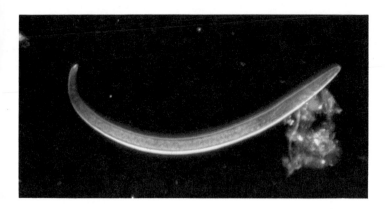

How Muscles Work

Light micrographs of striated muscle fibers show a very regular pattern, each pattern being repeated at intervals of a few micrometers (thousandths of a millimeter) along the fiber. Research in the early 1950s showed how this pattern could explain muscular contraction. There are two kinds of filament (thick and thin) running lengthwise along each muscle fiber (1). The thick filaments consist of the protein myosin and have projections known as cross-bridges; the thin filaments consist largely of the protein actin and lack cross-bridges.

When a muscle is stimulated to contract, the cross-bridges of the thick filaments attach to the thin filaments around them, pulling on them so that they slide between the thick ones. The fiber shortens like a telescope (2) so that the filaments totally overlap when seen in cross-section (3). As the muscle fibers shorten, the cross-bridges repeatedly detach and then re-attach further along the thin filaments.

Vertebrate striated muscle has thick and thin filaments about 2 micrometers long and can exert stresses (force per unit cross-sectional area) up to 0.3 megapascals (equivalent to the force exerted by a 3kg weight resting on one square centimeter). Some invertebrate muscles have longer filaments with more cross-bridges, with the result that larger stresses can be exerted. The strongest known muscle is found in mussels and can exert a force of 1.4 megapascals. Such strength, however, is obtained at the expense of speed of action. Even muscles with short filaments vary greatly in speed of contraction—finger muscles of mice (which are among the fastest known muscles) contract 15 times faster than the leg muscles of tortoises. Wing muscles of insects and small birds, contracting repetitively at very high frequencies, have a high power-to-weight ratio (about 200 watts per kilogram, compared to about 175 W/kg for an electric drill).

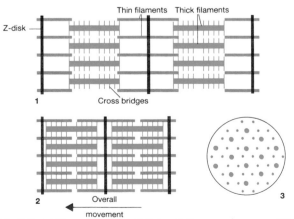

Skeletons

Muscles often act on skeletons which may be essential parts of the apparatus of movement. A vertebrate body without a skeleton would be like a blob of jelly, incapable of precise movement. Typical vertebrate skeletons are constructed of bone, which consists of calcium phosphate crystals (70 percent) embedded in the protein collagen (30 percent). The shells of crabs and other crustaceans consist of 60–90 percent calcium carbonate with protein and a fibrous carbohydrate (chitin). Mollusk shells consist of calcium carbonate with (usually) less than 5 percent protein. Insect cuticle contains no inorganic crystals, but is a composite of protein and chitin. In most cases the composite structure (crystals plus protein) is important because the crystalline material alone would be too brittle and the protein alone would be flexible and rather weak.

Bones and shells can be likened to fiberglass, which is a strong, tough material although it consists of glass, which is brittle, and a plastic resin which is not particularly strong. Bone and insect cuticle are about as strong and stiff as hardwood. Mollusk shell is weaker but stiffer.

Antagonistic action of muscles. The only active movement that a muscle can make is to shorten. It can be stretched, but it cannot lengthen itself and it cannot of itself twist or bend. How, then, can muscles cause the complex movements of living animals? One of the most important principles involved is antagonism. Two muscles are antagonistic if each reverses the effect of the other. Contraction of muscle A causes a movement and stretches muscle B. Contraction of B then reverses the movement and stretches A. Almost every muscle has an antagonist.

In many animals (those with so-called hydrostatic skeletons) antagonism depends on the incompressibility of water. Body tissues and fluids cannot be compressed like air in a bicycle pump, but have essentially constant volume. Imagine a sausage-shaped animal with two sets of muscles. One set runs hoop-like around the body (circular muscles) and the other set lengthwise along the body (longitudinal muscles). Contraction of the circular muscles makes the sausage thinner, but also makes it longer because its volume cannot be changed. Contraction of the longitudinal muscles makes it shorter and fatter. Thus, the two sets of muscles are antagonistic. Now suppose that the longitudinal muscles of the left side contract while the circular muscles keep constant length. The animal bends to the left and the longitudinal muscles on the right are stretched. Thus, the muscles of the two sides can act as antagonists. Our simple animal can lengthen, shorten and bend from side to side although it has no skeleton. Earthworms are like this, but have their bodies divided into segments. One group of segments can lengthen or bend to the left while another group shortens or bends to the right. Internal partitions cross the liquid-filled body cavity between segments.

In some animals, such as nematodes (roundworms), the circular muscles are replaced by an inextensible cuticle which prevents swelling. These animals can bend from side to side, or in a vertical plane, by contracting appropriate longitudinal muscles, but they cannot lengthen or shorten.

Snakes are similar in shape to earthworms and nematodes but, like other vertebrates, they have a backbone of bony, jointed vertebrae. Contraction of longitudinal muscles on one side bends the snake and stretches the muscles on the other side because the vertebrae cannot be compressed.

A few muscles do not have other muscles as antagonists. For example, the two halves of a clam shell are joined by an elastic hinge, which makes them spring open when the muscles holding them together relax. Part of the muscle that closes the clam is specialized to maintain tension for long periods with little expenditure of energy.

These principles of muscle contraction, antagonism and their actions on various kinds of skeleton are used by whole animals to move them through their environment.

Crawling

Crawling is usually taken to mean movement overland without legs. Most major groups of animals have members which practice it. The feature common to all is that forward movement is caused by rhythmic waves of activity traveling along the body. In a crawling earthworm, segments in some parts of its body are short and fat and others long and thin. As it crawls, the thickenings move backwards along its body. When a snake crawls, bends start at the head and travel to the tail.

When an earthworm is burrowing, the thick part of the body is jammed firmly in the burrow. Segments in front of the thickening elongate, pushing the head forward, and segments just behind the thickening shorten pulling the tail forward. These changes propel the body forward and also cause the thickening to travel backwards along it. Similar movements also serve for crawling on the surface of the ground, aided by the ratchet-like effect of tiny bristles (chaetae) that project from the body. They point backwards, making it easier for the body to slide forwards than backwards.

A snake cannot shorten or lengthen its body because it has a backbone. Instead, it curves its body into bends around stones and other irregularities on the ground. As the bends travel backwards along the body they push against the stones and drive the snake forwards.

Snails crawl on a long foot that is covered with slimy mucus. Although some of the small species are propelled by cilia, most make use of waves of muscular contraction that travel along the foot. Like earthworms, they depend on a ratchet, but here the rachet is the mucus, which resists gentle pressure as if it were a solid but, if pressed hard enough, gives way and behaves like a liquid. The muscular waves of snails' feet are so proportioned that the stress under the parts that are pushing forward is enough to liquefy the mucus, but the stress under the parts that are pushing back is not.

Walking and Running

Soft-bodied animals, such as earthworms and slugs, can crawl and burrow effectively, but complex jointed skeletons (see box) are generally required for walking and running. Humans and other terrestrial mammals walk to travel slowly and run to go faster. A walking person does not lift one foot until the other has been set down, so there are brief stages when both feet are on the ground simultaneously. In contrast, running involves stages when both feet are off the ground. A similar distinction applies to four-footed animals: in walking, but not in running, there are always at least one forefoot and one hind-

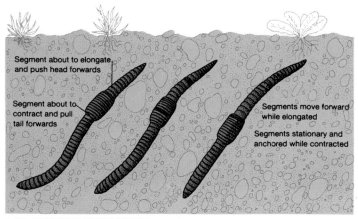

Segment about to elongate and push head forwards

Segment about to contract and pull tail forwards

Segments move forward while elongated

Segments stationary and anchored while contracted

CRAWLING MOVEMENTS

▲ **Movements of earthworms** through soil.

▶ **Locomotion in snakes.** In the usual serpentine movement, the sides of the body press against irregularities, and, as the waves pass back, the snake glides forward.

▶ **Sidewinding.** OPPOSITE In this bizarre method of locomotion, *Bitis peringueyi*, makes a series of parallel tracks in the sand.

▼ **Locomotion in slugs and snails.** The trail of slime left behind is essential for their movement. Where the body is extending the mucus liquefies to allow movement, but is rigid when the body is contracted.

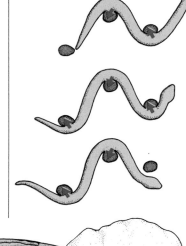

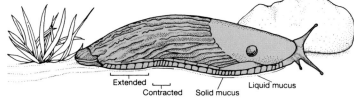

Extended   Liquid mucus
Contracted   Solid mucus

foot on the ground. Another important difference between human walking and running is that, in walking, each leg is kept fairly straight while the foot is on the ground. In running, the knees bend much more.

Most four-footed mammals walk at low speeds, but use several kinds of run at higher speeds. As horses and dogs increase speed they change successively from a walk to a trot to a canter and finally to a gallop, but many mammals omit one or more of these gaits. The sequence of footfalls in the gallop, in which the two forefeet are set down at one stage of the stride and the two hindfeet at another, makes it possible for back muscles as well as leg muscles to contribute to the work.

Walking and running have evolved to keep energy costs as low as possible, in very different ways. The principle of human walking is the principle of the pendulum, which requires very little energy to keep it swinging, although the bob is repeatedly rising and falling, speeding up and slowing down. As the bob swings down it loses height (and so potential energy) but gains speed (and so kinetic energy). As it swings up the reverse happens. Energy is swapped back and forth between the potential and kinetic forms. Similarly, a walking person slows down and

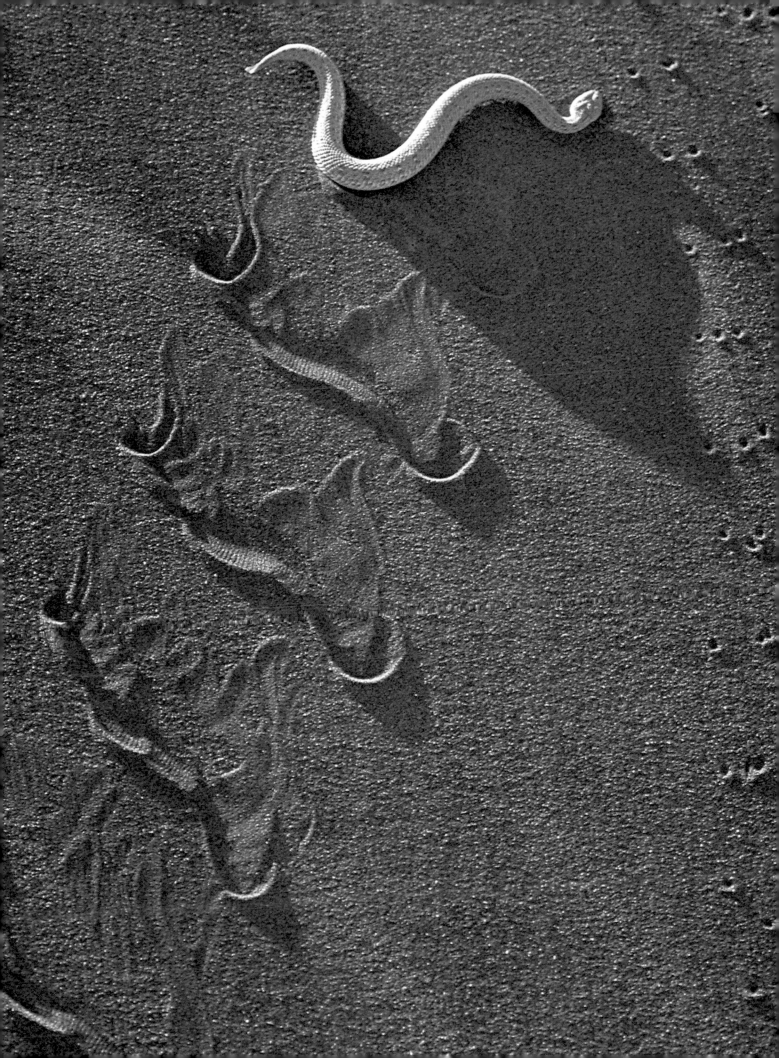

rises in the first half of each step but speeds up and falls in the second half. Ideally, the total mechanical energy (potential plus kinetic) should remain constant. This is not quite achieved, however, and the leg muscles have to do work at one stage of the step (increasing the mechanical energy of the body) and act like brakes at another (getting rid of mechanical energy by converting it to heat). Nevertheless, human walking is reasonably economical of energy. This is also true of the somewhat more complicated walking of four-footed mammals.

The principle of running is the principle of the bouncing ball, which will make many bounces without a fresh input of energy. When the ball hits the ground it is brought to a halt, losing its kinetic energy, but the energy is returned in the elastic recoil that throws it back into the air. The principal elastic structures in the legs that give them their bounce are the tendons, especially the Achilles tendon, which connects the calf muscles to the heel. It has been calculated that the Achilles tendon of a running human stretches and recoils by about 18mm (0.7in) at each footfall.

Swimming

Organisms that swim range from flagellate protozoans a few micrometers long to giant Blue whales more than 30m (100ft) long. Their mechanisms of propulsion use the principles of the

Jointed Skeletons

To enable an animal to walk, run, swim or fly, a system of solid levers is required. This is provided by jointed skeletons, of which there are two kinds—an endoskeleton which provides a system of levers inside the body and an exoskeleton which encloses the body like a suit of armor. Vertebrates have endoskeletons, but insects, crabs and other arthropods have exoskeletons. Knee joints of typical arthropods (4) and mammals (5) are shown below.

The skeletons of vertebrates are made of bone or, in sharks and so on, cartilage, which is softer. Individual bones meet at joints, the surfaces of which are covered by a thin layer of cartilage impregnated with a lubricating fluid—synovial fluid. The surface of cartilage is not particularly smooth, but this seems to improve lubrication, which depends on quite different principles from those used in engineering. The coefficients of friction in mammal leg joints are satisfactorily low, by engineering standards. Arthropod joints have no special lubrication and do not need it, because any pivots

involved have very small diameters. Similarly, toy cars are made with thin axles to minimize the effect of friction.

Bones linked by hinge joints, like the human knee (1), have flexor muscles to bend them and antagonistic extensor muscles to extend them. Joints like the wrist (2) and hip (3) that allow more freedom of movement are moved by correspondingly more muscles.

Some muscles attach directly to the skeleton, but others are joined to it by means of tendons made of collagen (in vertebrates) or by apodemes (pennate). This internal projections from the cuticle (in arthropods). Some muscles have all their fibers running parallel to one another, lengthwise along the muscle, but others have fibers running obliquely to tendons or apodemes (pennate). This pennate arrangement can increase the force a muscle can exert because numerous short fibers exert more force than a few long ones. However, the extra force is obtained at the expense of range of movement, because striated muscle fibers cannot shorten by much more than half their extended length.

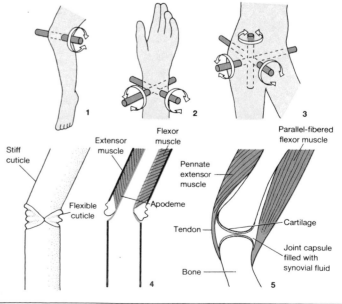

Stiff cuticle

Flexible cuticle

Extensor muscle

Flexor muscle

Pennate extensor muscle

Apodeme

Parallel-fibered flexor muscle

Tendon

Cartilage

Joint capsule filled with synovial fluid

Bone

▼ **Walking and pendulum analogy.** At stage (1) of their movements, man and pendulum are at their highest points. Hence, potential energy is high. However, their speeds (hence kinetic energies) are lowest at this stage. At stage (2) speed (and kinetic energy) are high but height (and potential energy) are low. Stage (3) is like (1) again. Thus, wastage of energy is avoided by converting energy back and forth between the kinetic and potential forms.

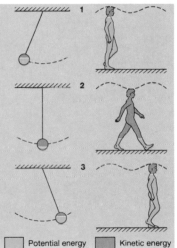

Potential energy   Kinetic energy

oar, of the propeller, of body undulation and of jet propulsion.

The essential difference between oars and propellers is that oars push in the direction of movement, but propellers exert forces at right angles to the movement of their blades. Thus, the thrust of an oar is derived from drag as it pushes backwards on the water, but the thrust of a propeller is derived from lift created as the blades (hydrofoils) move through the water. When a hydrofoil moves through water, tilted at a small angle of attack to its direction of motion, the force that the water exerts on it has two components: drag acting backwards along the direction of motion and lift acting at right angles to it. If the hydrofoil is suitably shaped and the angle of attack not too large, lift is much larger than drag.

To see how this applies to animals, compare a water beetle to a penguin. Both swim under water using paddle-like limbs. The water beetle has legs fringed with bristles and uses them as oars. It pushes the legs backwards with the bristles spread and then brings them forward again with the bristles folded so as to retard its motion as little as possible. The penguin swims with its wings; it does not move them backwards and forwards

as an oar, but up and down, using them as hydrofoils. Because it is moving forwards, the wing tips take an undulating path through the water. The angles of attack are adjusted so that lift acts forwards and up in the downstroke, forwards and down in the upstroke. The upward and downward components cancel out and the net effect is forward thrust.

Many fish row themselves along using their fins, especially when swimming slowly. Ciliate protozoans and many of the larvae in marine plankton row themselves along with vast numbers of tiny cilia. Whales are propelled by up and down movements of the tail flukes, in much the same way as penguins are propelled by their wings. Some fish, including tunnies, have hydrofoil-shaped tails, but move them from side to side, not up and down.

Many animals swim by undulation, making movements like a crawling snake. Just as the irregularities of the ground make it easier for the snake's body to slide forwards along its own length than to slide sideways, so does water resist sideways movement of a swimmer's body more than lengthwise movement. Therefore undulations traveling backwards along the

▶ **With fins extended like wings,** a shark (*Trienodon obesus*) maneuvers near the sea bed. Sharks obtain lift from their fins and tail.

▼ **Fish swimming.** Tracings from a film of a butterfish swimming showing the body positions at 1/20 second intervals. Undulations travel from head to tail, driving the fish forward.

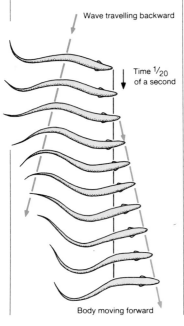

Wave travelling backward

Time 1/20 of a second

Body moving forward

body push the animal forwards. Water snakes, eels, leeches, flagellate protozoans and spermatozoans (male gametes) swim in this way.

The swimming techniques of fish grade imperceptibly from the undulation of eels to the hydrofoil action of tunnies. Many fish swim slowly by undulating their fins and for some, such as the sea horse, it is their only method of swimming. Cuttlefish (which are mollusks, not fish) swim slowly by undulating their fins and quickly by jet propulsion. They are related to the squids, which also use jet propulsion. They draw water into their mantle cavities and squirt it out forcefully forwards (to swim backwards) or backwards (to swim forwards).

Buoyancy. Muscle, bone, shell and most of the other tissues that make up animals are denser than water, making them tend to sink. Flatfish are denser than water and swim upwards to counteract sinking. Tunnies and many sharks swim with fins extended like airplane wings to give lift at the front end of the body, while their tails give lift at the rear. Many other swimming animals have their densities adjusted to match the

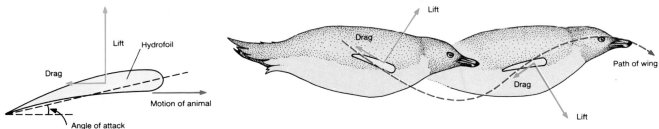

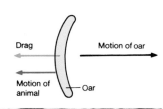

▲ **Swimming by hydrofoil.** To swim, the penguin uses its wings as hydrofoils, much as birds use their wings in flight. Unlike flying birds, however, the penguin reverses the angle of attack on the upstroke.

◄ **Swimming by oar action.** As the oar is moved backwards, it creates drag which projects the animal forward. This method of propulsion is used by water beetles (*Dytiscus marginalis*) BELOW.

▼ **Crashing through the waves,** a pair of Common dolphins (*Delphinus delphis*) swimming at the surface.

Swimming of Dolphins

Dolphins are among the fastest of swimming animals, propelling themselves by up-and-down movements of their tail flukes, but their apparent speed is sometimes deceptive. A dolphin keeping pace with a ship may be getting a free ride by resting in the wave that the ship is pushing along with its bows. The fastest record of unaided swimming is 40km/h (25mph), achieved by a trained dolphin chasing a lure which was towed by a winch across a lagoon in Hawaii. It has been calculated that this required at least twice as much power as can be produced by a human athlete of similar size. It has been suggested that the shape of dolphins and the properties of their skin have evolved to minimize drag, but it also seems that dolphin muscles must be more powerful than human ones.

water by some buoyant material. For example, some deep-sea sharks have huge quantities of squalene (a hydrocarbon) in their livers, the coelacanth and some of the oceanic lantern fish have wax esters widely distributed in their bodies and the cranchid squids have swollen body cavities filled with an (impure) ammonium chloride solution which is less dense than sea water although it has the same osmotic concentration.

Large quantities of all these materials are needed because their densities are not particularly low. Gas-filled floats can be much more compact. Many bony fish have gas-filled sacs (swimbladders) in their body cavities. These have flexible walls and are compressed by the increasing pressure as the fish swims deeper, so that more gas has to be added if the density of the fish is to be kept constant. Oxygen and other gases can be secreted from the blood into the swimbladder as required, or withdrawn again, but these processes are very slow. Cuttlefish and some other cephalopods have rigid shells divided into chambers, from which they extract the water to leave a partial vacuum. Because the shell is rigid there is no need to adjust for depth changes but, if the mollusk were to swim too deep, the pressure would make its shell collapse.

Gliding

Insects, birds and bats are the only animals that can make long flights, but some other animals glide for short distances. Flying phalangers from Australia have webs of skin between their fore and hind legs that enable them to glide from tree to tree. The same is true of the flying squirrels of Asia and North America and the flying "lemur" of Southeast Asia.

Flying fish, such as *Exocoetus* spp, have large fins that can be spread as wings. They emerge from the sea and travel for some distance with fins spread but with their tail still beating the water to increase their speed. Then they take off and glide for several seconds. The South American hatchet fish, such as *Carnegiella* spp, are small river-dwelling fish which are capable of leaping from the water and gliding for distances of about 10m (33ft). As well as large pectoral fins that function as wings, they have huge fin muscles and may beat their fins like insect wings. There seem to be no films that confirm this, but a buzzing noise has been heard as they fly past.

The weight of a glider (animal or machine) is supported by lift on its wings, but drag tends to slow it down. Nevertheless, it can maintain constant speed in still air by gliding on a downward gradient. Lift depends on speed and on the angle of attack of the wings, so the glider can travel quickly with a small angle of attack or slowly with a large one and get the lift needed to support its weight in either case. There is a minimum speed below which it cannot get enough lift and another higher speed at which drag is at a minimum and it can glide farthest.

As a general rule, the larger the aircraft the greater these speeds are. For instance, the minimum drag speed is about 90km/h (55mph) for a typical glider and 30km/h (18mph) for

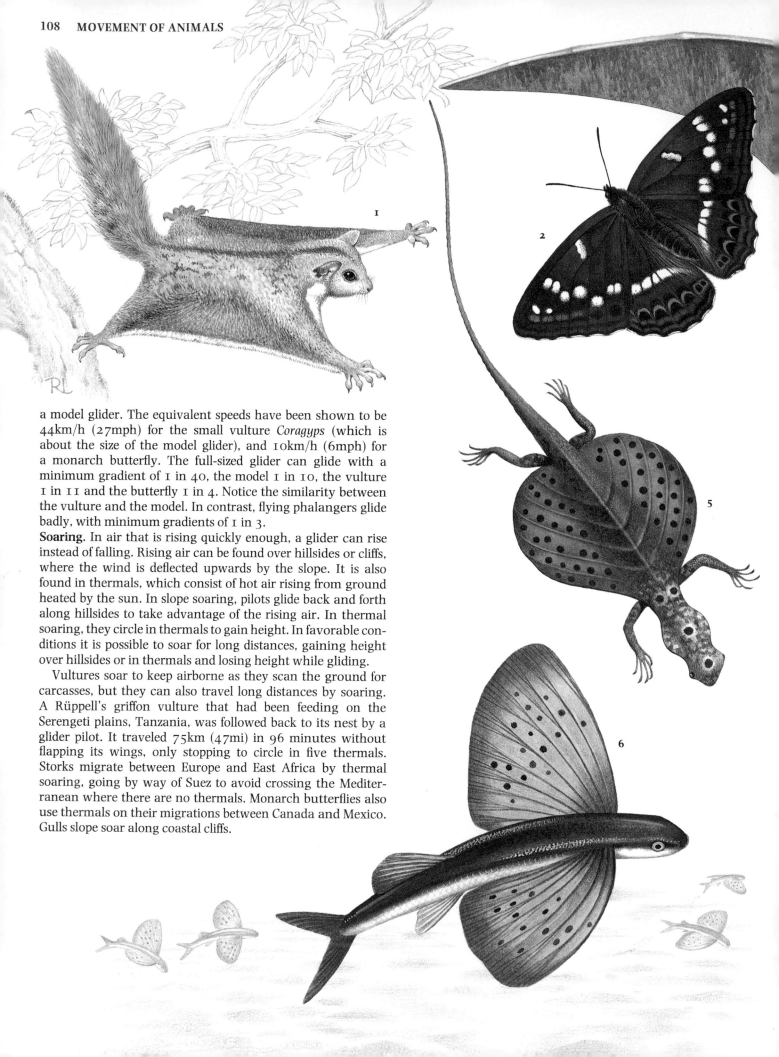

a model glider. The equivalent speeds have been shown to be 44km/h (27mph) for the small vulture *Coragyps* (which is about the size of the model glider), and 10km/h (6mph) for a monarch butterfly. The full-sized glider can glide with a minimum gradient of 1 in 40, the model 1 in 10, the vulture 1 in 11 and the butterfly 1 in 4. Notice the similarity between the vulture and the model. In contrast, flying phalangers glide badly, with minimum gradients of 1 in 3.

Soaring. In air that is rising quickly enough, a glider can rise instead of falling. Rising air can be found over hillsides or cliffs, where the wind is deflected upwards by the slope. It is also found in thermals, which consist of hot air rising from ground heated by the sun. In slope soaring, pilots glide back and forth along hillsides to take advantage of the rising air. In thermal soaring, they circle in thermals to gain height. In favorable conditions it is possible to soar for long distances, gaining height over hillsides or in thermals and losing height while gliding.

Vultures soar to keep airborne as they scan the ground for carcasses, but they can also travel long distances by soaring. A Rüppell's griffon vulture that had been feeding on the Serengeti plains, Tanzania, was followed back to its nest by a glider pilot. It traveled 75km (47mi) in 96 minutes without flapping its wings, only stopping to circle in five thermals. Storks migrate between Europe and East Africa by thermal soaring, going by way of Suez to avoid crossing the Mediterranean where there are no thermals. Monarch butterflies also use thermals on their migrations between Canada and Mexico. Gulls slope soar along coastal cliffs.

Albatrosses seldom flap their wings, but soar for hours over the oceans by a special technique that depends on the wind being slower close to the sea than it is higher up. They glide downwind, losing height but gaining speed, then turn into the wind and rise. As they rise they slow down relative to the sea, but, because they are rising into faster wind, the speed of the wind over their wings remains high enough to give the lift needed to keep them rising. After rising about 12m (40ft) they turn and repeat the process.

Gliding birds tilt their bodies to suit different gliding angles by swinging their wings forward or sweeping them back, altering their position relative to the center of mass of the body. They bank to make a turn by giving one wing a higher angle of attack than the other, so that it gets more lift. They normally fly with their feet retracted among the feathers, but they lower them when a braking effect is required.

The extinct pterosaurs probably soared like gulls and albatrosses. These winged reptiles, which lived at the time of the dinosaurs, in the Jurassic and Cretaceous periods (190–65 million years ago) included the largest known flying animals. Among them, *Pteranodon* had a wing span of 8m (26ft), and a few fragments of a considerably larger pterosaur have been found. The largest wing span among birds is about 3.4m (11ft), in the Wandering albatross. Pterosaurs seem to have had relatively small wing muscles but *Pteranodon* was so lightly built that its total mass was probably only about 17kg (38lb) and it could have taken off by spreading its wings and facing into a light breeze.

Powered Flight

When soaring is not feasible, power is needed for flight. Aircraft use propellers or jet engines, but animals flap their wings. There are two main kinds of flapping flight. In hovering flight, the animal's body is more or less stationary and its wings move very quickly. Hummingbirds and many moths hover in front of flowers while feeding on nectar, and dragonflies hover while watching for insect prey. In fast forward flight of birds, bats and large insects, the body travels forward at a speed which

◄▲▼ **Gliding animals**—species, past and present, which use gliding flight. (1) Sugar glider (*Petaurus breviceps*) in which gliding is achieved by use of a thin, furred membrane (patagium) that stretches from wrist to ankle. (2) Poplar admiral (*Limenitis populi*); butterflies use flapping flight for most of their movements, but over long distances, such as migrations, they often glide, frequently at the mercy of wind movements. (3) Pterosaurs, such as this *Pteranodon*, probably soared like gulls and albatrosses. (4) Large mouse-eared bat (*Myotis myotis*); bats have flaps of skin positioned similarly to those of the Sugar glider, but they can flap these and are thus capable of powered as well as gliding flight. (5) A flying dragon *Draco spilopterus*, which glides from tree to tree using a membrane joining the fore- and hind-limbs. (6) The Flying fish *Cypselurus californicus* has large fins which can be spread as wings that enable it to glide above the sea for short distances. (7) A flying frog *Agalychnis spurrelli*, which has large webs between its toes that enable it to glide between trees.

is comparable to the maximum speed of the wing tips. Small insects such as flies (Diptera) fly in a manner which is intermediate between hovering and fast forward flight.

In fast forward flight the wings beat up and down, taking a wavy path as the animal moves forward through the air. On the downstroke, lift acts forwards and upwards, propelling the animal forward and supporting its weight. For the upstroke, the angle of attack is decreased so that little or no lift is produced except possibly near the base of the wing (lift acting upwards, at right angles to the path of the wing, would have a backward component and so would tend to slow the animal down). In contrast to fast forward flight where lift is produced only on the downward stroke, in a penguin swimming with its wings, lift is produced on the upward as well as the downward stroke.

Animals use several different hovering techniques. In hummingbirds, moths, bees and many other insects, the wings are beaten horizontally, backwards and forwards. They turn upside-down for the backward stroke and the angle of attack is adjusted so that the lift always acts upwards.

Most hummingbirds beat their wings at frequencies of 20 to 50 cycles per second, a little above the lower limit of the range of frequencies of audible sound. For this reason, they emit a humming sound as they hover. Small insects beat their wings at higher frequencies, as indicated by the buzz of bees and the high-pitched whine of mosquitoes.

Each beat, up or down, of a mosquito's wing lasts less than one thousandth of a second. No ordinary muscle can contract so fast, but mosquito wings are worked by a special kind called fibrillar muscle. Other flies (Diptera), wasps etc (Hymenoptera), beetles (Coleoptera) and bugs (Hemiptera) also have fibrillar flight muscles. The special property of this muscle is that, so long as it is kept active by occasional nerve impulses (action potentials), it vibrates at the resonant frequency of the system.

A fibrillar muscle attached to a tuning fork would keep the fork vibrating. Tuning forks and many other mechanical systems have resonant properties because they have mass and elastic stiffness. Similarly, the mass of an insect's wings and the elastic properties of the thorax combine to make a resonant system which fibrillar muscle can drive. A simple experiment illustrates this; if the wings of a fly are shortened they beat at a higher frequency because their mass has been reduced.

▲ ▼ **Hovering.** A sequence BELOW showing the movements of a hummingbird's wings during hovering. Note that the underside of the wing is turned upward at one stage of movement. ABOVE A Costa's hummingbird (*Calypte costae*) hovering to suck nectar from a flower.

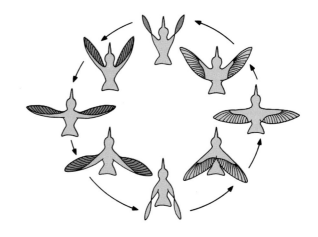

▶ **Insect hovering.** A Hummingbird hawkmoth (*Macroglossum stellatarum*) hovers over a scabious flower.

◀ **Clap and fling.** Diagram of a hovering insect using the clap-and-fling technique. The circulation of air around the wings as they separate following the clap gives enhanced lift.

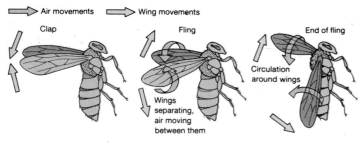

Air movements   Wing movements

Clap   Fling   End of fling

Wings separating, air moving between them

Circulation around wings

Lift

Drag

Drag

1

2

▲ **Flight sequence.** A duck's wing is an aerofoil which supports the bird in the air as well as propelling it (**1**). Unlike the hydrofoil of a penguin, the upstroke produces no lift (**2**), but drag is minimized.

▶ **Feather power**—a Blue tit (*Parus caeruleus*) in flight. The force of the air on the wings is indicated by the spreading and bending upward of the primary wing feathers.

In many insects, the elasticity of the resonant system seems to be mainly the elasticity of the muscles themselves. In others, the elastic properties of the skeleton are also important. Many have parts of the cuticle of the thorax made of resilin, a protein with properties like rubber. These serve to adjust the resonant frequency to the required wing-beat frequency.

The resonant qualities of the thorax are important even in insects with non-fibrillar wing muscles because a resonant system needs relatively little power to keep it vibrating. The kinetic energy of the wings is not lost at the end of each stroke, but is made available for the next stroke by the elastic rebound.

Unsteady Aerodynamics
It has been said that science has proved bumblebees cannot fly. Science has, of course, proved no such thing. What scientists have shown is that conventional aerodynamics is incapable of explaining the flight of many insects. The lift on their wings, calculated for each stage of the wing beat cycle from the standard aerodynamic equations, is far too small to support their weight. The explanation is that the equations refer only to wings or propeller blades moving steadily at constant speeds. Flapping wings stop and accelerate again between one stroke and the next, making it possible to exploit "unsteady" effects unknown in engineering.

There is still a lot of uncertainty about the aerodynamics of insect flight. There is no satisfactory, quantitative explanation of the hovering flight of dragonflies and hoverflies, which use rather small, roughly vertical wing movements instead of the usual large horizontal ones.

One of the unsteady effects used by insects (and some birds) was discovered in 1973 by Professor Torkel Weis-Fogh of Cambridge University, who called it the "clap and fling." The wings are clapped together, back to back, at the end of the upstroke. The air flowing into the growing space between them, as they separate again, sets up a circulation of air which gives greatly enhanced lift. For a short time, the lift is far greater than would act on the wings if they were moving steadily at the same speed. The clap and fling is used by many insects and also by some birds when hovering or flying slowly. The wings of pigeons can be heard clapping together, when they take off. RMcNA

Record Breakers

Speeds on land

The only animals whose top running speeds are known accurately are the three that race for sport: humans, the greyhound and the racehorse. In sprint races men reach speeds of about 36km/h(22.5mph). Greyhound races of about 0.4km (0.25mi) around the track are run at about 58km/h (36mph) and horse races of up to 1.5km (1mi) are run at about 61km/h (38mph).

It is often stated that cheetahs can run at over 110km/h (70mph), but this seems unlikely. It is difficult to measure accurately the speeds of wild animals in their natural habitats and estimates are often exaggerated. In the course of research, vehicles have been used to chase many species of mammal across the East African plains. The fastest speed measured in this way was 52km/h (32mph) for Thomson's gazelles and zebras; ostriches seem to be a little faster but technical difficulties prevented accurate measurement. Both larger and smaller animals are slower. The top speed of chipmunks is about 13km/h (8mph) and there do not seem to be any really reliable records of elephants running faster than approximately 16km/h (10mph).

Although the dinosaurs are extinct, study of fossil footprints can be used to estimate the speeds they traveled at. Most of the estimates are between 3.5 and 7km/h (2.25 and 4.5mph), but these represent habitual speeds, not top speeds. One set of footprints has been interpreted as having been made by a moderately sized dinosaur running at 43km/h (27mph), but there is no evidence of large dinosaurs running as fast.

Among arthropods, cockroaches can run at 3km/h (1.8mph) and an exceptionally fast crab at 7km/h (4.5mph). A snail's pace is about 10m/h or 0.006mph.   RMcNA

▼ **Galloping across the Etosha Plains,** Namibia, these gemsbok (*Oryx gazella*) have been frightened by an aircraft. They are probably running no faster than about 50km/h (31mph). The INSETS show a sequence of a racing greyhound at full speed. When galloping, dogs set down their two forefeet together (or in a rapid sequence), as they also do with the two hind feet. As well as the important role of tendons and muscles in the legs, those of the back are also involved since at one stage of the stride the back bends, and at another it straightens.

Coordination and Control

CONSIDER the many complex processes involved in playing a golf stroke. Firstly, the position of the hole must be located visually (if the hole is close enough to see). Then its distance and direction from the player must be assessed. The ball is placed accurately on to the tee. An appropriate club is selected from the many that may be carried and removed from the bag. The handle of the club is grasped correctly in both hands and the head lined up with the ball. The club is then drawn back and swung downwards so that its head strikes the ball with sufficient accuracy and weight to carry the ball through the air towards the hole. And, an experienced and skillful player may sometimes be able to direct the ball with one shot into the hole, which is only a few centimeters in diameter, over a distance of more than a hundred meters. And even a well-coordinated novice may be able to hit the ball to within a few meters of the hole after a little practice. Looked at in this way, such a series of actions is a remarkable achievement of coordination and control.

Without really considering the processes involved, the player must be able to sense and process a wide range of bits of information, such as the distance and direction of the hole, the lie of the land, any obstacles that may be present, the speed and direction of the wind, the weight and aerodynamics of the ball, the power and angle of lift of the club, and so on. He or she must then be able to grasp the club and swing it, using complex movements of the hands, arms, trunk, and legs, with such precision that its head strikes the ball in exactly the right place and with exactly the right force to carry it through the air and along the ground into the hole. Thus, information is gathered, processed, and then used to stimulate the body into carrying out a series of coordinated and cooperative actions. And so it is with every movement made by an animal, which has to use, in a coordinated fashion, its senses, nervous system, brain and motor systems.

◄ **Golfer in action**—Tony Jacklin about to strike a golf ball. The light traces show the path of the club head (red) and right hand (white) during the preceding practice stroke.

Coordinated movement in Amoeba *and* Paramecium. . .
Nerve nets in jellyfish. . . Nerve cells. . . Complex behavior of
sea anemones. . . Nerve tracts of sea stars. . . Nerve
impulses—the action potential. . . Animals with heads. . .
Connecting links—the synapses. . . Animal brains and the
central nervous system. . . Specialization within brains. . .
Brains in insects and crustaceans. . . How does the brain
work. . . Reflexes. . . Levels of complexity. . . Learning and
animal communication. . . Chemicals in the brain. . . The
neuro-endocrine system. . . Hormones. . .

FROM the simple, single-celled *Paramecium* to humans, animals have bodies which are designed to move and this is the one great advantage that they enjoy which plants do not. How they move, by contracting their bodies, beating their cilia or extending and flexing their limbs, has already been explained (see Movement of Animals), and the examples show that the movements of animals are superbly coordinated and controlled. This miracle is achieved by structures unique to animals, the nerve cells, which are connected together to form a rapid communication and central processing system. Information from the environment is collected, filtered (see Senses) and transmitted to the brain for processing. Commands are issued, movements monitored and, if necessary, adjusted. Coordinated and controlled actions are the end product of this sequence.

Inside Information

Unlike plants, if animals find themselves in an unsuitable environment they can move away and look for something better. This apparently simple action of moving, however, requires more than a set of appendages to move the body because to move away from unpleasant surroundings and towards a more comfortable situation, means that the goal must be identified, and the movements steered, so that the animal moves in the right direction. Thus, an animal, no matter how small or large, needs to get its appendages to cooperate and, through this cooperation, to propel its body in a chosen direction. This seemingly trivial fact is often taken for granted because haphazard and non-directed activity is very rarely seen in animals unless they are badly hurt.

One of the simplest animate life forms, an amoeba, moves in a coordinated way; one part of the apparently amorphous body extends tentacle-like, in a particular direction. The rest of the creature flows in this direction, following the leading "arm." There is no "contest" between the "leading" and "following" part of the animal. Different parts of the amoeba do not set off in different directions, and pull the animal in two. The communication system within an amoeba is probably chemical.

A second example of the cooperative and coordinated movements of body parts may be seen in the single-celled *Paramecium*, which is a slipper-shaped animal, only a few tenths of a millimeter long. These protozoans propel themselves through the water by beating many thousands of small cilia which cover their bodies. Paramecia can be watched through a microscope, and their smooth movements through the water are interrupted now and then by stops, reverses and turns. The movements of the cilia are always beautifully synchronized. No activity occurs in one half of the animal while the cilia in the other half are still. The animal is never seen to oscillate back and forth, being pulled first in one direction and then in the other by opposing groups of cilia.

Throughout the animal kingdom, this synchronous and coordinated movement of the appendages is the rule. Earthworms contract their bodies in a very special sequence (see Movement of Animals). Starfish move their many hundreds of sucker feet to propel the animal in a particular direction. Millipedes move their legs in a precisely controlled sequence and they never trip over their own feet. Shore crabs scamper over rocks, always in complete control of their eight walking legs which never tangle or bump into one another. Cooperative, and coordinated movements are to be seen everywhere in the living world.

Obviously, to achieve such coordination, the different parts of the animal need to be in communication with one another. The cilia at one end of a *Paramecium* must receive some signal when those at the other end begin to move, or they must all be supplied with a common signal controlling the direction of their beat. A comparison of the anatomy and the behavior of the larger multicelled animal types reveals the nature of this communication system. It also provides clues to the way the nervous systems and brains of the larger animals evolved.

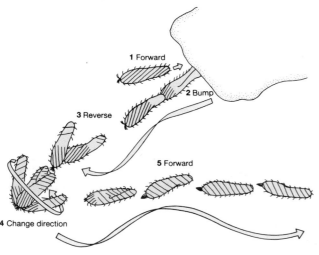

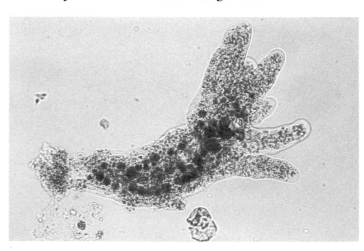

Cell to Cell Communication

There are several ways in which the different cells of the body could communicate with one another: by chemical substances diffusing from cell to cell; by mechanical "bumping" from cilium to cilium; or by the conduction of electrical potentials—and this is the method that has evolved. It is represented in the simplest possible form in the swimming bells of a hydrozoan jellyfish. Some jellyfish, known as siphonophores, are made up of clusters of cells (zooids), which are specialized in their function. Some of these are solely concerned with catching prey, some with digesting it, some with reproduction and some, the "swimmming zooids," with the propulsion of the freely floating animal, through the water.

Nerve nets. The swimming zooids are bell shaped and hollow. They propel the animal through the water by contracting circular and radial muscles and squirting the water contained in the bell, out at the base. The bells respond to being touched, and a resting animal will begin to swim if one bell is bumped. But the remarkable feature about the swimming bells of these jellyfish is that they have no special system of nerve cells over the surface of the bell to conduct the tactile information to the muscles. Instead, measurements with small electrodes show that touching the bell initiates a nerve impulse (action potential—see box) which spreads through the sheet of flat epithelial cells covering the surface of the bell. Muscular contractions follow when the action potentials reach the base of the bell and excite nerve cells there.

The difficulty with a cell-to-cell communication, spread over the surface of the body is obvious; each action potential is conducted to all cells. In many animals, though, it is important to be able to send communication signals to a few selected muscles. At an early stage in the long evolutionary history, special cells appeared, the neurons (see box) which serve this purpose. The present-day jellyfish, modern representatives of these early stages in the history of life on earth, still have these neurons, which function as well now for the limited requirements of jellyfish as they did so many millions of years ago.

How are these nerve cells in the jellyfish organized to form the communication system? The behavior of jellyfish can be observed: they swim, keep upright and respond to touch. Staining the cells so that they can be seen under the microscope, reveals a confusing, apparently randomly arranged and

▲ **Goal-orientated movement** in sea anemones—animals that are normally considered sedentary. When its territory is threatened, the red Beadlet sea anemone (*Actinia equina*) slowly approaches the yellow form TOP, with the latter beating as hasty a retreat as it can manage BELOW.

◄ **Movement in miniature.** The movements of the single-celled amoebae LEFT and paramecia FAR LEFT are controlled to the extent that the animals do not attempt to move in two different directions at the same time. Also, if paramecia bump into an obstruction they will reverse, alter direction and then move forward again. The cilia of *Paramecium* move in coordinated waves across the animal.

► **Nerve nets:** (1) Contractions of the swimming bells of a siphonophore hydrozoan are produced by muscles, synchronized by nerve pulses that spread through the outer wall of the bell. (2) The nervous system of the jellyfish consists of seemingly randomly connected nerve cells spread over the surface of the body. Swimming forms have two nerve nets, one for locomotion and the other for feeding.

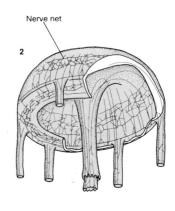

Float

Swimming bell

Water squirted from swimming bell propels colony

Main gastrozooid

Nerve net

1

2

interconnected mass of special nerve cells. (see box). Such a system is called a nerve net.

For simple swimming, where sequential contractions of the body muscles are required, the nerve net is a sensible system. Action potentials spread through the net and arrive at selected muscles which then contract. It has been discovered, though, that the first action potential to arrive at a muscle does not cause a contraction; a second action potential, if it arrives within a certain time span, will. This simple device of needing more than one stimulation, called facilitation, is of great importance to the animal because it "filters" out stray signals in the net, and allows muscle contractions of different intensities.

The puzzling aspect of the nerve net, however, is that some sea anemones (which have nerve nets like those of jellyfish) perform slow but quite complex goal-directed behavior. The best-known and described is that of an anemone which attaches itself to the shell of a hermit crab, apparently to the advantage of both animals. The hermit crab obtains a certain measure of camouflage; the anemone a mobility which more sedentary types do not enjoy. How the nerve net directs and controls the sequential patterns of muscular contractions which are necessary to bring about the transfer of the anemone to the shell of the crab is not known. It may be that, in a sense, the net is a "peripheral brain" capable not only of carrying out cooperative contraction of selected muscles, such as folding all the tentacles around a captured fish, but also of organizing a series of different movements in a particular sequence, like a computer which runs down a series of commands in its program. But, so far as is known, there is no central processing unit, no "brain" where the program is stored and "read" and then transferred to the selected muscles.

Nerve tracts. Not all animals are satisfied with the slow movements of the jellyfish. There is an advantage in being able to move more quickly, and the next stage in the evolution of the nervous system could well have been that now seen in the starfish. Starfish have many hundreds of tube feet on the undersides of their appendages. These tiny tubes are extended and retracted in a step-like way. The stepping movements of the tube feet are not synchronized, but are coordinated in such a way that they do not work against one another. This may not seem to be remarkable, but the starfish body has five or more arms, and can move in any direction. At all times, all the tube feet are cooperating. In addition the animals can change direction fairly rapidly, can right themselves if they are turned on their backs and can open mussel shells by pulling the two halves apart.

Starfish have nerve cells, and peripherally, these are arranged in a net-like way. In addition, though, the sea stars have tracts of nerve cell fibers (axons) which conduct action potentials along their lengths. Such "through-conducting" systems are important for the coordinated control of all the tube feet. If such a tract is surgically interrupted, the tube feet in the arm, no longer connected by nerves with the other arms, are also not coordinated with them. The tube feet within the neurally isolated arm still cooperate with one another, but not necessarily with those in the other arms. A dramatic demonstration of this "uncoupling" of the communication system in some starfish occurs when the ring nerve which binds all

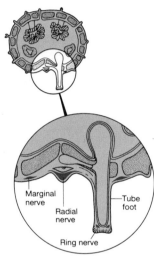

Marginal
nerve
Radial
nerve
Tube
foot
Ring nerve

▲ **Tube feet and spines** of a Crown-of-thorns starfish (*Acanthaster planci*). Coordination of movement of the tube feet is achieved by nerves lying on the ventral surface of the arms.

▶ **Regenerating arms** on a Common starfish (*Asterias rubens*). If the nerve ring is cut in two places, it is possible for the two halves simply to walk away from each other, and the wounds will heal.

◀ **Arms and tube feet** of a starfish. The starfish nervous system has developed a stage further than that of jellyfish in that, to the peripheral nerve net, has been added a central collection of nerve tracts—the radial and marginal nerve cords and the nerve ring.

Nerve Cells

The bodies of multicelled animals are made up of many millions of small cells which take on a variety of different shapes and sizes depending upon their function. The cells which make up the nervous systems of animals are essentially of two kinds—the nerve cells, or neurons, and the packing or glial cells which are wrapped around and between the nerve cells.

Information, which is so important for coordination and control of movement in animals, is carried along the nerve cells in the form of electrical potentials (see box). No wonder then, considering this unique function, that nerve cells also have a special shape, characterized by tube-like extensions of the cell

membrane. These tubes, which are many centimeters long in large animals, are called axons and it is along these that the information from the sense organs is conducted to the brain, and back to the various body muscles.

The axons usually end in fine branches, and these fine branches make special contacts, synapses (see box), with other nerve cells, or with muscles. The information is passed on only through these special contacts, and can only be transmitted in one direction across them.

Nerve cells are arranged in connected chains through the nervous system and, for most nerve cells, it is possible to identify an input, where information comes into the cell,

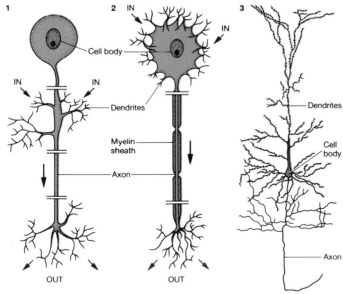

▲ **Types of nerve cell.** (1) Crayfish motor neuron. (2) Human motor neuron.
(3) Vertebrate brain (inter) neuron. All have a cell body, an axon and dendrites.
Information comes into the cell over the dendrites and passes out along the axon.

and an output, where the information is passed out of the cell and on to the next cell or to a muscle. The inputs and outputs of nerve cells can be separated by axons ranging in length from a few hundredths of a millimeter in some brain cells, to over a meter in neurons carrying information down the spinal cord of vertebrate animals.

For convenience, nerve cells can be classified into three broad groups: the sensory neurons carry information from the periphery to the central nervous system; interneurons collect the information from the sensory neurons and distribute it to appropriate motor neurons. The motor neurons carry the information to the muscles, and their concerted action produces behavior. It is the timing of the discharges in the motor neurons that is so critical to coordinate—and this is essentially the function of the interneurons.

The principle underlying the action of the nerve cells in all animals, from insects and crayfish to monkeys and humans, is the same. Although the shapes of neurons in crayfish and humans are somewhat different (in the crayfish the cell body is smooth while in humans the cell body is covered with fine branches) the essential functional features are present in both: an input through synaptic contacts; an axon to transport the information; and an output to pass on the information to the next cell.

the radial nerves together is cut in two places, thus disconnecting one half of the animal from the other. Such animals slowly pull themselves into two—each half simply walking away from the other. Fortunately for the starfish, this drastic behavior is not fatal. Their remarkable powers of regeneration allow each half animal to heal, and slowly to regrow the missing half.

Animals with "Heads"

Jellyfish and starfish are animals without a definite head or tail, and the emergence of animals with a bilateral symmetry, and a definite "front end" had an important effect in the evolution of the nervous system. Logically, if one particular body part always leads, the sense organs which direct the movement of the body are going to be concentrated there. The animal needs to see, feel or smell where it is going. Secondly, having grouped its sense organs in one part of the body, the animal needs to coordinate the inputs from these before it sends messages down the through-conducting systems to the muscles which are going to propel it towards the selected goal. Thus, in the flatworms a "head" and a collection of special sense organs (statocyst or eye) are developed. A cluster of nerve cells, also in the "head" receives information from the peripheral sensory systems, coordinates them and issues commands to appropriate motor nerve cells. The ground plan for the nervous system of all the higher animals was laid down at this stage.

Peripheral nerve nets were abandoned and a system to satisfy the needs of more complex and rapidly moving animals was adopted. In this new system three parts are combined: a peripheral sensory system, with neurons conducting information

BRAINS

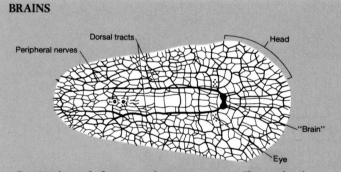

▲ **Primitive brain** of a flatworm and its nervous system. The peripheral nerves converge on two dorsal (shown here) and ventrally situated longitudinal nerve tracts that end in the brain. Rudimentary eyes are found near the brain, and a statocyst for detecting the vertical pull of gravity is contained within or just behind the brain in some species.

▼ **Vertebrate brains**—the relative sizes of the brain regions in vertebrates from fish (1) through amphibians (2), reptiles (3), birds (4), and mammals (5) to humans (6). Notice the increase in the size of the cerebellum, responsible for coordination and control of the motor systems, and the enormously expanded cerebrum of the human in relation to that of the lower vertebrates.

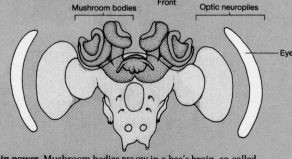

▲ **Bee brain power.** Mushroom bodies BELOW in a bee's brain, so-called because of their resemblance to mushrooms in section, are believed to be important areas of the brain for learning and remembering the way to a food source and back to the hive. ABOVE A honeybee (*Apis melifera*) collecting pollen.

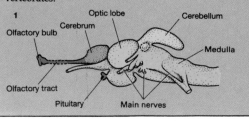
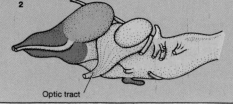

from an array of finely tuned sense organs or receptors; a central nervous system where these inputs are collected and correlated; and the motor nervous system which carries messages from the central nervous system to the muscles to move the limbs or body of the animal. Finally, and critically important for the coordinated movements, there is a system of sensory cells which detects the positions and motions of the animal's own body and limbs, and thus allows the central nervous system to adjust and correct inappropriate commands.

Animal Brains

What is a "brain?" Can we talk about "brains" in crayfish, in flies? The answer in the case of crayfish and flies is a very definite "Yes." To clarify the meaning of brain as comparative physiologists understand the term, there is perhaps a rather arbitrary, but necessary, definition. A collection of neurons which are neither collecting information from the outside (sensory), nor producing muscle action (motor), does not necessarily constitute a brain but is referred to as a ganglion. Thus, the peripheral nerve cells collected around the statocysts of jellyfish are not really brains but ganglia in which the two nerve nets of this animal interact.

Brains are found only in animals with a bilateral symmetry; there is only one brain in each animal, and this is always situated at the front. Associated with the brain are a number of ganglia which are often distributed back down the animal. The ganglia are subsidiary to the brain and, together with it, form the central nervous system. The evolution of the invertebrate brain and central nervous system probably passed through a series of stages not too different to that seen in modern animals, extending from the flatworms along two lines—one leading to the arthropods (insects etc) and the other to the mollusks. The vertebrate brain and central nervous system have a similar evolutionary history, culminating in animals with extremely large brains—humans.

The long association of the brain with special sense organs has resulted in certain areas of the brain being set aside to receive axons from predominantly one or other receptor organ. In the crayfish, for example there are areas in the brain which receive axons from the receptors of taste and smell in the antennules (feeler-like sensory appendages), areas which collect the signals from the eyes; and other areas which are concerned primarily with the inputs from the receptors sensitive to mechanical stimulation on the antennae, or on the head. Similarly, in vertebrate animals, special brain areas are associated with particular sensory inputs.

Brains also have centers which control specific outputs. In crayfishes these motor centers are grouped with their sensory inputs. Thus, the motor neurons which move the eyes are closely associated with inputs from the eyes and the balance organs. Motor neurons moving the antennae lie, together with the sensory inputs, in the antennal lobe. In vertebrates, a separate part of the brain is set aside to oversee the motor control of the body itself, particularly during locomotion and postural adjustments. This center does not contain motor neurons, but dedicated interneurons which send commands to clusters of motor neurons in the spinal cord. Crayfish also have interneurons which command specific groups of motor neurons

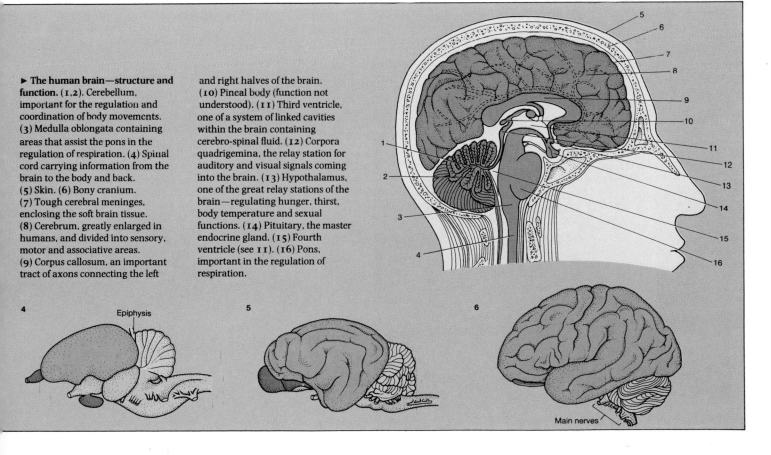

► **The human brain—structure and function.** (1,2). Cerebellum, important for the regulation and coordination of body movements. (3) Medulla oblongata containing areas that assist the pons in the regulation of respiration. (4) Spinal cord carrying information from the brain to the body and back. (5) Skin. (6) Bony cranium. (7) Tough cerebral meninges, enclosing the soft brain tissue. (8) Cerebrum, greatly enlarged in humans, and divided into sensory, motor and associative areas. (9) Corpus callosum, an important tract of axons connecting the left and right halves of the brain. (10) Pineal body (function not understood). (11) Third ventricle, one of a system of linked cavities within the brain containing cerebro-spinal fluid. (12) Corpora quadrigemina, the relay station for auditory and visual signals coming into the brain. (13) Hypothalamus, one of the great relay stations of the brain—regulating hunger, thirst, body temperature and sexual functions. (14) Pituitary, the master endocrine gland. (15) Fourth ventricle (see 11). (16) Pons, important in the regulation of respiration.

Epiphysis

Main nerves

that, in turn, control the leg and body motions of the animal.

The nature of the animal's way of life is mirrored in the size of the different lobes or divisions of the brain. In the brains of sharks and rays the anterior lobe of the brain is still concerned largely with the processing of information coming from the chemoreceptors in the nose. The optic lobe is relatively small and the deeply folded hemispherical lobes or cerebellum, which contains the control centers for locomotion, is one of the largest areas of the brain. A series of brains ranging through frogs, alligators, birds, horses and humans shows how the anterior part of the brain has expanded and become folded in upon itself, allowing space for greater and greater numbers of nerve cells. In humans this number reaches 10,000,000,000 and the cerebrum, or frontal lobes, cover the entire brain.

The development of invertebrate brains is less clearly defined than in vertebrates. At the top of the arthropod line, the insects and crustaceans have relatively large brains (about 100,000 neurons). Areas which have become highly developed in bees to control learning stem from the centers of smell. These mushroom bodies in the bee brain are most likely to be associated

Nerve Impulses—the Action Potential

The most fundamental and important property of the membrane around nerve cells is the generation of an electrical potential difference between the inside and the outside of the cell, and the conduction of temporary changes in polarity, called action potentials.

The potential difference across the cell membrane is brought about by the semipermeability of the membrane. In other words some kinds of electrically charged atoms, or ions, are allowed a freer passage through the membrane than others; some are prevented from passing through. The result is that electrically charged atoms of sodium, chloride and potassium distribute themselves across the membrane according to two forces—those of concentration and those of electrical charge. Equilibrium is reached when the tendency for the positive potassium ions to move from high concentration inside the cell to a low concentration outside, is balanced by the electrical attraction of negative ions

trapped inside the cell.

An action potential is a very rapid and short-lived reversal of the resting potential (the potential difference that exists across the cell membrane of a non-conducting neuron) so that, for a few thousandths of a second, the inside of the neuron becomes positive with respect to the outside. The nerve membrane then returns to its original state. This remarkable event is caused by a sudden, and not entirely understood, change in the properties of the nerve membrane. For a very short period the nerve membrane becomes very permeable to the sodium ions. Before the event, and in its resting state (1), the nerve membrane is relatively impermeable to sodium. The sudden reversal of polarity of the membrane, then, is the result of a movement of the positively charged sodium ions into the cell (2). Equilibrium is restored when the membrane regains its impermeability to sodium, and becomes suddenly more permeable to potassium ions. These leave the cell (3),

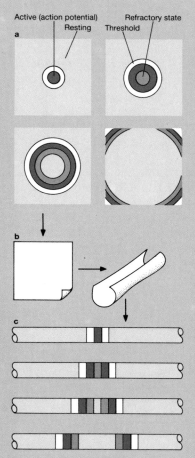

and the inside again becomes more negatively charged relative to the outside, with slight initial hyperpolarization (4). In the resting state, the sodium and potassium ions which are exchanged during the action potential, plus those ions which have leaked through the membrane, are actively "pumped" back to their appropriate sides (5).

The action potential is the basic digital signal used by the nervous system to code information. Obviously, the signals must be conducted in some way along the axons of the nervous system to their destinations. The conduction of the action potential along the nerve is not quite the same as the conduction of an electrical signal in a copper wire. In nerve axons, the action potential rolls forward from one patch of membrane to the next, rather like ripples spreading across a pond (a). In the nerve cell the depolarization in a patch of membrane spreads to the neighboring patch and depolarizes it until it also becomes active and produces its own action potential.

Our analogy with the pond can be carried further if we imagine being able to roll (b) the surface of the pond, like a membrane, into a tube (c). The splash in the middle of the pond now travels along the tube. And so it is in the axons of nerve cells which are no more than membrane tubes.

Action potentials can move in both directions along an axon, but, because the synapses between nerve cells allow action potentials to pass in only one direction, action potentials going the wrong way in a nerve cell never get beyond the cell in which they occur.

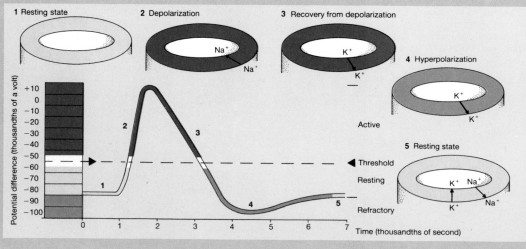

too with complex social behavior used in communicating the position of a food source to other worker bees.

The most remarkable brain in the invertebrate world, however, is that of the octopus. Lacking an external skeleton, and having eight flexible and muscular arms, the octopus needs an extensive control system. The brain lobes associated with vision and smell are large. Octopus, with their large brains, can perform fairly complex tasks requiring true associative learning and memory, and a special area of the brain controls this activity. If this part of the octopus's brain is removed, the animal's ability to learn is destroyed. An interesting aspect of these experiments is that, in all animals, the ability to learn seems to depend on the numbers of cells in the "learning" brain lobes. If cells are removed piecemeal from this area, the ability declines proportionately, but there is no correlation with the removal of specific cells.

In all the higher animals which learn, such as arthropods, mollusks or the vertebrates, the "learning" lobes contain large numbers of small cells, which may indicate why they have often developed from the primitive centers of smell that always have large numbers of very small neurons.

Coordination, Control and the Central Nervous System

But how does the brain work? The brain consists of a large collection of single nerve cells. The paths of sensory neurons can be traced into special areas, and from these special areas a certain command is issued. But this input/output system must be able to control and coordinate all the information which is continually pouring into it. It somehow ensures that the movements of animals are graceful and are not a sequence of puppet-like, jerky, consecutive limb movements, like those of assembly-line robots.

It is difficult to imagine how and where an exploration of something as awesome as the brain can begin. The approach has been, logically, to start with the simple systems.

Reflexes. There is a kind of movement that all animals, including humans, make without "thinking." A loud noise or flash of light causes the eyes to blink. A sharp blow on the tendon below the knee causes the leg to swing out. A tap on the carapace of a crab makes it pull its stalked eyes quickly into protective sockets. And there are many other examples. These reactions are called reflex responses, and it was found that many reflex systems will work in isolation. The input sensory systems can be easily identified, and only a single motor system is directly involved.

Studies of these reflex systems have provided much significant information about how the lower levels of the nervous system work. It has led, for example, to the knowledge that there is a constancy of neuron numbers and types in any one species of animal. In the invertebrates this is carried to an extreme. Many individual motor neurons in the invertebrates have been specifically identified according to their shape and function. This finding has had a very great impact on any thinking concerning the way in which nervous systems work. Looking at the tangled neurons in the brain, it may have been justified to consider that there was no recognizable anatomical order, but it is now known that many neurons have very definite forms and functions and always occupy the same places

▲ **Intelligent octopuses.** Octopuses have the most complex brain of invertebrates with considerable capacity for muscle coordination, sensory ability and learning. Shown here is the Lesser octopus (*Eledone cirrhosa*).

▼ **A simple reflex system.** Placing a weight in a person's hand causes it to move downward extending the joint at the elbow. This stretches the muscle spindle organ which produces a nerve impulse. In the spinal cord, the sensory input from the muscle spindle organ is connected to the motor neuron that commands the muscles to move the arm up, thus compensating for the added weight.

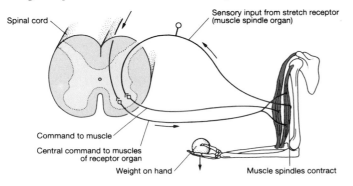

Spinal cord

Sensory input from stretch receptor (muscle spindle organ)

Command to muscle

Central command to muscles of receptor organ

Weight on hand

Muscle spindles contract

in the brain. The two motor neurons which produce the eye blink in crabs, for example, are always found in the same place in different individuals of the same species, and always have the same form. This has been found to be true for a large number of invertebrate motorneurons in a wide range of species. Suddenly, it was realized that the circuitry and the components of one brain type are all the same. Therefore, it is possible to study many individuals of the same species, and slowly build up not only a component list, but also a real circuit diagram, for any particular animal, knowing that the circuit will be the same in all individuals of that species.

The problem facing those investigating the brains of animals can now be likened to someone who is presented with a computer, and is asked to explain how it works. In the case of the invertebrates, these are perhaps more like programmable pocket calculators than fully fledged computers. Thus, it has now been recognized that all those pocket calculators coming from a particular firm, have not only the same circuit, but that the components are always to be found in the same place. Therefore, the circuits can be drawn up with confidence. There comes now, though, a conceptual leap. It may be possible to observe the operation of limited parts of the entire circuit, and even to understand how inputs are added or subtracted and an answer provided. On the calculator, 2 + 2 and = is keyed in, and the result 4 appears. And, a tap on the carapace of a crab produces an eye blink. These operations are all "wired in." But the behavior of an animal is far more than the adding together of reflexes. For example, the "2 + 2" reflexes in animals are not necessarily as inflexible as in pocket calculators. In an active, and moving animal, "2 + 2" may give "5." In a quiet animal "2 + 2" may give "3." Somewhere between the input and the output there is an amplifier, and the control of this amplifier is correlated with the activity of the animal.

The analogy between the calculator and the brain can be taken a step further. A programmable calculator has an added level of complexity in it—the program. Thus, a single input may, or may not, release a complex sequence of actions which depends upon the program that is stored in the calculator. So it is too with animals, and understanding the behavior of animals cannot be achieved just by drawing up the circuits of the nervous system. It is necessary to be able to read the programs which are stored, but this is difficult. The methods

▲ **Blinking fiddler crab.** The retraction of each eye stalk is under the control of just two motor neurons, which, in different individuals, are always in precisely the same place in the brain.

◄ **Many legs to coordinate.** Keeping its legs in coordinated motion is clearly a problem for all land animals, but particularly so for this giant millipede.

available are few but it is possible to measure the small changes in electrical potentials in less than 1 percent of brain cells, and then usually from only three or four simultaneously. The brain can be disrupted by cutting or injecting it with chemicals and the effect observed.

Nevertheless, even with such crude tools, some of the rules followed by brains and a picture of coordination and control of bodily movements are emerging. In the apparently simple matter of an insect walking, years of careful research have established that the generation and maintenance of the back-and-forth movement of the individual legs are the result of activity in central driving interneurons, which will oscillate, given the appropriate feedback from receptors monitoring the leg positions. The feedback from these nerve endings, called proprioceptors, in all the legs must be cross connected in some

way to prevent "mistakes." An obvious "mistake" would be to lift all the legs on one side simultaneously. This does not happen. It is important to grasp that large numbers of neurons are acting and interacting, and that many behaviors, such as walking, are "automatic." The connections between the neurons are extensive, however, and not only can be inhibitory or excitatory but also modulatory, that is, exerting a bias instead of an "all-or-nothing" response. A problem not yet adequately understood, is volition. An insect, which has been sitting still for some time, will suddenly begin to walk. No apparent stimulus has been given—and, quite feasibly, the walking has been initiated purely from within the animal by slow, long-term changes (see below).

The analogy between the "programs" in brains and a computer highlights an important aspect of brains: programmable calculators are limited in the numbers of "steps" they are able to perform, and cannot carry out tasks requiring very long programs. Animal brains have similar limitations, particularly in terms of their ability to learn. Bees, for example, can be taught to discriminate between different colors, a task obviously important in their natural search for nectar. Tasks which are inappropriate to this activity, such as rolling over on their backs, are never learned. Such behavior-specific learning suggests that there are certain things that various animals cannot learn, and certain concepts they are unable to grasp. A domestic cat, for example, knows the surroundings of the house in which it lives far better than the owners do. It probably experiences and sees things people never will. But it cannot so easily grasp the concept of the entire world with all the lands, cultures, and people in it. No amount of experience of those lands and people will ever lead it to this because the cat's mind has certain boundaries.

For centuries people have been trying to discover the boundaries of the human mind and to find out whether or not it will ever be capable of grasping the meaning of the Universe. There is an enormous disparity in the size and capabilities of the brains of different animals. One interesting possible reason for this is that the development of the brain goes hand in hand with the ability to communicate with the individuals of the same species. The subject of animal communication is very diverse but communication between individuals of a species ranges from the simple, basic actions of defense and mating to the sophisticated exchange of abstract ideas. Communication necessarily requires a transmitter of some kind and a receiver. Fiddler crabs signal to attract females, not only by waving one large claw, but by drumming on the sand. Birds call to one another, and emphasize their actions with brightly colored feathers. Apes communicate with noises and gestures. Humans speak. Through this series, it can be appreciated that the signals which are transmitted range from the very simple to the enormously complex. The range of vibration patterns transmitted by the fiddler crabs is narrow; that achieved by the human tongue extremely broad. The range of "message types" which can be transmitted by the fiddler crab is limited; in humans extensive. The fiddler crab signals his willingness to mate. The human can exchange abstract ideas.

Chemicals in the Brain

So far, the brain has been likened to a computer with describable electronic circuits. The coordination and control of the movements are achieved by signals passing rapidly back and forth between the brain and the periphery. There is a level of control, however, which is not so easily explained by such circuitry, and that is the control of long-term changes in behavior. Such changes can only be described as changes of "mood." By their actions, animals can show that they are angry, afraid, alert or sleepy. At a more complex level, it is evident that, during the spring, birds carry out elaborate courtship and nesting behavior, but not in winter. All the processes taking place in the brain which have been considered so far, happen very rapidly. Reflexes act in fractions of a second. Messages are transferred along axons with great speed. But, the brain also brings about long-term changes, where entire behavior patterns, such as nest building, are "turned on" at the appropriate season.

There is a system of neurons and glands, collectively called the neuro-endocrine system, and an important part of this system are the neurosecretory cells. Like motor neurons, neurosecretory cells are output cells representing the final common path of the integrated activity of many neurons. Unlike the motor neurons, however, the neurosecretory cells do not end on muscles. Instead, they end in special organs that bring their nerve endings directly in contact with the blood system. These organs are called neurohemal organs. Neurosecretory

Connecting Links—the Synapses

Synapses are the connecting links between nerve cells, where information is passed from one cell (the presynaptic cell) to the next (the postsynaptic cell). The anatomy of this junction between nerve cells has been revealed by the electron microscope and is essentially much the same in the nervous systems of all animals.

The presynaptic branch ends in a rounded knob which is in close contact with the postsynaptic cell (1). The membranes of the two cells are separated by a gap (the synaptic cleft). A number of round vesicles are usually present in the presynaptic terminal and these contain a chemical called a "transmitter."

An action potential in the presynaptic cell is conducted along the axon and invades the presynaptic terminal (2a). The change in potential results in the release, through the membrane and into the cleft, of the transmitter substance. On the postsynaptic membrane, special sites, sensitive to the transmitter, change their permeability to the various ions situated inside and outside the membrane. The result is a short depolarization of the cell, called a postsynaptic potential. Much smaller than an action potential, the synaptic potential spreads passively through the postsynaptic cell.

If enough synapses are simultaneously excited by presynaptic inputs (2b), the postsynaptic potentials sum and raise the membrane of the axon to threshold. The membrane, however, does not have the ability to produce an action potential, except at the base of, and along, the axon.

The input branches of the cell

▼ Synapses—their structure (1) and operation (2)—see box for details.

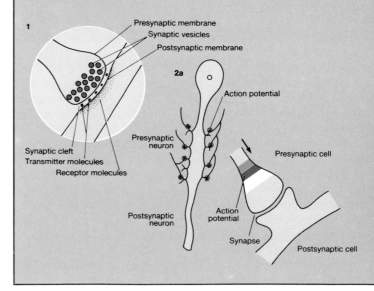

1
Presynaptic membrane
Synaptic vesicles
Postsynaptic membrane

2a
Action potential

Synaptic cleft
Transmitter molecules
Receptor molecules

Presynaptic neuron

Presynaptic cell

Action potential

Postsynaptic neuron

Synapse

Postsynaptic cell

▶ **The neuroendocrine system in humans.** (1) The master endocrine gland, the pituitary, is located just below the hypothalamus. (2) Different regions of the tripartite pituitary produce different hormones.

cells have contact points or synapses (see box) on them like any other neuron. They also conduct action potentials along the axons which lead to the neurohemal organ. Like other nerve cells, the action potentials invade the axon terminals and cause the release of a chemical. But, whereas in a normal central neuron, the secreted chemical is directed to a single receiving synapse, the products of the neurosecretory cells are

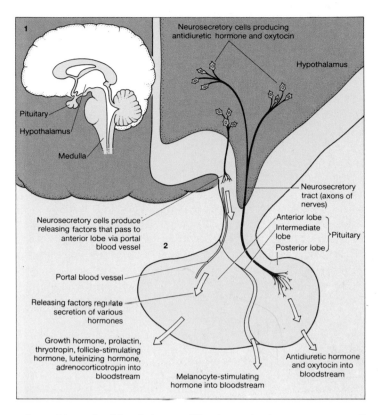

and the cell body then return (2c) to the resting potential, ready for the next invasion from the presynaptic neurons.

Vesicles containing transmitter substance occur only in the presynaptic terminals, and receptors only on the postsynaptic membrane. Thus, synapses allow the passage of information in only one direction. Also, the released transmitter substance is very rapidly broken down by a special enzyme after its release into the synaptic cleft. Thus, a single presynaptic action potential releases only a short depolarization in the postsynaptic cell.

An important variation of the above scheme is also found: some transmitter substances produce not a depolarization of the postsynaptic membrane, but an increase in polarization. Thus, the postsynaptic cell is forced into a state where it is less likely to produce an action potential. This is called inhibition. Most brain cells receive both excitatory and

inhibitory inputs and each cell can, therefore, play a role as a decision maker. Whether it discharges an action potential or not, depends on the balance between the excitatory and inhibitory synapses which are active at any particular moment.

A special type of synapse is sometimes found between cells in the nervous system of animals, such as crayfish and squid, which have fast-action escape systems. Here the presynaptic cell is pressed even closer to the postsynaptic cell and no synaptic vesicles are found. An action potential in the presynaptic neuron passes straight across such a synapse with a minimum delay. Thus, such a synapse has been called an electrical synapse. Some electrical synapses conduct action potentials in only one direction. This ability rests in the membranes of the pre- and postsynaptic neurons which rectify, or allow current to pass in one direction more easily than in the other.

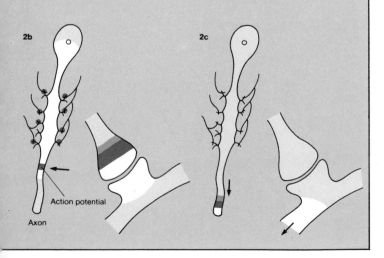

released into the blood stream. The important consequence of this is that these chemicals, called neurohormones, are transported by the blood to all parts of the body, including the brain. The targets for the neurohormones can be other neural systems, or glands that are then activated to produce yet a greater variety of active chemicals—hormones.

Hormones can also be released from their glands by activity in neurons which are in themselves not necessarily neurosecretory, but which directly stimulate the endocrine gland. Essential for the operation of the neuro-endocrine system are the feedbacks from the endocrine glands to the brain, from which the initial stimulus comes (see box). The types of behaviors which can be controlled by the neuro-endocrine system range from simple to complex. Changes can be produced in the animals' actions which last a few seconds, to several weeks—long after neurosecretory activity has ceased.

In vertebrates the "master gland" is the hypophysis. Neurosecretory cells release their products in this gland and their action results in the release of six different hormones which circulate in the blood and exert a fundamental control over major aspects of the animal's life.

Knowing that small quantities of chemical substances released into the blood stream can so powerfully affect the behavior of animals, it is understandable why great care should be taken when humans introduce chemicals into the blood stream. There are very familiar changes in mood which can be caused by certain euphoric drugs such as alcohol, and devastating effects may be produced by overuse. Given the sensitivity of the brain to chemicals and the fine balances which must be struck between the neuron populations' behavior, it is remarkable that it withstands the treatment often imposed upon it.   DCS

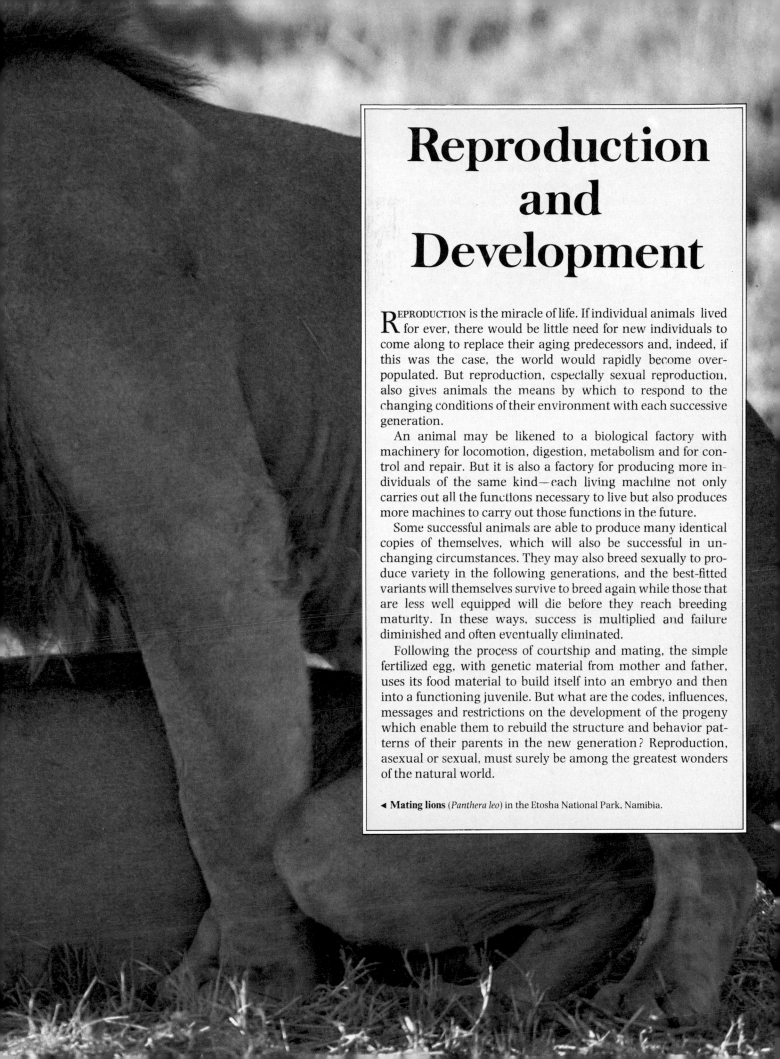

Reproduction and Development

REPRODUCTION is the miracle of life. If individual animals lived for ever, there would be little need for new individuals to come along to replace their aging predecessors and, indeed, if this was the case, the world would rapidly become over-populated. But reproduction, especially sexual reproduction, also gives animals the means by which to respond to the changing conditions of their environment with each successive generation.

An animal may be likened to a biological factory with machinery for locomotion, digestion, metabolism and for control and repair. But it is also a factory for producing more individuals of the same kind—each living machine not only carries out all the functions necessary to live but also produces more machines to carry out those functions in the future.

Some successful animals are able to produce many identical copies of themselves, which will also be successful in unchanging circumstances. They may also breed sexually to produce variety in the following generations, and the best-fitted variants will themselves survive to breed again while those that are less well equipped will die before they reach breeding maturity. In these ways, success is multiplied and failure diminished and often eventually eliminated.

Following the process of courtship and mating, the simple fertilized egg, with genetic material from mother and father, uses its food material to build itself into an embryo and then into a functioning juvenile. But what are the codes, influences, messages and restrictions on the development of the progeny which enable them to rebuild the structure and behavior patterns of their parents in the new generation? Reproduction, asexual or sexual, must surely be among the greatest wonders of the natural world.

◄ **Mating lions** (*Panthera leo*) in the Etosha National Park, Namibia.

What is reproduction. . . Multiplication and reproduction. . .
Cell division—mitosis and meiosis. . . Eggs and
spermatozoa. . . Sex and variety. . . Alternation of asexual
and sexual generations. . . Reproduction in jellyfish and sea
anemones. . . Reproduction in parasites. . . Reproduction
without sex—parthenogenesis. . . Mushroom flies. . . Egg
production. . . Fertilization. . . The beginning of
development. . . What controls early development?. . . The
unfolding genetic program. . . Reaching juvenile size. . .
Metamorphosis. . . Yolk and live birth. . . Tarantula wasps. . .
Live birth—viviparity. . . Nests. . . Growth and the stages to
adulthood. . .

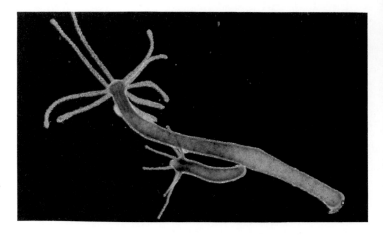

REPRODUCTION is not simply the process of producing more individuals: a cat having kittens has not reproduced; only when a pair of cats replaces a pair of cats, or a kitten replaces a kitten, has reproduction taken place. The offspring of cats and sharks resemble their parents and mostly need only to grow, but many other creatures produce offspring apparently unlike themselves: the maggot is the offspring of the fly, the tadpole of the frog, and these larvae have different lifestyles from those of their parents. Some offspring never resemble their parents: jellyfishes are the products of the polyp stage of the life cycle, and breed polyps in their turn.

Cycles of Reproduction
There is always multiplication at some stage of the reproductive cycle, and, almost always, there is reduction to match it. In a stable population, two parents in a given generation are replaced by two parents in each future generation, but many offspring may die to achieve this balance. A female European starling lays about 16 eggs in her life; of these only two, on average, survive to breed and 14 die without breeding. A female plaice may lay 20 million eggs in her life and, of those, only about two will breed—otherwise the world would be knee-deep in starlings or plaice!

Some animals, such as albatrosses (about four eggs per female) or rhinoceroses (about six offspring per female), seem to put much of their reproductive effort into producing more creatures of the same kind; others, such as oysters (40 million eggs per female) or even mice (as many as 50 offspring) seem to put most of their reproductive work into feeding other animals with their offspring! This contrast is between investing

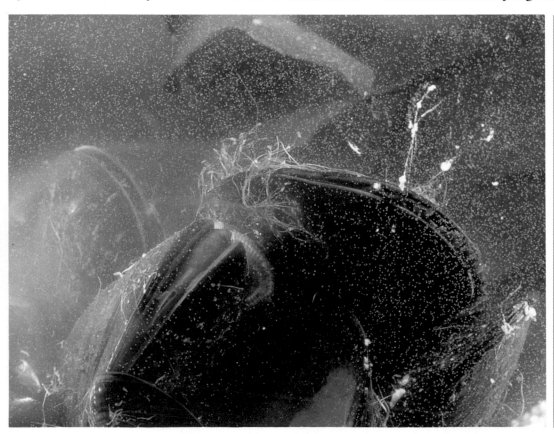

▲ **Reproduction without sex.** Asexual reproduction in many invertebrate animals occurs by simple budding of new individuals from the parent, as in this *Hydra*. The offspring have an identical genetic makeup to the adults.

◄► **Two parents produce two young**—strategies of reproductive effort. LEFT Many animals, such as this spawning mussel (*Myrtilis edulis*), produce millions of eggs and show no parental care; the majority of the offspring merely become the food of other animals. RIGHT Animals, such as lions, produce few offspring and invest considerable time and effort in rearing them. However, for both groups, whether gross mortality of young is high or low, the net aim is for two parents to produce just two new individuals for the next generation. If they do this they have been reproductively successful.

heavily in a few offspring or producing myriads, each of which has little chance of survival. Animals which do the former are usually well adapted to their ecological niches, take a long time to develop and grow to a large size. The more profligate, on the other hand, are usually generalists, pioneers which breed early and often.

Similarity or Variety

Animal cells can divide in two basic ways: the original cell, with all its chromosomes, can be multiplied as copies by the process of mitosis; or cells can perform meiosis in which the chromosomes are shuffled and recombined so that, ultimately, half the number of copies are produced in each of the four cells. Fertilization between two such assorted, reduced sets produces a new kind of double set (see box). Animals use mitosis to multiply similarity (asexual reproduction), but meiosis and fertilization (sex) to generate variety. The cells produced by meiosis, which fuse at fertilization, are of two kinds. There are enormous numbers of (usually) tailed, swimming spermatozoa or fewer immotile eggs, most often packed with energy and food reserves, and with a structure which ensures that they begin the development of the embryo. Male animals produce spermatozoa and females produce eggs, but there are many species in which eggs and spermatozoans can be produced by one animal. Spermatozoa may meet eggs in the water in which the animals live, or they may be passed into the female by the male during copulation. This need for the two sexes to come together is often a major difficulty, and sexual aberrations which do not require mating, but still produce some variety, are often found.

Hydra, and even our cousins the sea squirts, use mitosis to multiply cells to make each body; they can also make more genetically identical whole bodies in this way by producing so-called buds. As the bodies of most animals develop, however, some of these progeny cells, which result from mitosis, are set aside from the other developing cells and become the germ cells for sexual processes; they multiply by mitosis until the final, meiotic, stages of gamete formation. Multiplication of these cells puts an upper limit to the number of variant progeny that an animal can produce sexually, but these upper limits are only approached in some very simple creatures. Some rotifers produce only 10 to 16 eggs, all of which are fertilized from the male's 64 spermatozoa. In humans, as in most higher animals, millions of potential eggs and millions of millions of spermatozoans are produced; yet people produce tens of offspring at most. There is usually "wastage" of nearly all the sexual products of animals: the male rotifer produces four times too many sperms, a human male some 100,000,000,000 times too many; the female starling produces eight times too many eggs and the female plaice 20 million times too many (not even

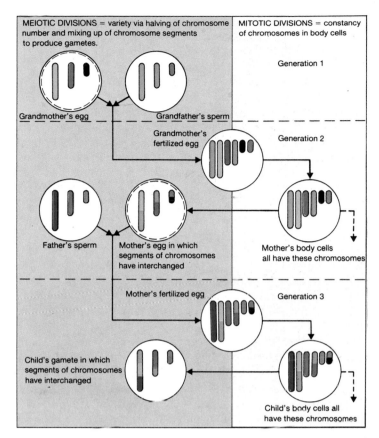

▲ **Similarity or variety** of genetic makeup—a diagram illustrating how the structure of chromosomes either remains the same during mitotic divisions or their genes are reassorted during meiotic divisions. The sequence follows the pattern of change of chromosome structure through three generations (although only three pairs of chromosomes are shown, humans actually have 23 pairs).

counting germ cell deaths in their ovaries). The deaths of most baby starlings and plaice certainly occur because most of them have the "wrong" genetics; whether this is so for the losses of spermatozoans and eggs is not so clear.

Sex produces variety, leading to this "necessary" wastage, but many animals use asexual multiplication for part, at least, of their reproductive cycles; then there is no such waste. This multiplication produces many copies of a well-adapted genetic combination produced by, and selected from, a previous sexual generation of variety. All its brothers and sisters may have died, but one well-adapted organism can multiply and exploit a new resource; when algae start growing in ponds in the spring, water fleas hatching from sexual ("winter") eggs multiply parthenogenetically (without fertilization—indeed, without

Lions – Parents

Offspring

Only two offspring survive to maturity.

males) and a few clones take over each pond. Mushroom flies find a new crop of mushrooms, lay their many eggs and the maggots multiply and compete until all the mushroom is eaten. Only a few clones survive, a few then turning into sexual flies and again generating variety (see box).

Alternation of Generations

There are many very successful animals in which the reproductive cycle includes an asexual multiplication phase alternating with a sexual generation of variety. Coral reefs are communities of many kinds of organisms but most of their solid structure is made up of the hard skeletons of the sedentary forms, known as polyps, of cnidarians (coelenterates). The structure of these polyps is similar to that of a sea anemone, and the polyps develop originally from fertilized eggs. These eggs become small (1mm) swimming larvae, called planulae, which search for a patch of well-lit, hard substrate on the reef on which to settle. Those few that find a suitable place settle and transform into little polyps; only a small number of these polyps seem to have the right kind of genetic makeup to enable them to grow well, in the site they select, but the successful ones grow and bud vigorously to produce thousands or millions of polyps which secrete a massive skeleton that shades nearby competitors.

The symbiotic algae in the tissues of corals need light, and the corals require moving sea water containing the plankton on which they feed. Thus, competition between the colonies is fierce. Large colonies, with plenty of light and food, produce eggs or spermatozoans (which pass between the colonies in the moving sea water); planulae are released after a period of "brooding" in the parent polyp and, once again, only a very few will survive to make colonies in their turn.

The marvellous siphonophores, such as the Portuguese man-

▲ **Ghostly colonies of the planktonic world.** Siphonophores, such as *Physophora hydrostatica*, are colonies of individual, but connected, organisms, derived from a single planula-like larva. Unlike the constancy of form of polyps in an *Obelia* colony, polyps of a siphonophore show considerable variety of form and function.

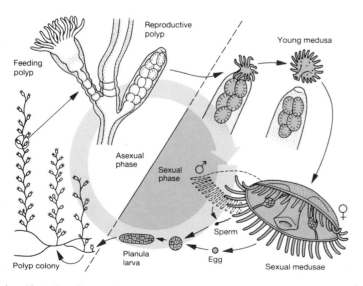

▲ **Alteration of generations.** Coelenterates, such as *Obelia*, reproduce asexually by producing more polyps to form a colony. However, some polyps become reproductive and bud off many medusae, which float freely in water. Eventually the medusae produce either eggs or sperms. After fertilization, the resulting larva swims for a while before settling to produce a new polyp generation.

◄► **Superindividuals of a coral reef.** Many corals, such as *Monastrea cavernosa*, shown LEFT, consist of many separate polyps. In brain corals, such as *Diploria strigosa*, RIGHT, however, individuals may not separate but form incomplete polyps in intimate association. Each polyp association is demarked by a closed system of ridges which may be small or large, as can be seen here. The detail of *Diploria labyrinthiformes* INSET shows the outline of one association.

of-war are also cnidarians which developed colonies of individual, but connected organisms, each colony derived from a planula-like larva. Siphonophores are large, transparent carnivores with many specialized kinds of polypoid or medusoid (free-swimming) individuals produced from the original larva. All of those in one colony are genetically identical but they are very diverse in form: some are just stomachs for digestion; some are floats or swimming bells; while others have long tentacles and are specialized for stinging or trapping prey. Some types of colony can multiply by fragmentation: pieces or individuals torn off by struggling prey or in rough seas can regenerate the whole varied set of specialized individuals.

Large, well-fed colonies always have sexual individuals, too, which generate a variety of larvae and a few will take their places in the planktonic world.

Many parasites have an asexual multiplication phase in their reproductive cycles. Like corals, tapeworms multiply their sexual individuals (segments) to produce more eggs. In contrast, flukes multiply their successful larvae and so increase the chances that adults will result from some larval genetic type. The adults produce millions of genetically diverse eggs sexually, and a few of these invade the first host again and multiply.

All these organisms multiply asexually by mitosis to generate many repeats of the successful structure. This is a good way for an organism with the "best-fitted" genetics to exploit a habitat. Stagshorn coral produces lots of little polyps like sea anemones, but brain corals simplify the process by not splitting the polyps one from another, and the result can be seen either as one very extended branched polyp or as many incomplete polyps in intimate association. In contrast, the siphonophores have specialized their genetically identical units in different directions; each becomes an "organ" of the "superindividual"; they separate more than brain coral polyps do, and each seems

to have a life of its own in the colony. The adult colony can catch and digest prey which is much bigger than a single polyp could manage, just as the brain coral knob can dominate tens of cubic meters of reef.

Tapeworms exploit a large area of the host's gut in the same way, by multiplying the sexual organs (although it is a major puzzle why a large tapeworm, which is nearly always solitary, should concern itself to produce such complicated devices to mate with another bit of itself!) On the other hand, flukes saturate the larval environment with a few clones so that the final sexual stage is attained by at least some of them.

Multiplied Successes–Parthenogenesis

Corals and flukes multiply their polyps or their larvae from genetically identical cell masses produced by mitosis. The sexual apparatus itself can be used for generating copies instead of variations, and there are many animals which have reduced the sexual process so that it does not generate variety. Eggs are produced rather than nonsexual cell masses, but they develop without fertilization, by parthenogenesis.

There are many examples showing different degrees of such reduction from sexuality, and most biologists believe that some kinds of sexual species often produce parthenogenetic forms which are short lived, on an evolutionary scale, compared with the variable parent stock. Many of today's parthenogenetic forms, as well as some which are on their way to losing sex, are hybrids which means that they result from crosses between forms that are genetically not alike. There is a species of Central American fish, *Mollienisia (Poecilia) formosa*, which is a hybrid between two (possibly three) other species of *Mollienisia*; it is basically *triploid* which means that its cells contain three times the haploid, or unpaired, number of chromosomes. Although its eggs do not require, or use, a male genetic contribution, they do still need to be penetrated by spermatozoa to start development, but the male nucleus degenerates—males of various sexual species all seem happy to oblige! This process has been called amazonogenesis after the mythical Amazon tribe of women. Some earthworms and even some lizards are triploid hybrids, too, and, like *M. formosa*, have retained meiosis—they double up their chromosomes before meiosis so that late reproductive cells (oogonia and oocytes) are hexaploid, that is, they contain six times the haploid number of chromosomes. This is then reduced in the final eggs to their normal triploid number by a regular meiosis. These parthenogenetic organisms with meiosis do exchange genetic material between chromosomes by crossing-over so a little variation is open to them, but the resultant recombinant chromosomes all derive from one parent so it is like the most extreme inbreeding.

Most parthenogenetic animals, such as *Carausius*, the common Indian stick insect, have lost meiosis as well as fertilization so that eggs are produced by mitosis and are all alike.

Those organisms which reproduce both sexually and by parthenogenesis are most informative about the differences between the two methods. In temperate climates, water fleas and many other freshwater crustaceans, as well as rotifers and many insects, all show parthenogenetic multiplication when living conditions are good. They also produce sexual variety at the end of the good times when summer heat or winter ice

interrupts their habitats. *Daphnia* females hatch from "winter eggs" in the early spring and feed on the start of the algal bloom. They produce eggs which begin development directly, and each female accumulates growing babies in its brood pouch. As the ponds warm up, tens of babies are produced each week and, in their turn, breed about a week after release. Thus, thousands of clones, each the progeny of one original female, compete in the special conditions of each pond. If the pond dries in the summer, and in any event at the approach of winter, competition becomes much more intense as the algal supply fails. Males

Mushroom Flies

The maggots of mushroom flies of the family Cecidomyidae live in stalks of fungi. The maggots multiply to exploit this temporary but very nutritious source of food. The ovary appears early in the transformation of larva to fly so that eggs are available for parthenogenetic development in the older maggots. The new larvae consume their mother larva's body first and then eat the fungus tissue. Competition between these groups (clones) is most intense when the supply of fungus is dwindling, and some maggots produce progeny which can pupate. These pupae hatch to become "normal" male or female flies which mate, and then the females find new food sources on which their variant eggs can try out their developmental programs.

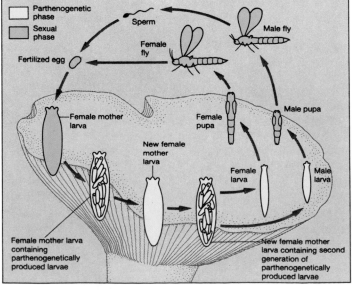

Parthenogenetic phase

Sexual phase

Sperm

Male fly

Female fly

Fertilized egg

Female mother larva

Female pupa

Male pupa

New female mother larva

Female larva

Male larva

Female mother larva containing parthenogenetically produced larvae

New female mother larva containing second generation of parthenogenetically produced larvae

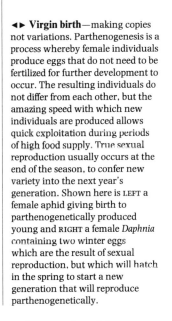

◄► **Virgin birth**—making copies not variations. Parthenogenesis is a process whereby female individuals produce eggs that do not need to be fertilized for further development to occur. The resulting individuals do not differ from each other, but the amazing speed with which new individuals are produced allows quick exploitation during periods of high food supply. True sexual reproduction usually occurs at the end of the season, to confer new variety into the next year's generation. Shown here is LEFT a female aphid giving birth to parthenogenetically produced young and RIGHT a female *Daphnia* containing two winter eggs which are the result of sexual reproduction, but which will hatch in the spring to start a new generation that will reproduce parthenogenetically.

are then produced from some of the females, and others produce eggs which after fertilization acquire thick, brown shells that can survive freezing or even desiccation. Presumably, some of these variants will be adapted for the new problems of the pond's next spring.

Aphids (greenfly etc) exploit the growing higher plants by parthenogenetic multiplication in the spring and early summer. Many species have acquired a complex life history, however, involving a succession of different forms and more than one host plant.

Parthenogenesis may also be employed to produce males. Many different organisms, from bees to *Daphnia* to rotifers, make use of parthenogenesis for this purpose. In some insects, Hymenoptera, fertilized eggs become females, while unfertilized eggs always become males. This peculiar sexual stratagem has many biological consequences and must have a bearing on the success of hymenopterans both as social insects and as "species flocks" of parasites and hyperparasites (parasites of other parasites). The haploid genome is "tested" in the production of males—any genetic material likely to cause the death of the organism is weeded out—and the mother's genetic makeup is also tested in male functions. The peculiar kin selection relationships, by which daughters of a queen contrive that more of "their" genes contribute to the future if they help their mother to have more daughters than if they breed themselves, are also a direct consequence of this male haploidy. Termites, in which both sexes are diploid, show that male haploidy is not obligatory for social insects.

Sexual Reproduction

Egg production. The eggs of all animals are produced in special organs called ovaries. These may be long tubes in which the egg-producing cells, or oogonia, are situated at one end of the tube and then there is a succession of egg maturation stages along the tube. This type of ovary occurs in nematode worms and in insects. In mammals, however, the ovaries are solid organs which release mature eggs into the abdominal cavity where they are picked up into tubes called oviducts, ready for fertilization. The cytoplasm, or non-nuclear living material, which is finally included in the egg cells is usually of a special kind, known as germ plasm, which was not involved in embryonic development and differentiation.

Most animal eggs spend a very long time in the first stage, or prophase, of the first meiotic division and, during this time, the nucleus is very active. A "fuzz" of long DNA threads extends out from all the chromosomes and a very large proportion of the genetic information is converted, or transcribed, into messenger RNA (mRNA). The resulting mRNA is packaged in various ways, because most of it is not used until the development into the new animal has begun (see box). During the long oogenesis, which is the process of formation of the ova, the egg also acquires a special structure to its cytoplasm, and special membranes and yolk are formed, often by cooperation between the egg cell itself and the surrounding follicle cells which contain the developing ova. Human eggs begin this long oogenesis in the three-month female fetus, and must wait for at least tens of years before ovulation. Frog eggs take some two

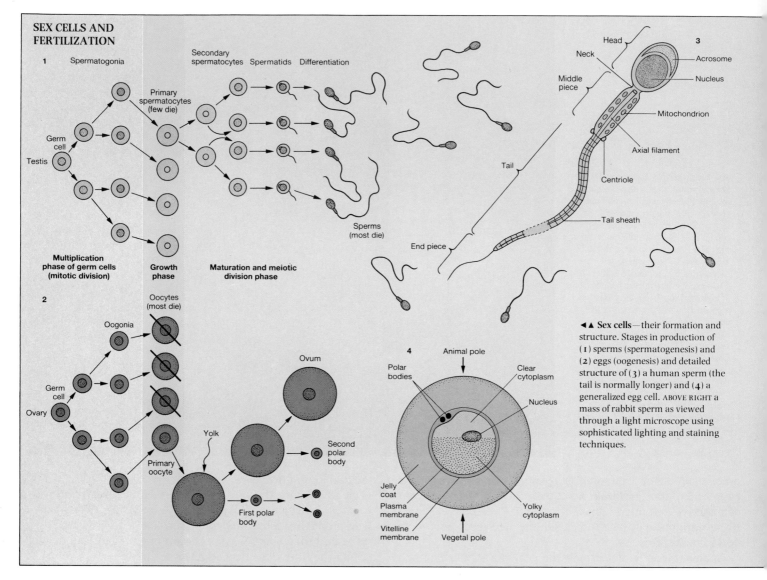

SEX CELLS AND FERTILIZATION

◄▲ **Sex cells**—their formation and structure. Stages in production of (1) sperms (spermatogenesis) and (2) eggs (oogenesis) and detailed structure of (3) a human sperm (the tail is normally longer) and (4) a generalized egg cell. ABOVE RIGHT a mass of rabbit sperm as viewed through a light microscope using sophisticated lighting and staining techniques.

years to develop, but the eggs of some worms and echinoderms can complete oogenesis in just months. Because of the yolk food reserves, the mature egg may be thousands (or in birds and sharks, millions) of times bigger than the original oocyte which started oogenesis. Some eggs, such as those of placental mammals, have no yolk and receive their nutrients in other ways during development.

Fertilization. Spermatozoans (sperms) are produced in a testis, usually of a different individual from that which produces the ova. There are many ways in which the spermatozoa can come into contact with the eggs. In some organisms, such as marine worms, echinoderms, and most fish and amphibians, eggs and spermatozoans are released into the water around the animals, where they meet randomly, and the spermatozoans pass through the membranes of the eggs—at least the sperm's head, with its nucleus, passes into the cytoplasm of the egg cell. Only the spermatozoans of hydroids, and perhaps some fish, are chemically attracted to their eggs.

Nearly all land-living organisms copulate, so that the male's spermatozoa are deposited in the reproductive tract of the female, often into a special sac, called a spermatheca, in

which they are stored. Thus, the female has a source of "foreign" spermatozoa inside her which she can then use to fertilize her eggs at a convenient time. Copulation avoids the necessity for the two sexes to synchronize the release of their reproductive cells, or gametes, and means that sexual congress can take place in very different conditions from egg laying. It also permits the female to retain eggs in her body so that they can develop in a safe and suitable environment.

The beginning of development. After fertilization, the eggs of most multicellular animals begin mitotic division or cleavage. The nuclei of the egg and the spermatozoan mix their chromosome sets into the first egg nucleus, but only the egg's centriole and mitochondria contribute to the cell which results from the fusion of the gametes (the zygote). The genetic contribution of the spermatozoan has no control over the earliest stages of development, either. The cleaving egg usually forms a spherical mass of cells, or the cells form part of the spherical surface of the yolk. When cleavage has divided the cytoplasm into cells in which the ratio of the nuclear to the cytoplasmic material approaches that of the adult cells of the organism, there is usually a series of cell movements, often involving the folding of

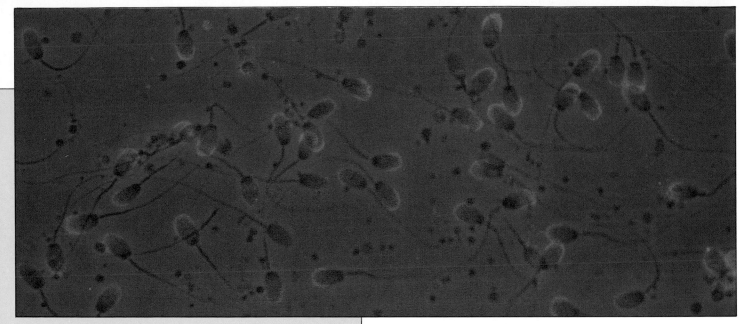

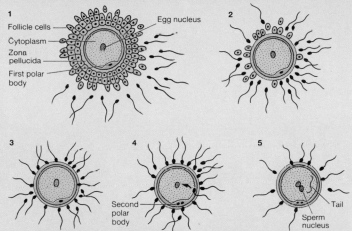

1	2

Follicle cells
Cytoplasm
Zona pellucida
First polar body
Egg nucleus

3	4	5

Second polar body
Sperm nucleus
Tail

▲ ▼ **Coming together** of egg and sperm—the act of fertilization. ABOVE Events leading to fertilization. (1) Sperms reach the ovum. (2) Follicle cells disperse. (3) Sperm penetrates zona pellucida. (4) A single sperm enters the egg cytoplasm; egg nucleus completes division and second polar body formed. (5) Sperm nucleus and egg nucleus fuse. BELOW Egg with sperm inside visible on the right.

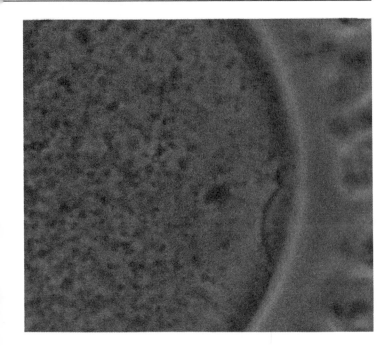

cell layers, so that the embryo becomes multilayered. The gut, and even other organ systems such as the flexible supporting rod, or notochord of vertebrates, the nervous system and heart are in position after this.

Life Histories

The unfolding genetic program. The earliest development of most animals results from the programming of the egg during its development in the ovary. This leads to a simple embryonic structure which is, nevertheless, the framework for all later embryonic development. This is called the "phylotypic stage." All of the complicated growth of nerves, blood vessels, skeleton and tubes uses this framework, as each cell responds to its position by turning on some of its genes. Although all of the nuclei have the same array of genes available, different sets are turned on in the different circumstances found in the various parts of the phylotypic stage: muscle cells turn on that gene array which includes lots of the proteins myosin, actin and calmodulin, as well as the other materials used in contraction; nerve cells specialize in those gene products which produce, receive and regulate neurotransmitters, and so on. Very few cells acquire their final properties early in their embryological development but groups, and sometimes clones, of cells progressively become differently specialized (differentiated).

One way of understanding this process is to consider the original architecture of the phylotypic stage as a three-dimensional map. The cells are all located in different places on the map and each responds to the information conveyed by its position by developing into one of a few kinds of cell. Each kind of cell usually appears in many places in one embryo—there is not a unique response to each "map reference!" Nevertheless, front and back legs of four-legged animals have somewhat different patterns of such cells, for example, and experiments with regenerating limbs in embryos (and young amphibians) have shown the influence of local positional factors on transplanted rudiments.

Reaching juvenile size. Few animal lifestyles can operate over a wide range of sizes—most animals grow much less than ten times linearly, or 1,000 times in mass, from time of birth or emergence from the eggs. However, some parasites, the giant snakes, many fish and other creatures do. These animals either absorb their food "chemically" or they eat food which is

What Controls Early Development?

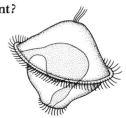

Much recent investigation has yielded the surprising conclusion that, in most animals, the nuclear genetic program of the fertilized egg contributes little to this laying down of the framework of the embryo. It is accomplished mostly as a result of the complex architecture, together with the molecules carrying information (messenger RNA), which are acquired during the long oogenesis—the nuclei are just "passengers" until they find themselves in the different organs of the simple embryonic body plan. The period of development during which the genetic program of the zygote is taking over the organization of the embryo is called the phylotypic stage.

For example, some marine animals, especially polychaete worms and echinoderms, produce very many eggs, each of which has only a little yolk. They must feed and fend for themselves early in development. The first, ciliated, free-swimming feeding larva of many worms is called a trochophore (ABOVE) while that of most starfish and sea urchins is known as a dipleurula. In both these cases, these are phylotypic stages and the development of the egg to this point has been determined by events during egg formation, and not by the fertilization nucleus. Thus, all of the eggs of a mother starfish are guaranteed by *her* genetics to be able to develop this far, and the yolk has provisioned them. They find themselves in the rich pastures of the spring plankton as their nuclei take over control of development. Only then can their own genetic programs be tested—very few of these larvae will metamorphose and most will be food for other creatures. Presumably, those genetic programs which make the best-fitted later larvae survive; and those mothers which produce the best phylotypic stages will contribute the most "raw material" for these programs.

graduated in size. The egg's cytoplasm is always only a tiny proportion of the mother's mass, so that there must be enormous growth before the mother's lifestyle can be adopted by the juvenile animal. Basically, there are two ways of achieving this: either several successive lifestyles can serve as steps (larvae) on a ladder of size; or the mother can donate enough yolk or other food to the embryo so that it can develop into a juvenile without feeding itself by its own efforts. There are intermediate solutions: for example, the tarantula wasp mother gives her offspring a paralyzed spider to eat (see box); the first whelk hatchling's first act is to eat all his more tardy brothers and sisters. Nevertheless, there is a broad distinction between independent and privileged early stages of the life histories of animals.

Metamorphosis. In the case of those animals for which the mother provides little for her offspring, they are usually produced in vast numbers, and usually into an environment (such as the plankton) where "life is cheap;" nearly all are eaten but a few survive to metamorphose to the next stage. Sometimes, as in the case of the echinoderms and marine worms, the first metamorphosis coincides with the phylotypic stage, when the zygote's own gene set is taking over control of its development. Sometimes, the first body plan is retained for a long time, with modifications, as in the tadpole, and the major change is then from a well-developed larva to a juvenile of adult form. The tadpole's tail degenerates as its cells respond to the hormones

of metamorphosis by programmed suicide; skin, gut and many other tissues change, and the skull is completely remodeled; new blood cells appear which make a different, adult, form of hemoglobin suitable for life on land.

Many planktonic larvae, such as those of starfish or nemertean worms, only make the juvenile from a small part of the larva. Insects, such as true flies, butterflies, moths and beetles, make most of the adult's limbs, wings and genitalia from tiny thickenings of the larva's epithelium, known as imaginal disks, although much of the larval nerve system and internal organs are only modified in the pupa.

The hormonal control of development of these successive stages has been sufficiently well investigated for it to become clear that this is not the major problem. But how can one genetic program result in the production of two very different forms? Where one form is detemined by the egg structure, as it is in the polychaete worms and, to a large extent, in tadpoles, there is less of a problem. In other cases, however, where a major change of form occurs at puberty, converting the animal from a vegetative to a reproductive stage, as in the mayfly, there are clearly two very differently adapted creatures. The larva is produced from the structured egg, considerably modified by the action of the zygote genes; but the adult results from the action of a peculiar balance of hormones on the late larva. This is, however, no less or no more remarkable than the

▲ **Privilege.** Soon after birth or hatching, many juvenile animals closely resemble the form of their parents, only differing in size from them. The mother donates enough yolk or other food to the embryo that it can develop into a juvenile without feeding itself. Shown here is a hatching Johnston's crocodile (*Crocodylus johnstoni*).

► **Independent life and metamorphosis**—two stages in the life cycle of mayflies (*Ephemera danica*). ABOVE A nymph which hatches from a yolkless egg and lives in water. BELOW An adult which enjoys a short aerial existence after emerging from the pupa before laying its eggs under water.

▼ **The first division** of the fertilized egg of a frog divides it in half. Further divisions produce a solid ball of cells, followed by the formation of a hollow sphere-like blastula. After this the form of the final animal starts to develop.

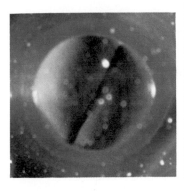

development of antlers by male deer or of beards by human males; or, the development of the first larva from the egg.

Privilege—Yolk and Live Birth

All higher animals "invest" much energy and material in their offspring, usually giving each enough to guarantee its early survival. Sometimes, however, the mother may produce large numbers of eggs and invest little in each one. When mature animals are in reproductive condition, they are able to make gains of energy and materials during their metabolic processes which then become available for reproduction. The gains made usually take the form of stored food products which can be transformed into yolk for the eggs—as in the case of locusts, for example. On the other hand, such gains may also free the animal from the need to feed so that it then has time and energy for reproductive behavior; animals that die after breeding ("terminal breeders"), such as eels, salmon, mayflies and silk moths, function in this way, as does the tarantula wasp (see box).

Mature animals which do need to feed usually have spare time and energy which can be devoted to caring and providing for the offspring. It is clear that animals which have genetic programs that enable them to give greater care to their offspring are more likely to be better represented among the breeders of the next generation. In other words, more care may be much more effective than more offspring. It has been shown, for example, that for songbirds, simply laying more eggs does not increase their contribution to the future and that, for each species, there is an optimum number of eggs at a particular place in a given year. If the bird lays too many eggs, the parents are unable to feed the chicks adequately but, if there are too few, the contribution to the next generation falls short of the number required for replacing the parent birds because of the low rates of survival of songbirds. In this case, therefore, natural selection operates in favor of parent birds which produce an adequate number of offspring with greater privilege.

The eggs of some animals, such as most insects and reptiles, contain large amounts of yolk but the parents devote relatively little care to their developing progeny. Birds usually devote a lot of care as well by maintaining an even temperature in the nest and by feeding the hatchlings until they are big enough to fend for themselves. The size range over which a given species of bird can fly effectively is usually very small, and some nestlings may actually weigh more than the adult.

Live birth—viviparity. In viviparous animals, the embryo develops within the mother's body, resulting in live birth. Many different kinds of animal have adopted viviparity as a way of providing care, nutrients and a favorable environment for the developing embryos, with the mother's own physiology maintaining them. Contrast the eggs of a European Common frog with those of a guppy, for example. The frog's eggs may develop for several days at temperatures between 0° and 5°C (32° to 41°F) or between 25° and 30°C (77° to 86°F) depending on the spring weather—nights at 5°C (41°F) and days at 25°C (77°F) are not rare! The eggs of the fish, however, which are much the same size and complexity of those of the frog, are maintained in the ovaries of the female as they develop. She avoids extremes of temperature, as well as predators, and the eggs receive oxygen and the other benefits of a good blood supply. Some fish, called mouth brooders, care for their young by holding them in the mouth and, compared with their egg-guarding relatives, they have some of the advantages of viviparity.

Placental mammals are the masters (mistresses?) of viviparity. The female's uterus is certainly one of the best-controlled stable environments in this solar system! The eggs have little or no yolk and undergo the early stages of development in the nutrient-rich fluids of the oviduct and uterus. The eggs interact subtly with the prepared mucus membrane lining

◀▲ **Parental care in birds.** It is not worth songbird parents, such as this European robin (*Erithacus rubecula*) ABOVE, trying to raise more than four young in each brood, as this is the maximum number they can adequately feed. Penguins, such as these King penguins (*Aptenodytes patagonicus*) OPPOSITE, only raise one young each season. Before leaving the nest the chick will weigh more than each parent; the store of fat will be used to sustain it during the first weeks of its independence.

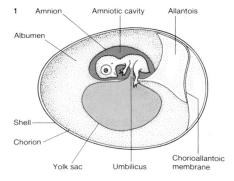

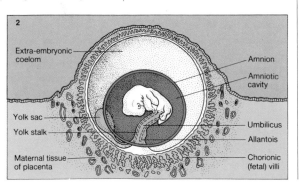

◀ **Egg and placenta structure compared.** Structure of (1) a bird's egg with developing chick inside and (2) a mammalian embryo within the uterus. Note that both embryos are enclosed in similar membranes, the chick connected to the yolk sac for nourishment and the embryo to its mother via the placenta.

the uterus so that their outer layer, known as the trophoblast, invades the tissues of the mother and a metabolic exchange takes place. Only then does the development of the embryo proceed. The eggs of a mammal derive little of their organization from the mother and it is a puzzle how, from a few cells in the inner mass of cells, they reach the stage at which the typical vertebrate zygote's genetic program takes over the organization of the embryo. As the embryo becomes more complex and a blood system develops, the interaction with the surface of the uterus also becomes more complicated, and a *placenta* results. This allows metabolic molecules to be exchanged between embryo and mother while preventing the embryo's tissues, which are usually foreign to the mother, from being attacked by antibodies. Some antibodies, and even some cells, do cross the membranes of the placenta, however, especially during the birth process, resulting in conditions such as rhesus incompatibility in human babies.

There is every degree of viviparity. No bird is really viviparous although bird eggs all begin their development while they are still in the oviduct. At the other end of the spectrum, baby wildebeest, giraffes and guinea pigs can lead near-adult lives very soon after birth. The tsetse fly maggot is retained in its mother's "uterus" for all of its larval development; it is "born," burrows and pupates, then emerges a full-size fly. *All preadult growth occurs in utero.*

Nests. Many animals make use of nests to protect eggs or young which are unable to fend for themselves. A nest may be as simple as a mucus-filled crevice, in which a snail lays its eggs, or the stone surface used by a cichlid fish. Nests may be mechanically complex, such as those of some weaver birds or the egg basket of the octopus, *Argonauta*, known as the "paper argonaut." Otter holts, rabbit warrens, mice nests and human homes all serve complex nesting functions; in these cases the most important of the functions is in the instruction of their young.

Growth

Juvenile animals need to reach a minimum size before they can adopt the life style of their parents. The range of sizes between the fertilized egg and the minimum may be climbed on a "ladder" of different larval forms, as it is in many crustaceans, with growth occurring at the molts between stages. Alternatively, enough nutrient may be provided for the offspring that they only achieve independence when they have almost reached the size of their parents. In the case of these highly privileged embryos, their development must be modified so that they can make use of the yolk, and they usually have special organs to enable them to cope with nutrition, to respire, to excrete waste products and to deal with their water economy.

Even when these animals are hatched or born, however, only rarely are they immediately able to adopt fully the lifestyle of their parents. Many land snails, lizards and snakes and some birds, such as ostriches, do, and some kinds of rodents, such as guinea pigs, as well as ungulates, are almost effective at birth. Most mammals and birds, however, require a relatively long period of further care before they can become independent. Baby mammals are suckled on milk secreted by the mother's mammary glands, and have special adaptations to their guts

▼ **Larder for its young.** A tarantula wasp (*Cryptocheilus* species) carries a paralyzed spider to its burrow TOP which provides food for its larva BOTTOM (see box).

▶ **Bubble nest** of Siamese fighting fish (*Betta splendens*). After courtship and shedding of eggs or sperm under the water, the male collects the fertilized eggs (as here) and places them under the "nest" of air bubbles he has produced.

▶ **Protection in a nest.** BELOW Young deer mice (*Peromyscus maniculatus*) spend their first weeks of life protected in a grassy nest and are fed by their mother on milk.

Tarantula Wasps

The reproductive arrangement of tarantula wasps is very peculiar. The female digs a burrow and then searches for a spider (each species of wasp attacks only a very restricted number of kinds of spider). It engages the spider in a short battle, usually resulting in the wasp stinging and paralyzing the spider with its venom. The wasp then drags the spider to its burrow (or may dig another), lays an egg on it, buries it and then disguises the entrance. It may repeat this process tens of times. When the egg hatches, the maggot penetrates the still-living spider's cuticle and slowly eats it, leaving vital organs, such as the heart, until last. Then it pupates and hatches as a fully provided adult; if it is female it digs its way out to find males already waiting for it (perhaps the mother leaves a chemical scent marker). It mates once and never feeds for all its food and energy have come from the spider.

to enable them to deal with it. Baby birds are also specially adapted: many have a strikingly colored gape, special behavior or, as in the pigeons, even a "suckling" response to milk glands. They grow during this period although the rate of growth is usually slower than that of the embryo. Most importantly, their shape changes and there is further development of their organs. Newborn puppies, kittens or humans are very different in shape from the adults, and their temperature regulation is ineffective as it is in newly hatched chicks.

Snails and other gastropods grow faster as they age so that their shells grow in an ever-increasing spiral; there is little change of proportion, however. This kind of growth is unusual, and most animals change shape gradually, but dramatically, as they grow, changing in proportions, so that, at each stage, the organs are of the appropriate size in relation to the functions they perform at the time.

Even those animals which do not metamorphose so markedly as insects or frogs do, nevertheless, show many changes of shape which herald the entry into the reproductive phase of life. These are referred to as pubertal changes and occur in most animals although they are particularly evident in humans (at least to our eyes and brains). At the very least, as in the case of echinoderms, the sex glands mature and the animal's internal "plumbing" develops to deal with their release. Commonly, there are also differences between the sexes which result from the responses of the various tissues to different hormones which are released from the nervous system or from the gonads themselves as they develop and reach maturity.   JC

Bibliography

The following list of titles indicates key reference works used in the preparation of this volume and those recommended for further reading. The list is divided into categories corresponding to those of the volume.

General

Arms, K. and Camp, P.S. (1982) *Biology*, Saunders College Publishing, Philadelphia.

Gordon, M.S., Bartholomew, G.A., Grinnell, A.D., Jørgensen, C.B. and White, F.N. (1982) *Animal Physiology, Principles and Adaptations*, (4th edn), Macmillan, New York.

Maynard Smith, J. (1975) *The Theory of Evolution*, (3rd edn), Penguin, Harmondsworth.

Roberts, M.B.V. (1982) *Biology: A Functional Approach*, Nelson, Walton-on-Thames.

Schmidt-Nielsen, K. (1972) *How Animals Work*, Cambridge University Press, Cambridge.

Schmidt-Nielsen, K. (1983) *Animal Physiology: Adaptation and Environment*, (3rd edn), Cambridge University Press, Cambridge.

Villee, C.A., Solomon, E.P. and Davis, P.W. (1985) *Biology*, Saunders College Publishing, Philadelphia.

The Animal Kingdom

Alexander, R.McN. (1979) *The Invertebrates*, Cambridge University Press, Cambridge.

Alexander, R.McN. (1981) *The Chordates*, (2nd edn), Cambridge University Press, Cambridge.

Attenborough, D. (1985) *The Living Planet: a Portrait of the Earth*, Reader's Digest, London.

Barnes, R.S.K. (ed) (1984) *A Synoptic Classification of Living Organisms*, Blackwell, Oxford.

Barrington, E.J.W. (1979) *Invertebrate Structure and Function*, (2nd edn), Nelson, London.

Barth, R.H. and Broshears, R.E. (1982) *The Invertebrate World*, Saunders College Publishing, Philadelphia.

Hildebrand, M., Bramble, D.M., Liem, K.F. and Wake, D.B. (eds) (1985) *Functional Vertebrate Morphology*, Harvard University Press, Cambridge, Massachusetts.

Wells, M.J. (1968) *Lower Animals*, Weidenfeld & Nicolson, London.

Young, J.Z. (1981) *The Life of Vertebrates*, (3rd edn), Clarendon, Oxford.

Molecules and Cells

deDuve, C. (1984) *A Guided Tour of the Living Cell*, Scientific American Books, New York.

Kimball, J.W. (1984) *Cell Biology*, (3rd edn), Addison-Wesley, Reading, Massachusetts.

Rees, A.R. and Sternberg, M.J.E. (1984) *From Cells to Atoms*, Blackwell, Oxford.

Rose, S. (1979) *The Chemistry of Life*, (2nd edn), Penguin, Harmondsworth.

Welsch, U. and Storch, V. (1976) *Comparative Animal Cytology and Histology*, Sidgwick & Jackson, London.

Feeding and Digestion

Brafield, A.E. and Llewellyn, M.J. (1982) *Animal Energetics*, Blackie, Glasgow.

Jennings, J.B. (1972) *Feeding, Digestion and Assimilation in Animals*, (2nd edn), Macmillan, London.

Jørgensen, C.B. (1966) *Biology of Suspension Feeding*, Pergamon, Oxford.

Morton, J. (1979) *Guts*, (2nd edn), Arnold, London.

Gas Exchange and Circulation

Jones, J.D. (1972) *Comparative Physiology of Respiration*, Arnold, London.

Weibel, E.R. (1984) *The Pathway for Oxygen. Structure and Function in the Mammalian Respiratory System*, Harvard University Press, Cambridge, Massachusetts.

Widdicombe, J. and Davies, A. (1983) *Respiratory Physiology*, Arnold, London.

The Internal Environment

Davenport, J. (1985) *Environmental Stress and Behavioural Adaptation*, Croom Helm, London.

Hardy, R.N. (1979) *Temperature and Animal Life*, (2nd edn), Arnold, London.

Hardy, R.N. (1983) *Homeostasis*, (2nd edn), Arnold, London.

Rankin, J.C. and Davenport, J.A. (1981) *Animal Osmoregulation*, Blackie, Glasgow.

Stanier, M.W., Mount, L.E. and Bligh, J. (1984) *Energy Balance and Temperature Regulation*, Cambridge University Press, Cambridge.

Senses

Gregory, R.L. (1978) *Eye and Brain*, (3rd edn), McGraw-Hill, New York.

Lythgoe, J.N. (1979) *The Ecology of Vision*, Clarendon, Oxford.

Rosenberg, M.E. (1982) *Sound and Hearing*, Arnold, London.

Movement of Animals

Alexander, R.McN. (1982) *Locomotion of Animals*, Blackie, Glasgow.

Gray, J. (1968) *Animal Locomotion*, Weidenfeld & Nicolson, London.

Margaria, R. (1976) *Biomechanics and Energetics of Muscular Exercise*, Clarendon, Oxford.

McMahon, T.A. (1984) *Muscles, Reflexes and Locomotion*, Princeton University Press, Princeton, New Jersey.

Rüppell, G. (1977) *Bird Flight*, Van Nostrand Reinhold, New York.

Coordination and Control

Buckle, J.W. (1983) *Animal Hormones*, Arnold, London.

Messenger, J.B. (1979) *Nerves, Brains and Behaviour*, Arnold, London.

Mill, P.J. (1982) *Comparative Neurobiology*, Arnold, London.

Scientific American (1979) *Hormones and Reproductive Behavior*, Freeman, San Francisco.

Usherwood, P.N.R. (1973) *Nervous Systems*, Arnold, London.

Young, J.Z. (1978) *Programs of the Brain*, Oxford University Press, Oxford.

Reproduction and Development

Calow, P. (1978) *Life Cycles*, Chapman & Hall, London.

Cohen, J. (1977) *Reproduction*, Butterworth, London.

Cohen, J. and Massey, B. (1982) *Living Embryos*, (3rd edn), Pergamon, Oxford.

Picture Acknowledgements

Key: *t* top. *b* bottom. *c* center. *l* left. *r* right.
Abbreviations: AN Agence Nature. ANT Australasian Nature Transparencies. BA Biophoto Associates. BCL Bruce Coleman Ltd. CAH C.A. Henley. NHPA Natural History Photographic Agency. NSP Natural Science Photos. OSF Oxford Scientific Films. P Premaphotos Wildlife/K. Preston Mafham. PEP Planet Earth Pictures/Seaphot. SAL Survival Anglia Ltd. SPL Science Photo Library.

1 SPL/Dr. L.M. Beidler. 2 Mansell Collection Ltd. 3t BCL/G.D. Plage. 3b AN/Lanceau. 4–5 AN/Chaumeton. 5 NSP/P. Ward. 6–7 BCL/K. Taylor. 8 PEP/D. George. 9t PEP/P. Atkinson. 9b PEP/C. Pétron. 10 CAH. 11 PEP/K. Vaughan. 12–13 SAL/J. Foott. 14 Ardea/V. Taylor. 16–17 BCL/G. Zeisler. 17 BCL. 18t, 18–19, 19 CAH. 20–21 Sinclair Stammers. 22–23 SPL/E. Gravé. 23tl SPL/M. Abbey. 23br BA. 23cr SPL/Dr. Mia Tegner. 23br BCL/G. Cox. 23bl SPL/E. Gravé. 26t SPL/Dr. R. King. 26bl, 26br, 27tl BA. 27bl SPL/Dr. D. Fawcett. 27br, 29t, 29c, 29b BA. 30 SPL. 31 SPL/Dr. G. Murti. 32 SPL/Anderson-Simon. 32–33 SPL/Prof. S. Cohen. 33 SPL/Dr. E. Cook. 34–35 John Visser. 36 Eric and David Hosking/D.P. Wilson. 37 NHPA/Bill Wood. 38 inset BA. 38t OSF/G. Thompson. 38b CAH. 39 SPL/Dr. T. Brain. 40t Sinclair Stammers. 40c, 40b PEP/C. Pétron. 40–41 G. Frame. 42 ANT/K. Atkinson. 43 OSF/G. Bernard. 45t Biofotos/H. Angel. 45b SPL/M. Sklar. 47 NHPA/P. Johnson. 50–51 AN/Chaumeton. 54t R.W. van Devender. 54b C. Howson. 55 OSF/P. Parks. 56–57 OSF/J. Dermid. 57 BCL/J. Burton. 58–59 William Ervin, Natural Imagery. 60 NHPA/S. Dalton. 61 PEP/N. Greaves. 66–67 Peter Veit. 68–69 B. Hawkes. 69t NSP/D. MacCaskill. 72b PEP/N. Sefton. 72–73 PEP/K. Amsler. 73b PEP/C. Roessler. 74 NSP/I. Bennett. 76 BCL/C. Hughes. 77 AN/Grospas. 78–79 ANT/G. Fyfe. 80b NHPA/S. Dalton. 80–81 G. Frame. 81b Ardea/J. van Gruisen. 82–83 BCL/J. & D. Bartlett. 83b BCL/K. Taylor. 84–85 P. 86–87 ANT/G.D. Anderson. 88–89 B. Hawkes. 89b OSF/G. Bernard. 90t PEP/J. Lythgoe. 90b BCL/C. Frith. 91 Dwight R. Kuhn. 93t NHPA/Bill Wood. 93b BCL/H. Reinhard. 94b Leonard Lee Rue III. 94–95 PEP/J. Hudnall. 96l G. Mazza. 96r, 96–97 NHPA/A. Bannister. 97r PEP/N. Greaves. 98–99 PEP/K. Ammann. 100 J.D. Currey. 101 OSF/P. Parks. 103 A. Bannister. 104–105 CAH. 106 AN/Chaumeton-Lanceau. 106–107 AN/Gohier. 107t NHPA/S. Dalton. 110t BCL/B. & C. Calhoun. 110b P. 111 David Hosking. 112–113 NHPA/A. Bannister. 113b A.S. Jayes. 114–115 Ken Adwick. 116 G. Mazza. 117 OSF/G. Bernard. 118 PEP/Bill Wood. 119 P. 123 Ardea/P. Morris. 124b NHPA/S. Dalton. 124–125 Ardea. 128–129 NHPA/P. Johnson. 130t NHPA/M. Walker. 130b OSF/J. Cooke. 132t Biofotos/Heather Angel. 132b OSF/L. Gould. 133 OSF/F. Ehrenström. 134 Dwight R. Kuhn. 135 BCL/K. Taylor. 137 Dr. J. Cohen. 138–139 NSP/C. Banks. 138bl BA. 139tr Peter Gathercole. 139br OSF/G. Bernard. 140 NHPA/B. Hawkes. 141 Eric Hosking. 142 CAH. 143t G. Frame. 143b SAL/J. Foott.

Artwork

All artwork Oxford Illustrators Limited unless stated otherwise below.
Abbreviations: SD Simon Driver. RL Richard Lewington.

8b, 11, 12, 15cl, 15b, 38 SD. 48, 49 RL. 58 SD. 64, 65, 108, 109 RL. 110t, 111t Ad Cameron.

GLOSSARY

Abdomen that part of the trunk of a mammal which is POSTERIOR to the ribs and diaphragm and that contains the LIVER, STOMACH, INTESTINES and other viscera. Also, the third of the three parts (HEAD, THORAX and abdomen) into which the trunk of an insect is divided. Also, that part of the body of a crustacean which is posterior to the walking legs.

Abiotic describing the physical factors, such as water and temperature, in the environment of an organism.

Acclimation non-genetic changes in the physiological functions of an animal in response to long-term, continuing changes in the environment.

Achilles tendon the tendon that connects the calf MUSCLE to the heel. It can be felt through the skin, behind the ankle. It is so named because the heel was the only vulnerable part of the legendary Greek hero, Achilles.

Actin a PROTEIN which is the main constituent of the thin filaments of MUSCLE. When muscle contracts, the cross-bridges on the thick filaments attach to the actin molecules on the thin ones and exert tension. Actin has also been detected in amoebas and probably plays a part in their movement.

Action potential a change in the electrical voltage which travels the length of a stimulated nerve fiber in an animal and which stimulates activity either in other NERVE CELLS or in other cells such as MUSCLE fibers. An action potential is usually very brief and fast moving.

Active transport the process in which, with the expenditure of energy, a substance is pumped across a membrane in the direction opposite to that of DIFFUSION.

Adaptation a characteristic that fits an animal for a particular way of life. For example, the long proboscis of a butterfly or moth is an adaptation for feeding on nectar hidden deep within flowers.

Adenosine triphosphate (ATP) the principal energy currency of cells. A fixed amount of energy is stored in each ATP molecule. This energy is released when ATP is broken down to **adenosine diphosphate (ADP).**

Adrenaline a HORMONE produced by the adrenal gland of higher vertebrates, serving different functions in different tissues.

Advanced see PRIMITIVE.

Aestivation a period of torpidity which helps an animal to survive a period of either heat (in summer) or dryness.

Alveolus the functional unit of the LUNG of a mammal. Oxygen and carbon dioxide are exchanged through the walls of the alveoli between alveolar air and pulmonary capillary blood. The alveoli are small, spherical chambers that lie at the ends of a progressively dividing system of tubes. The system begins at the TRACHEA which divides to form the **bronchi**. Division then proceeds through many stages in **bronchioles** and **alveolar ducts** before the **alveolar sacs**, which are completely covered with alveoli, are reached.

Amino acid a chemical compound containing amino (NH_2) and carboxyl (COOH) groups, and from which PROTEINS are formed.

Anerobic describes an organism which is capable of living in the absence of oxygen. Also describes an environment in which oxygen is absent.

Anerobic metabolism the process taking place in cells in which nutrients, such as CARBOHYDRATES, are decomposed ENZYMATICALLY in the absence of oxygen to yield energy. The products of this type of decomposition are substances such as LACTIC ACID. The energy produced by anerobic processes is much less than that produced by the OXIDATIVE METABOLISM of an equivalent amount of nutrient.

Antagonism the situation in which two MUSCLES have opposite effects, each tending to reverse the action of the other. For example, the biceps muscle bends the elbow and is antagonistic to the triceps muscle which extends it.

Anterior towards the front end of the body.

Antibody a substance formed by the IMMUNE SYSTEM to react with and inactivate a specific ANTIGEN. This process provides an important defense against infection.

Anticoagulant a substance, such as heparin and hirudin (found in leeches), which prevents the coagulation of blood.

Antigen a substance which activates the IMMUNE SYSTEM to produce an ANTIBODY against the antigen, ultimately eliminating it from the body.

Anus the posterior opening of the digestive tract.

Apodeme one of the structures in arthropods that serve the same function as the TENDONS of vertebrates: they connect MUSCLE to skeleton. They project in from the cuticle like turned-in fingers of a glove, and consist of similar materials to the cuticle.

Aquatic describing an organism which lives in water.

Arterial blood blood which flows from the HEART to the tissues of the body. Such blood is high in oxygen and low in carbon dioxide. Note that the pulmonary vein contains arterial blood which has just been oxygenated in the lungs.

Artery a blood vessel with thick, elastic walls that carries blood from the HEART to the tissues. Blood pressures in the arteries are high and oscillate between certain limits as the heart beats, causing the diameters of the vessels to change. This movement can be felt in certain regions as the **pulse**.

Autotrophic describes those organisms (plants) which form CARBOHYDRATE, PROTEIN and fat from carbon dioxide and inorganic compounds.

Axon a prolongation of the cell body of a NERVE CELL along which ACTION POTENTIALS or other potentials may be transmitted.

Biosphere that part of the earth containing living organisms.

Blood corpuscle a cellular element of the blood consisting of two main types – the red cells or **erythrocytes** and the white cells or **leucocytes**.

Bone the main material of the skeletons of most vertebrates. It consists of approximately equal volumes of COLLAGEN fibers (the fibers from which TENDONS are made) and crystals of bone salt (containing calcium phosphate and hydroxide). Bone is much denser than wood but resembles hardwoods, such as oak, in its strength and elastic properties.

Brain a collection of NERVE CELLS usually at the ANTERIOR of the animal. It is often formed from the fusion of several anterior GANGLIA and consists of several lobes or nuclei associated with the inputs from the major senses of vision, smell, hearing and touch.

Buccal cavity the cavity into which the mouth opens and which is, therefore, the first part of the alimentary canal. In many animals the buccal cavity is part of the respiratory as well as of the alimentary tract and may also contain the openings of the nostrils and glottis. In mammals the respiratory tract is separated from the buccal cavity by the palate.

Capacity adaptation a physiological ADAPTATION in an animal involving changes in the animal's rate of doing something, such as a change in the amount of blood pumped by the HEART per unit time.

Capillary a vessel of the blood circulation system. Capillaries are the smallest vessels of the system with walls only one cell thick. They form extensive, branching networks in almost all tissues of the body. Materials of all types, salts, nutrients and water, are exchanged through the thin capillary wall between blood and tissues.

Carbohydrate a compound of carbon, hydrogen and oxygen. Sugars and the POLYSACCHARIDES built from the sugars are carbohydrates.

Carnivore any meat-eating organism; alternatively, and more specifically, a member of the mammal order Carnivora, many of whose members are carnivores.

Catch muscle a MUSCLE which is capable of maintaining tension over a prolonged period with very little expenditure of energy. Bivalve mollusks (clams etc) have catch muscles to hold their shells closed.

Cecum a blind pouch in the alimentary canal of an animal. The cecum is vital to the digestive system of HERBIVORES. Mammals are not usually able to digest cellulose which makes up a large part of the diet of a herbivore but the cellulose is broken down by bacteria in the cecum and can then pass into the bloodstream of the animal.

Cell membrane a double layer of LIPID and PROTEIN molecules which envelopes cells.

Central nervous system that part of the nervous system of an animal which receives input from the sensory nerves and which issues commands to the MUSCLES, thus exerting an important controlling influence over the animal's body. It usually consists of an aggregation of interconnected NEURONES, the BRAIN, joined by AXON connectives to a number of subsidiary GANGLIA.

Chemoreceptor a cell which produces electrical signals when stimulated by the presence of particular molecules making contact with its membrane. These cells are responsible for the senses of smell and taste.

Chitin a POLYSACCHARIDE found in combination with PROTEIN in the skeletons of arthropods (insects etc), in the bristles of annelid worms, in the outer casing of some hydrozoans, in the teeth of the tongue-like organs of mollusks and in various other animal structures.

Chloride cell a specialized cell found in the GILLS of most fish and which is largely responsible for the ACTIVE TRANSPORT of salts, especially chloride salts, across the gills.

Chromosome one of the bodies that appear in the nucleus of a cell during division. The chromosomes consist of DEOXYRIBONUCLEIC ACID, which contains the genetic plans of an organism, as well as many kinds of PROTEINS. All the cells, except for SPERMATOZOON and EGGS, of every individual in a species have the same number of chromosomes.

Cilium a hair-like growth from a cell. When present in large numbers on surfaces exposed to water, the beating cilia can produce currents in the surrounding water (see also FLAGELLUM).

Class a group of related organisms, such as the class Insecta (the insects) or the class Aves (the birds). Most classes consist of several ORDERS and most PHYLA contain several classes.

Cleavage the division of an EGG into smaller cells. The nuclei multiply by MITOSIS, all the products being equivalent initially, but the cytoplasm divides into different, or potentially different regions.

Click mechanism a mechanism which has two stable positions. If it is set in one position, it will resist forces tending to push it towards the other position but, if it is pushed more than half way, it will click suddenly to the that second position. The two winged-flies of the ORDER Diptera have a click mechanism in the THORAX. Their wings are stable in the "up" and "down" positions and click from one to the other.

Cloaca the common opening for the intestine and urinary tract in all vertebrates apart from mammals.

Clone a population of cells or organisms which share common descent from only a single ancestor.

Collagen the group of PROTEINS of which TENDONS are made. They are also important constituents of BONE, cartilage, skin and many other tissues. They are rare in arthropods (insects etc) but plentiful in most animal PHYLA.

Community any naturally occurring group of different organisms which live and interact in a particular environment.

Compound eye an eye made up of many separate optical systems rather than the single one found, for example, in humans. Typically, arthropods, such as insects and crustaceans, have compound eyes.

Conditioned reflex a REFLEX RESPONSE elicited by a stimulus substituting for the normal one; for example, the salivation by a trained dog in response to the ringing of a bell.

Conformer an animal which changes its internal state (temperature, body fluid composition) in conformity with changes in the external environment.

Consumer an organism that feeds upon another organism, or consumes food, the nature of which indicates the position of the organism in a FOOD CHAIN.

Contractile vacuole the ORGANELLES of excretion used by many single-celled organisms.

Copulation the act by which SPERMATOZOA are transferred between animals, usually from the male into the female.

Core temperature the temperature of the central parts of the body of an animal.

Counter current the flow of liquids in opposite directions in adjacent channels, for example, the flow of water and blood in many GILL systems.

Crossing over the exchange of segments between CHROMOSOMES during production of GAMETES, before MEIOSIS, so that most gamete chromosomes contain mixtures of parental segments.

Cuttlebone a stiff, lightweight structure found in cuttlefish. It is a stack of gas chambers enclosed by thin walls of calcium carbonate and PROTEIN. It gives the cuttlefish buoyancy, adjusting its density to match the seawater it swims in.

Deformation the bending or stretching of a surface. Deformation functions as a stimulus for most mechanically sensitive receptors.

Dentine the BONE-like material in teeth, also called ivory. It has the same constituents as bone but grows differently; the cells that make bone become enclosed in the bone they have made but those that make dentine retreat and avoid being enclosed.

Deoxyribonucleic acid (DNA) the carrier of GENETIC plans in all cells. DNA molecules consist of two long, unbranched chains of four small molecules called nucleotides. The two chains twist round each other in a double helix. The sequence of nucleotides in DNA contains the genetic information of the cell. When a cell divides, the two strands of DNA separate, and each directs the assembly of a new matching strand.

Differentiation the acquisition of functional and structural differences between tissues or cells in the EMBRYO or adult.

Diffusion the movement of substances resulting from the constant random bouncing of molecules. Diffusion tends to produce a uniform distribution of each substance so that its net effect is the transport of a substance from a region of higher concentration to a region of lower concentration. Diffusion is a spontaneous process and does not require the expenditure of energy.

Dipleurula the characteristic early LARVA of echinoderms (sea urchins, starfish) with gut and CILIA but before the development of arms. This is the PHYLOTYPIC stage.

Distal at a (greater) distance from the center of the body. Human fingers are the distal ends of the arms and wrists are distal to the elbows.

Dorsal towards the back (rather than the belly). For example, a saddle would normally be placed on the dorsal surface of a horse.

Ecosystem a COMMUNITY of plants and animals in their HABITAT. The concept is applied both to very small systems (such as a rock pool) and to very large ones (such as the open waters of an ocean or the Amazonian rain forest).

Ectoparasite a PARASITE that lives on the outer surface of its HOST organism.

Ectothermic describes an animal which derives from its surroundings most of the heat that determines its body temperature.

Egg the female reproductive cell with its provision of material and energy (usually YOLK), and instructions for early development. An egg usually needs to be fertilized before development can begin.

Electrical synapse a functional connection between two NERVE CELLS where ACTION POTENTIALS can pass from one cell to another without the mediation of a chemical transmitter substance.

Embryo the developing EGG, until it hatches. Developing mammals hatch very early inside the mother and are called embryos until they look baby-like (see FETUS).

Endocrine gland an organ or tissue without ducts that secretes a HORMONE into the blood circulatory system.

Endoparasite a PARASITE that lives inside its HOST organism.

Endoskeleton a skeleton that is enclosed within the body of an animal, such as the skeletons of humans and other vertebrates.

Endothermic describes an animal which derives from its own METABOLISM most of the heat determining its body temperature.

Enteroreceptor a receptor which signals the state of some internal variable, such as blood pressure or stomach distension.

Enzyme a PROTEIN molecule that speeds up a chemical reaction, without being changed itself, by recognizing and binding the molecules that are to react. There are many kinds of enzymes, each of which accelerates one particular chemical reaction.

Esophagus that part of the digestive tract between the PHARYNX and the stomach.

Euryhaline describing an organism which can tolerate a wide range of SALINITY in its environment.

Eurythermal describing an organism which can tolerate a wide range of temperatures in its environment.

Evolution the process by which new SPECIES are believed to arise as a result of gradual changes that occur in populations of organisms over a long period of time. Charles Darwin's theory of NATURAL SELECTION describes the most generally accepted mechanism.

Exafferent describes the sensory information which results from events or changes in the external surroundings (see also REAFFERENT).

Excretion the elimination of useless or harmful substances from the body of an organism, especially in the urine.

Exoskeleton a skeleton, such as that of a crab or any other arthropod, that encloses the body of an organism like a suit of armor.

Exteroreceptor a receptor, such as that for sight or hearing, which signals information about external events.

Extracellular outside the cells of the body.

Facilitation an increase in the ease with which an ELECTRICAL SYNAPSE will pass information as a result of its previous activation.

Family a group of related organisms, such as the family Felidae (cat family) which includes the lion, the tiger and all the smaller cats. Most families contain several GENERA, and families are grouped together into ORDERS.

Feedback loop the mechanism of control for a process in which the effects or products of a process act upon the process itself either to accelerate it (positive feedback) or decelerate it (negative feedback).

Fermentation the ANEROBIC breakdown of organic compounds by bacteria or other microscopic organisms, such as yeasts.

Fertilization the fusion of male and female GAMETES to initiate development in organisms which reproduce sexually.

Fetus the developing stage of a mammal within its mother's UTERUS, after the formation of limbs, "face" and baby-like body form but before birth.

Fibrillar muscle a type of STRIATED MUSCLE that operates the wings of flies, beetles and many other kinds of insects. Ordinary striated muscle needs nerve impulses to stimulate each individual contraction but a few nerve impulses arriving each second are enough to keep fibrillar muscle working at the very high frequencies that are needed for flight (up to several hundred contractions per second).

Filter feeder an aquatic animal which feeds by filtering the water surrounding it to obtain PHYTOPLANKTON and other suspended food particles.

Flagellum a long, hair-like structure on the surface of a cell, usually found singly or in small numbers and used for locomotion or feeding. In animals flagella have the same basic structure as CILIA but are longer. The flagella of bacteria are unrelated to those of protozoans and animals.

Follicle cell one of the cells which surround the growing EGG in the OVARY; follicle cells often contribute to the nutrition and organization of the egg.

Food chain a sequence of organisms, such as aphid-ladybug-blackbird-sparrowhawk, in which each organism in the sequence is food for a higher member of the sequence.

Food web a web of interconnected FOOD CHAINS.

Fossil any trace or remains of a long-dead organism, preserved in a rock or some other material. Usually only hard parts, such as the bones of mammals or the shells of mollusks, are preserved.

Gall bladder a sac which, in vertebrates, stores the bile secreted by the LIVER.

Gamete one of the cells (an EGG or a SPERMATOZOON) which fuse during FERTILIZATION.

Ganglion a collection of NERVE CELLS, subsidiary to the BRAIN, and linked to it and to other ganglia by connectives containing many AXONS. Ganglia also receive sensory inputs and/or send commands to muscles via MOTOR NERVOUS SYSTEM.

Gas exchanger any surface through which respiratory gases are exchanged between the environment and the interior of an animal's body. The structure may be relatively simple and unspecialized (such as the whole body surface) or may become very complex and specialized for gas exchange (many GILL and LUNG systems).

Gene the unit of hereditary information. Structural genes specify the sequence of single PROTEIN chains. Other genes contain information about when and where structural genes are to be expressed.

Genome the nuclear genetic complement of an organism, directing its development.

Genus a group of closely related SPECIES. For example, the lion and the tiger are placed in the same genus, *Panthera*, but the smaller cats are considered to be different enough to be placed in a different genus, *Felis*. The scientific name of a species consists of two words of which the first is the genus name and the second indicates the species within the genus. Thus, the lion is *Panthera leo* and the tiger is *Panthera tigris*.

Germ cell a group of cells, usually set aside early in the development of most multicellular animals, which produce the GAMETES and so are the only cells whose heredity extends indefinitely into the future.

Germ plasm either the reproductive cells of organisms, as opposed to their mortal bodies, or the special region of the cytoplasm of EGGS which determines that nuclei in this region go on to make GERM CELLS.

Gill an outward extension of the body used for gas exchange. Gills are usually present in animals that are entirely or mainly aquatic.

Glial cell one of the inexcitable cells associated with NERVE CELLS that function as packing and insulating elements in BRAIN tissue.

Golgi body a system of membranes used to collect and package substances produced by a cell for secretion.

Gonad the special organ of multicellular animals in which the GAMETES are made. (See also TESTIS and OVARY.)

Habitat the environment in which a plant or animal lives.

Head a distinct region at the ANTERIOR end of an animal containing the BRAIN and also the mouth and sense organs. Arthropods and vertebrates have well-defined heads but most simpler animals do not.

Heart the muscular pump that drives the blood through the vessels of the circulatory system. Its structure varies from a simple contractile tube, as found in annelid worms, to the multichambered hearts of vertebrates.

Heart muscle a type of MUSCLE which is peculiar to the HEARTS of vertebrates. It resembles SKELETAL MUSCLE in some aspects of its microscopic structure but its contractions are not under the control of the will.

Hemocyanin a blue, copper-containing blood pigment found in some mollusks and arthropods. Like HEMOGLOBIN, it is important in the transport of oxygen.

Hemoglobin a red, iron-containing blood pigment found in the red blood cells of vertebrates. It is responsible for the transport of oxygen in blood, taking the gas up in regions, such as the GILLS and LUNGS, where the PARTIAL PRESSURE is high and releasing it in the tissues where the partial pressure is low.

Herbivore an animal that feeds mainly or entirely on plant material, such as grass, herbs and leaves.

Heterothermic describes an animal which either has different temperatures in different parts of its body at a particular time (**regional heterotherm**) or has different overall body temperatures at different times (**temporal heterotherm**).

Heterotrophic describes an organism which obtains its nourishment from organic materials.

Hibernation a period of sleep-like TORPIDITY in which the METABOLIC RATE is reduced to help an animal survive cold winter conditions.

Homeothermic describes an animal which maintains an essentially constant body temperature even when the environmental temperature varies. Homeothermic animals are often referred to as being warm blooded.

Homologous describes structures which are believed to have evolved from the same structures in some ancestor. Thus, the arms of humans and the wings of birds are described as homologous because both are thought to have evolved from the forelegs of some early reptile that was ancestral to mammals and to birds.

Hormone a chemical compound which is synthesized and secreted by ENDOCRINE tissue and which has a specific effect on a target organ which it reaches via the blood circulation system.

Host the organism in which a PARASITE lives.

Hybrid an organism which results from the crossing of genetically unlike parents.

Hydrofoil a structure which produces large lift forces when it moves through water. The wings of penguins and the tails of dolphins function as hydrofoils. Oars are not hydrofoils.

Hydrostatic skeleton a fluid-filled cavity that enables one group of MUSCLES to work ANTAGONISTICALLY to another group. The body cavity of an earthworm is a hydrostatic skeleton. As the longitudinal muscles shorten the worm when they contract, they also make the worm fatter because the fluid in the body has a fixed volume. The circular muscles make it thinner and longer. Thus, contraction of either group stretches the other group.

Hyperosmotic describes a solution in which the OSMOTIC CONCENTRATION is higher than the osmotic concentration of another solution with which it is being compared.

Hyperparasite a PARASITE of a parasite. Many insects, especially certain social insects, lay their EGGS inside the eggs of LARVAE which parasitize caterpillars.

Hyperthermic describes an environmental temperature or a body temperature which is higher than the normal body temperature of the animal.

Hypoosmotic describes a solution in which the OSMOTIC CONCENTRATION is lower than that of another solution with which it is being compared.

Hypothermic describes an environmental or a body temperature which is lower than that of the normal body temperature of the animal.

Immune system the defense system of an organism, which takes effect by producing ANTIBODIES against foreign substances and organisms, including viruses, bacteria and parasites.

Immunity the ability to resist a specific infection by recognizing and eliminating foreign molecules. Vertebrates have two types of immunity – the ability to produce sets of specific ANTIBODIES and the recognition of foreign cells by specialized white cells in the blood. (See also IMMUNE SYSTEM.)

Inheritance the transmission of characteristics from parents to offspring.

Inhibition the process through which a NERVE CELL is brought to a state in which it is less likely to transmit information. Inhibition is also used to refer to the suppression of excitation in a nerve cell.

Interneurone a NEURONE resident in the BRAIN or GANGLIA but with no AXONS extending to the periphery. Interneurones can receive inputs from sensory axons, or interneurones, integrate these and pass on the information to the motor NEURONES, or back to other interneurones.

Intestine part of the digestive tract from the STOMACH to the anus.

Intracellular describes the interior of the cells of an organism's body.

Ion an electrically charged atom or molecule.

Ionic regulator an aquatic animal which regulates the concentrations of individual SOLUTES in its body fluids as the environmental concentrations of these substances change.

Isosmotic describes a solution with an OSMOTIC CONCENTRATION that is equal to the solution with which it is being compared.

Isothermic describes an animal or an object in which the temperature is uniform throughout.

Keratin the PROTEIN that is deposited in the epidermis of amphibians, reptiles, birds and mammals. It prevents the skin from being so easily damaged, and waterproofs it so that water loss by evaporation is reduced. Thicker layers of keratin form claws, nails, hooves and the outer covering of horns. The scales of reptiles, the feathers of birds and the hair of mammals are also made of keratin.

Kidney the main organ of the body of most animals for the elimination of excess body fluid and the waste products of METABOLISM.

Kinetic energy the energy which a body possesses as a result of its motion.

Krebs cycle named after the British biochemist, Sir Hans Krebs, and also referred to as the citric acid cycle, it is the set of chemical reactions which converts the products of the breakdown of sugar to carbon dioxide and water. In plant and animal cells, these reactions take place in the MITOCHONDRIA. The working of the Krebs cycle depends upon the presence of oxygen.

Lactic acid the major end product of ANAEROBIC METABOLISM in animals, usually resulting from high levels of activity of the MUSCLES. The capacity to accumulate lactic acid is often very limited, and fatigue quickly results. After activity, the lactic acid is eliminated from the cells and blood by oxidation.

Larva an immature stage in the life cycle of many animals. It is the stage in which these animals, such as butterflies, hatch from the egg and is usually very different in appearance (caterpillar) from the adult. Larvae are usually incapable of reproduction.

Lateral line the canal running along the flank of many fish and amphibians and which contains hair cells that respond to movements caused by currents in the surrounding water.

Ligament a flexible strap connecting two BONES, cartilages or other skeletal parts. Most of the moveable joints of vertebrates are held together by ligaments of COLLAGEN but the **ligamentum nuchae** that runs along the back of the neck of cattle and other hoofed mammals, helping to support the head, is made of a much more rubber-like PROTEIN called elastin.

Lipid any of a diverse group of compounds characterized by solubility in fat solvents, and insolubility in water. Lipids include fats, oils and waxes.

Liver an organ which opens into the gut. It has many functions, including an involvement with digestion, but its major purpose is to regulate the chemical composition of the blood.

Locomotion movement from one location to another. The different kinds of locomotion used by animals include walking, running, crawling, swimming and flight.

Lumen the cavity of a tubular part of an animal's body, such as the digestive tract, blood vessels etc.

Lung an internal chamber, almost always air filled, used for GAS EXCHANGE in animals. The structure varies from a simple, unfolded chamber in some amphibians to the complex systems of tubes in the ALVEOLAR lungs of mammals and the air CAPILLARY lungs of birds.

Macromolecule large molecules produced in living organisms from smaller units, such as PROTEINS from AMINO ACIDS, and cellulose and starch from glucose.

Macrophage a large phagocytic cell which may be fixed or capable of LOCOMOTION, or an animal that is capable of feeding on large food items.

Mammary gland a milk-producing gland found in a mammal; mammary glands include the breasts of women, the udders of cows etc.

Mechanoreception the reception of sensory information resulting from the mechanical disturbance of receptors (mechanoreceptors) that are sensitive to DEFORMATION. Touch and hearing are examples of mechanoreception.

Medusa a jellyfish, especially the small sexual stages of a hydrozoan coelenterate, such as *Obelia*. (See also POLYP.)

Meiosis two successive divisions of the nucleus of a cell during the formation of GERM CELLS. During meiosis, CHROMOSOMES are distributed so that each germ cell has half the amount of DNA and half the number of chromosomes as the other cells of the body. The full number of chromosomes and the full amount of DNA is restored when SPERMATOZOON and EGG come together at FERTILIZATION.

Mesic describes moderate ENVIRONMENTAL conditions.

Mesoglea a jelly-like substance sandwiched between the cell layers of the body wall of a sponge, sea anemone, jellyfish etc. It contains fibers of COLLAGEN embedded in a jelly that contains PROTEINS and POLYSACCHARIDES. It resists attempts to stretch it rapidly but can be stretched enormously by a small force acting for a long time.

Metabolic rate the rate at which the cells of an organism use energy. If the METABOLISM is entirely OXIDATIVE, then the rate of consumption of oxygen will give a measure of the metabolic rate. If the metabolism is entirely or partly ANEROBIC, it is also necessary to measure the rate of accumulation of end products, such as LACTIC ACID.

Metabolism the processes by which chemical compounds are built up and broken down in cells with the consumption of energy.

Metamorphosis the dramatic change of structure and way of life as a LARVA takes on adult form; sometimes, there is a resting stage, such as the PUPA of some insects.

Microfilament the thinnest fiber (diameter 7nm) of the cell skeleton. It is built from the globular PROTEIN, ACTIN. Microfilaments are important in cell movements, especially in changing their shape.

Microphage an animal that feeds on small food items.

Mitochondrion an ORGANELLE bounded by a double membrane and in which most of the energy of the cell is produced. Mitochondria contain the chemical apparatus needed to extract energy from food using oxygen.

Mitosis the division of the nucleus of a cell. The result of mitosis is that the nuclei of the two daughter cells each contain the same CHROMOSOMES as the parent cell.

Modality a type of sensory system defined by the nature of the energy of substance which causes stimulation. For example, the modality vision involves light energy and hearing involves sound energy.

Motor nervous system that part of the NERVOUS SYSTEM which is directly connected to the MUSCLES.

Mucus a slimy substance which consists mainly of water, with a small quantity of PROTEIN-sugar complex which makes it very viscous.

Multiplication the production of many effectively identical copies, by reproductive processes (eg cleavage nuclei, waterfleas or banana trees); in division the products are, at least, potentially different.

Muscle a material, composed largely of the PROTEINS, ACTIN and myosin, that is capable of exerting forces and of contracting. Most movements, among animals visible to the naked eye, are produced by muscles.

Muscle spindle a type of MECHANORECEPTOR found in the MUSCLES of vertebrates in parallel with the muscle fibers. Muscle spindles signal the state of extension of the muscle.

Mushroom body a set of NERVE CELLS found in the BRAINS of annelid worms and insects. They are gathered into lobes with three major divisions and which, in section, resemble the stem and cap of a mushroom. The mushroom body is thought to represent a higher center of the invertebrate brain.

Myoneme one of the contractile fibers in the surface of certain protozoans.

Myosin see MUSCLE.

Nasal salt gland a special gland in the HEAD of many marine and desert reptiles and birds. It has its opening in or near the nostrils and functions as an accessory organ of excretion in the elimination of excess salt.

Natural selection the tendency for some members of a SPECIES to survive and for others, with different inherited characteristics, to be eliminated. This process is popularly known as "survival of the fittest." Charles Darwin (1809-82) suggested it as the most important mechanism of EVOLUTION.

Nematocyst any of the capsules found in some of the cells of sea anemones and jellyfish etc. Each contains a long, hollow thread coiled up inside it. The threads can be extruded very rapidly to entangle small prey or to pierce the bodies of prey and inject venom.

Neotony the retention of juvenile characteristics in the adult, as the result of EVOLUTION. For example, adult ostriches resemble the chicks of more typical birds in having rudimentary wings and downy feathers.

Nephridium a type of organ of excretion found in the annelid worms and some other invertebrate animals.

Nerve cell a specialized cell which is able to transmit information in the form of electrical signals. Nerve cells are only found in animals. All aspects of animal behavior, from a simple eye blink, through the most complex bodily movements to abstract thought, are mediated by the action of nerve cells.

Nerve net a system of NERVE CELLS connected in the form of a net, and in which the connections between the individual cells do not appear to occur along restricted or directionally organized paths.

Neuro-endocrine system a system composed of specialized NERVE CELLS that liberate NEUROHORMONES when they are activated.

Neurohormone a hormone released by the NEUROSECRETORY CELLS.

Neurone see also NERVE CELL. Large numbers of interconnected neurones make up the nervous system of all animals. Neurones are specialized to conduct electrical messages, known as nerve impulses, or ACTION POTENTIALS, from one end of the cell to the other. The cell often has a long process, or AXON, projecting from its body so that action potentials can be conducted over a considerable distance. Many axons bound together in connective tissue form nerves.

Neurosecretory cell a specialized NERVE CELL which, when activated, releases NEUROHORMONES into the blood circulation system.

Notochord a flexible rod that functions as a backbone in the marine animals, known as lancelets (*Amphioxus*), in the larvae of sea squirts and in the embryos of vertebrates. Possession of a notochord at some stage of the life history is diagnostic of the chordates.

Nucleic acid any of the cellular MACROMOLECULES produced from units containing a sugar, phosphoric acid and a base. Nucleic acids function as carriers of GENETIC information.

Nucleus the largest ORGANELLE of a cell. Bounded by a double membrane, the nucleus contains almost all of a cell's GENETIC plans in a set of CHROMOSOMES.

Olfaction the sense of smell. The MODALITY concerned with the detection of airborne chemicals.

Omnivore an animal that includes both plant and animal material in its diet.

Oocyte the stage in the development of the GERM CELL of a multicellular animal between MITOSIS and MEIOSIS; an EGG from its earliest existence in the OVARY to FERTILIZATION.

Oogenesis the process of producing EGGS. The process includes the growth of the OOCYTE, the processing and packaging of YOLK and the development of the program of early development.

Oogonium the cell which gives rise to the OOCYTE; the GERM CELLS multiply to make oogonia or spermatogonia which, in turn, multiply to form OOCYTES and spermatocytes.

Operculum the GILL cover of a bony fish, or the plate that closes the opening of the shell of a gastropod mollusk.

Order a group of related organisms, such as the order Rodentia (rodents). Most orders consist of several FAMILIES and most CLASSES contain several orders.

Organelle a structure, such as the NUCLEUS, within a cell which has a particular function and is analogous to an organ of a body.

Osmoconformer an animal which changes the OSMOTIC CONCENTRATION of its body fluids more or less in conformity with changes in the external osmotic concentration.

Osmotic concentration the total concentration of dissolved SOLUTES in a solution, independent of the kinds of solutes present.

Ossicle a small skeletal element, especially the small blocks of calcium carbonate that make up the skeletons of sea urchins, etc. Also, one of the small BONES in the middle ear which transmit sound vibrations from the ear drum to the cochlea.

Ovary the organ in which OOGENESIS occurs, where EGGS are made.

Oviduct the tube through which the EGG passes on its way to laying; FERTILIZATION and early development occur in the oviduct in mammals and birds.

Ovulation the process in which the OOCYTE leaves the OVARY. In most vertebrates the eggs are shed into the peritoneal cavity; in most other animals, they are shed into the LUMEN of the tubular ovary.

Oxidative metabolism a process which takes place in cells in which oxygen reacts with compounds derived from CARBOHYDRATES, LIPIDS or PROTEINS to yield energy which is then used in other cellular processes. The byproducts of such oxidations are mainly carbon dioxide and water.

Oxygen debt the amount of oxygen needed to oxidize the products of ANEROBIC METABOLISM, such as LACTIC ACID, that accumulate in MUSCLES, the blood stream and other tissues during high levels of activity.

Pacemaker an electrically active group of cells in the HEARTS of vertebrates which triggers and determines the rate of beating of the heart.

Packing cell any of the cells that insulate, protect and nourish NERVE CELLS in the BRAIN and GANGLION.

Pancreas a large gland that secretes digestive ENZYMES, as well as water and bicarbonate, into the INTESTINE of vertebrates.

Parasitism a relationship between two organisms whereby one, the parasite, obtains its food from the other, the HOST. Ectoparasites, such as lice, attach themselves to the outer surfaces of their hosts, and **endoparasites**, such as tapeworms, live inside their hosts.

Parthenogenesis the development of an EGG without FERTILIZATION into a new individual. Eggs which develop in this way give offspring which are genetically identical to the parent.

Partial pressure the pressure that an individual gas in a gas mixture would exert in the absence of all the other components. Thus the total pressure exerted by a gas mixture is the sum of the partial pressures of all the components. When a gas mixture is in contact with a liquid, the gases dissolve in the liquid until, at equilibrium, the partial pressures of the gases in solution are identical to those in the gas mixture. Partial pressures can be given in any of the many different units that are used to measure pressure, although respiratory physiologists favor millimeters of mercury (mmHg). 1mm Hg = 1/760 atmospheres = 134 pascals = 13.6kg/sqm (or mmH$_2$O) = 1/52lb/sqin (psi).

Pepsin a PROTEIN-splitting ENZYME that requires a strongly acidic medium to be optimally active.

Peptide bond a mechanism that holds the individual AMINO ACIDS together in a peptide by uniting the amino group of one acid with the carboxyl group of another.

Peripheral sensory system that part of the NERVOUS SYSTEM which receives and transduces physical phenomena in the environment into nerve ACTION POTENTIALS and conducts these to the CENTRAL NERVOUS SYSTEM.

pH a symbol that indicates the acidity or alkalinity of a fluid. The degree of acidity or alkalinity is represented by a series of whole numbers from 1 to 14 with 7 indicating a neutral solution. Numbers less than 7 show increasing acidity, more than 7 increasing alkalinity.

Pharynx a part of the gut of invertebrates between the mouth and the esophagus.

Pheromone an air- or water-borne chemical which is used by animals for communicating certain sorts of information, such as sexual receptiveness.

Photon the smallest quantity of light energy that can exist.

Photoreceptor a receptor that responds to light energy.

Photosynthesis the use of light energy to build sugar molecules from water and atmospheric carbon dioxide gas. Almost all life depends upon this process: green plants produce food materials by photosynthesis, and animals obtain food either directly or indirectly, from eating plants or other animals.

Phylotypic describes the EMBRYONIC or LARVAL period during which control of development passes from the program in the EGG cytoplasm to the zygote's own GENOME. Within large animal groups (CLASSES and some PHYLA), diverse eggs converge so that all the organisms resemble one another at this time, then diverge towards their own juveniles.

Phylum a major group of living organisms, such as the phylum Mollusca (mollusks) or the phylum Platyhelminthes (flatworms).

Phytoplankton any of the single-celled microscopic plants which float in the sea and in freshwaters.

Pituitary gland a gland on the VENTRAL side of the BRAIN of vertebrate animals which produces or controls the release of many very important HORMONES.

Placenta especially in mammals, the organ which transports food, oxygen, hormones and waste materials between the mother's and the EMBRYO's blood.

Plankton organisms that float in mid-water in ponds, lakes or the sea. They are generally small organisms that are moved round more by water currents than by their own swimming.

Planula the simple, oval CILIATED LARVA of hydroids, jellyfish and corals.

Plasma the liquid that remains when the cellular components are removed from blood, for example, by centrifugation. Plasma contains materials, such as salts, CARBOHYDRATES, fatty acids and PROTEINS in solution.

Poikilothermic describes an animal whose body temperature depends largely on the temperature of its surroundings. Regulation of the body temperatures in such animals is generally very rudimentary. Poikilothermic animals are often referred to as cold blooded or are called ECTOTHERMS.

Polyp one of the two body forms (polyp and MEDUSA) of jellyfish, sea anemones, etc. Typical polyps are cylindrical animals with a mouth at one end surrounded by a ring of tentacles.

Polysaccharide any of the large molecules composed of sugar molecules, such as starch, cellulose, pectins etc.

Posterior toward the hind end of the body.

Potential energy energy possessed by a body as a result of its height.

Predator an organism which obtains its food by hunting and killing animals.

Prey an animal which a PREDATOR hunts and kills for food.

Primary producer an organism that constitutes a first link in FOOD CHAINS, usually a photosynthetic green plant.

Primary production the crop of PRIMARY PRODUCERS; mainly the green plants, constituting the basis of life on earth.

Primitive resembling ancestral members of the group. For example the ORDER Primates includes the lemurs, monkeys and apes. The lemurs are described as primitive primates because they have few monkey- or ape-like features. In contrast, apes and humans are advanced primates.

Prokaryotic describes primitive organisms, such as bacteria, lacking a membrane around the nucleus.

Proprioceptor any of the receptors concerned with monitoring the position of the body in space (eg semicircular canals), or of one part of the body relative to another (eg MUSCLE SPINDLES).

Protandrous describes an organism, such as the Slipper limpet (*Crepidula fornicata*) which is first effectively male and then becomes functionally female.

Protein a MACROMOLECULE built of AMINO ACIDS, constituting complex substances characteristic of living matter.

Protogynous an organism, such as the cleaner wrasse, which is first effectively female, and then becomes functionally male.

Proximal close (or closer) to the center of the body. Human shoulders are at the proximal ends of the arms, and elbows are proximal to the wrists.

Pseudopodium a temporary extension of the body of a cell, used in cell movement or in cell feeding by engulfing food.

Puberty the period during which an animal acquires reproductive abilities successively in contrast with METAMORPHOSIS where there is a radical, dramatic change.

Pupa a stage in the life history of advanced insects, such as butterflies and two-winged (dipteran) flies. These insects change their form and way of life dramatically between the LARVAL and adult stages. The pupa is the quiescent stage during which the larva, enclosed in a protective case, changes to an adult. The pupa of a butterfly is also called a **chrysalis**.

Reafferent describes sensory information which results from movements of the body itself, rather than from movements of objects in the external

Receptor see CHEMORECEPTOR. ENTERORECEPTOR, EXTERORECEPTOR. MECHANORECEPTION, PHOTORECEPTOR. PROPRIOCEPTOR.

Recombinant the GAMETE which results from CROSSING OVER so that the exchange of GENETIC material between the parents results in combinations and, thus, characteristics not found in the parents.

Rectal gland a type of gland found near the RECTUM in some sharks and related cartilaginous fish and which has a similar purpose to that of the NASAL SALT GLAND in a reptile or bird.

Rectum the part of the digestive tract in which waste material is stored before being released into the ENVIRONMENT through the ANUS.

Reflex response a simple form of response in which a stimulus almost always results in the same relatively simple motor action, independently of VOLITION.

Refractive index a measure of the amount by which a substance bends the path of light rays passing through it. Glass has a higher refractive index than water or air.

Regulation the ability of an animal to maintain more-or-less constant some important feature of its internal ENVIRONMENT, such as temperature or OSMOTIC CONCENTRATION, over a period of time.

Renal pertaining to the KIDNEY.

Resilin a rubber-like PROTEIN found in the THORAXES of many insects. Pieces of resilin serve as springs, stopping the wings at the end of each stroke and making them bounce back in the opposite direction. This reduces the power required to keep the wings beating. Fleas have no wings but have pieces of resilin that assist jumping.

Resistance adaptation a physiological adaptation in an animal permitting it to survive over a wider range of environmental conditions.

Respiration the processes involved in the production of energy within the cells of the body. More specifically, it is often used to refer to the uptake of oxygen and the release of carbon dioxide by an animal.

Resting potential the potential difference measured across the membrane of a NERVE CELL when it is not transmitting information.

Retina the layer of PHOTORECEPTORS and associated NERVE CELLS which receive the image in the eye.

Rhodopsin the chemical substance in the PHOTORECEPTORS which changes its form when it absorbs the light energy of a PHOTON. It is a combination of a derivative of vitamin A and a PROTEIN.

Ribonucleic acid (RNA) a long molecule used in several ways in carrying out a cell's genetic instructions. RNA is chemically similar to DEOXYRIBONUCLEIC ACID and consists of an unbranched chain of four nucleotides.

Salinity the total salt content of a volume of sea water, defined in a complex and precise way.

Sarcomere any of the large number of units set end to end in STRIATED MUSCLE fibers which give the muscle a striped appearance under the microscope.

Sense cell a cell responsible for converting the energy of a particular MODALITY into electrical signals which convey information to the BRAIN.

Sensory neurone a NERVE CELL that transmits information from peripherally located sensory RECEPTOR CELLS to the CENTRAL NERVOUS SYSTEM. Sensory neurones in invertebrates also function as receptors.

Seta a bristle-like structure, found in several groups of animals and plants.

Sex attractant a PHEROMONE molecule emitted by one sex to attract the other.

Skeletal muscle the type of STRIATED MUSCLE that works the skeletons of vertebrates and also works some soft structures, such as the human tongue. Unlike SMOOTH MUSCLE and HEART MUSCLE, it can be made to contract at will.

Smooth muscle MUSCLE that lacks the striations seen in STRIATED MUSCLE. Smooth muscle in the walls of the guts of vertebrates squeezes food along the gut. Smooth muscle in the walls of blood vessels adjusts their diameters, controlling the flow of blood to the tissues that they serve.

Solute a substance dissolved in a solution.

Solvent the liquid in which the SOLUTES dissolve in a solution.

Species a group of similar living organisms whose members can interbreed to produce fertile offspring but which cannot breed with other species.

Spermatheca a special SPERMATOZOON receptacle in the female which serves to keep venereal infection away from the EGGS and, often, to keep a sperm store for a succession of eggs.

Spermatozoon (sperm) the characteristic male GAMETE of an animal. Although the motile, tailed form is most common, non-motile or amoeboid forms are not unusual.

Spiracle an opening of the TRACHEAL system on the outer surface of an insect. Muscles control the size of the aperture and can close the spiracle completely.

Squalene a compound of carbon and hydrogen that has a much lower density than water. Some sharks contain huge quantities of squalene and this gives them buoyancy.

Statocyst a sense organ that is a receptor for gravity, acceleration and vibration. It is usually in the form of a capsule containing collections of MECHANORECEPTIVE hairs. These hairs either carry or surround a mass. Alteration of the orientation of the organ with respect to gravity results in changes in the shearing forces exerted by the mass on the mechanoreceptive hairs, which, in turn, signals this change.

Stenohaline describes an aquatic animal which is able to tolerate only a narrow range of SALINITIES in its ENVIRONMENT.

Stenothermal describes an animal which is able to tolerate only a narrow range of temperatures in its ENVIRONMENT.

Stomach that part of the digestive tract between the ESOPHAGUS and the INTESTINE.

Streamlining the adjustment of the shape of the body to reduce the drag which resists movement through a fluid.

Striated muscle vertebrate SKELETAL MUSCLE, HEART MUSCLE and some types of invertebrate MUSCLES which, under the microscope, can be seen to possess narrow stripes (striations) running across the fibers.

Substrate a substance acted upon by an ENZYME.

Surfactant a material contained in the thin layer of liquid which lines the insides of LUNGS. Surfactant reduces surface tension and stabilizes the fine, bubble-like structure of finer divisions of the lungs.

Swimbladder a gas-filled chamber found in the body cavities of most bony fish. It serves as a buoyancy organ.

Symbiosis a condition in which two organisms (symbionts) live in a mutually beneficial partnership, one often inside the other.

Synapse a connection between two NERVE CELLS across which electrical information is carried either directly (electrical synapse) or by the release of a chemical transmitter substance (chemical synapse).

Teleology explanation by reference to purposes. "Birds have wings for flying," is a teleological statement because it indicates that wings have a purpose. Such statements are often condemned as unscientific, apparently because they are thought to imply conscious purpose; to imply, for example, that a deity gave birds wings to enable them to fly. Many scientists, however, consider such statements to be entirely acceptable. Wings are for flying in the sense that they evolved because they gave birds the advantage of being able to fly.

Temperate moderate in temperature.

Tendon a cord- or strap-like structure that transmits the force exerted by a MUSCLE. Tendons connect muscles to the skeleton whereas LIGAMENTS connect parts of the skeleton together. Tendons of vertebrates consist mainly of COLLAGEN fibers, and are usually very flexible.

Test any of the protective outer coverings of the bodies of sea urchins and some other animals.

Testis the organ in which SPERMATOZOA are made; in most mammals, spermatogenesis cannot proceed at the deep body temperature, so testes are usually cooled in the scrotum.

Thermoregulator an animal which controls and regulates its body temperature relatively well.

Thorax in mammals, the chest (the part of the body enclosed by the ribs). In insects, the second of the three main regions of the body (HEAD, thorax, and ABDOMEN). The wings and legs of an insect are borne on the thorax.

Thyroid gland a large, ductless gland in the neck, or equivalent region, of vertebrate animals which produces two HORMONES that are very important in various aspects of METABOLIC control.

Torpid an inert state of a living animal, physiologically normal and closely regulated by the animal, which helps it to survive a period of adverse ENVIRONMENTAL conditions.

Trachea in vertebrates, the windpipe that leads from the region of the BUCCAL CAVITY to the region of the LUNGS where it divides into two bronchi serving left and right lungs. In insects, a tube leading from the environment, via the SPIRACLE, to the cells of the body. The tracheae branch repeatedly, and the finest branches, which often penetrate to the interior of the cells, are called tracheoles.

Transcription the transfer of the DEOXYRIBONUCLEIC ACID message sequence to "messenger" RIBONUCLEIC ACID; it is controlled by DNA sequences around the transcribed sequence itself, and involves "splicing" of mRNA, too.

Transduction the process by which a sense cell uses the energy of the stimulus (light, deformation etc) to produce an electrical signal for transmission to the BRAIN.

Trochophore the first LARVA of flatworms, most polychaete worms and some mollusks; after spiral cleavage, this CILIA-girdled sphere has a gut and a sensory apical tuft, and is the PHYLOTYPIC stage.

Ungulate a hoofed mammal, such as a horse or antelope.

Uterus the organ which receives and nurtures the EMBRYO in VIVIPAROUS animals, such as tse tse flies, some sharks and nearly all mammals.

Vein a thin-walled blood vessel, often of larger diameter than an ARTERY in the same region, in which blood flows from the tissues towards the HEART. Blood pressures in veins are low and the blood flow sluggish.

Venous blood blood flowing from the tissues to the HEART. Such blood is low in oxygen and high in carbon dioxide. Note that the pulmonary ARTERY contains venous blood on its way to the LUNGS.

Ventilation any of the processes by which ENVIRONMENTAL water or air is pumped through the GAS-EXCHANGING structure by breathing movements.

Ventral toward the underside of the body, or belly. The navel is described as being on the ventral surface of the body of a mammal whether it walks upright, like a human, or on all fours.

Viscosity a physical property of fluids which resists internal flow.

Visual acuity a measure of the fineness with which an eye can resolve a scene.

Vitamin a constituent of food which is needed in very small quantities to maintain health.

Viviparity the condition in which the EMBRYO develops within the mother's body and derives continuous nourishment by close contact with the mother's tissues. It results in the birth of live young, and occurs in most mammals.

Volition self-initiated or voluntary actions of animals, in the absence of applied stimuli.

Yolk a mixture of nutrient materials provided for most animal EGGS by maternal synthesis.

Zooid an individual of a colonial animal, such as coral or hydrozoan jellyfish.

INDEX

A **bold number** indicates a major section of the main text, following a heading. A single number in (parentheses) indicates that the animal name or subjects are to be found in a boxed feature and a double number in (parentheses) indicates that the animal name or subject are to be found in a spread special feature. *Italic* numbers refer to illustrations.

A

aborigines 81, 82
Acanthaster
 planci 118
Accipiter
 gentilis 48
acclimation 69, 78
acid
 acetic 39
 amino 28, 29, 30, 31, 33, 41, 42, 43, 45
 deoxyribonucleic—*see* DNA
 fatty 39, 41, 43, 45
 hydrochloric 45, 47
 lactic 40, 52, 58, 64, 100
 nucleic 28, 33
 propionic 39
 pyruvic 52
 ribonucleic—*see* RNA
Acinonyx
 jubatus 81
acoustico-lateralis system 92
Acraga
 moorei 80
actin filament—*see* microfilament
Actinia
 equina 117
actinopterygians 16
action potential 117, 118, (118), (122), 127
active transport 24, 25
adaptation
 and animal behavior 69
 and environmental conditions 68-70
 and migration 69, 69
 and multi-celled animals 68
 and temperature change 82-83, (82)
 and water conservation 76
 genetic 68
 non-genetic 68, 69
adenosine diphosphate—*see* ADP
adenosine triphosphate—*see* ATP
admiral butterfly
 Poplar 108
ADP 24, 24
Aepyceros
 melampus 104-105
aestivation 81, 83
Agalychnis
 spurrelli 109
Agnatha 15
air
 expired 53, 56, 59
 gas exchange—*see* gas exchange
 inspired 53
 oxygen capacity 55
albatross
 Wandering 109
albatrosses 109, 130
Alburnus
 alburnus 93
Alces
 alces 48
alciopids 90
alcohol 45, 52, 127
algae 12, 37, 39, 41, 74, 131, 32
 blue-green 25
 green 39
Alouata
 seniculus 96
alternation of sexual generation 132-134, 132
amazonogenesis 134
amino acid—*see* acid, amino
ammonia 41, 70
amoebas 5, 6, 6, 25, 116, 116
Amphibia 16
amphibians 3, 16
 anatomy 15
 circulation 62
 evolution 15
 fossils 5
 regeneration 137
 regulation of body fluids 75
 reproduction 136
 respiration 56, 59
 senses 94
amphioxus 15
amylase 45
anaerobiosis 58, 61, 64
anatomy
 of birds 16, 18
 of chordates 13
 of crustaceans 11
 of cuttlefish 12
 of dogs 19
 of ectothermic vertebrates 15
 of insects 10
 of mammals 19
 of mollusks 11
 of multi-celled animals 7
 of scorpions 10-11
 of sea urchins 12
 of segmented animals 9
 of spiders 10-11
 of worms 10
 see also skeleton
angel fish 72
animal behavior
 adaptation 69
 evolution 18
 patterns 126
Animalia 5
Annelida 9
annelids 9, 13, 62, 75, 89, 90

B

Anopheles
 stephensi 43
anteaters 19
antelopes 19, 40
Anthozoa 7
antibiotic resistance (33)
antibodies 43
antifreeze in animals (82)
antigens 43
ants 10, 10, 96
apes 19 126
aphid
 Rose 42
aphids 42, 134, 135
apnea 83
Aptenodytes
 patagonicus 64, 140
arachnids 11
Archaeopteryx 18
Argema
 mimosae 97
Argiope
 aetherea 49
Argonauta 142
Argyroneta
 aquatica 50
arms
 starfish 118, 118, 119
artery 62, 63
Arthropoda 10
arthropods 9-11, 13, 62, 70, 73, 75, 104, 113, 121, 122, 123
artificial selection 5
Artiodactyla 19
ascarids 42
Ascaris 43
Asio
 otus 88-89
associations
 aquatic animals–algae 39
 herbivores–decomposing microorganisms 39-41, 45
Asterias
 rubens 119
Asteroidea 12
atom 28
ATP 24, 24, 25, 26, 27
autotrophic organism 36
Aves 17
axon 118, (118)

bacteria 6, 8, 24, 25, 27, 28, 31, 32, 33, 36, 39, 40
bacteriophage 32
badgers 41
Balaenoptera
 musculus 65
balance 93, 95
barnacles 10
bass 57
bat
 Common bentwing 86-87
 Kitti's hog-nosed 19
 Large mouse-eared 109
bats 17, 19, 80, 83, 87, 88, 94, 107, 109
bears 19, 41
beavers 19
bees 90, 91, 92, 110, 122-123, 126, 135
 see also bumblebees
beetles 64, 76, 81, 110, 138
 diving 65
 scarab 78
 tiger 90
 water 105, 107
bends 54
Betta
 splendens 143
bilharzia 43
biotechnology 33
birds 17-18
 anatomy 16
 body fluids 73, 74
 brains 18
 circulation 62, 63
 classification 3
 communication 126
 evolution 16
 excretion 70, 74, 75
 feeding 68
 fossils 5
 growth 142
 movement 107, 109, 111
 muscles 101
 number of species 2
 reproduction 136, 141, 141, 142
 respiration 56, 58-59, 60, 61
 senses 94
 temperature regulation 79, 80, 81, 82
Bitis
 peringueyi 103
bivalves 44
Bivalvia 12
bleak 93
blood
 circulation 61-63
 composition 29, 86
 gas exchange in—*see* gas exchange, in body fluids
 parasites in 42, 43
 pigment (62)
 sucking 41-42, 43, 48
 vessel 62-63, 64
blowfly 20

C

body fluid
 chemical composition of 69, 72
 gas exchange in—*see* gas exchange
 regulation of 69-76
body temperature—*see* temperature
bradycardia 64
brains 13, **121-127**
 breathing 61
 chemicals 126-127
 evolution 116, 121
 in bees 122-123
 in birds 18
 in crayfish 121
 in humans 89, 121, 122, 126
 in mammals 18
 in octopus 123, 123
 in vertebrates 122, 123, 124
 peripheral 118
 reflexes—*see* reflexes
 sensory messages 86-87, 121, 123
 size 127
Branchiostoma 15
breathing 51, 56, 59, 60, 61, 83, 86
 see also gas exchange *and* respiration
breeding success 5
brittlestars 12
bryozoans 7, 8
budding 131
buffalo 76
bugs 64, 96, 110
bullfrog
 American 94
bumblebees 80, 81, 111
bumping 117
buoyancy **106-107**
burrowing
 and temperature changes 79, 81
 in worms 102
bustards 18
butterfish 106
butterflies 10, 79, 90, 111, 138

caecilians 16
calcium 28, 46, 76
Callimorpha
 jacobaeae 40
Calypte
 costae 110
camel
 Dromedary 75-76
camels 19, 40
cancer (32)
capacity 68-69
capillary 62, 63
carbohydrase 44, 46
carbohydrate 28, 41, 43, 44, 45, 52
carbon 28, 36
carbon dioxide 52, 53, 53, 54, 55, 56, 59, 61, 63, 86
Carcharodon
 carcharias 14
Carnegiella 107
Carnivora 3, 19, 41
carnivores 36, 40-41, 41, 46, 73
Cat
 domestic 41, 126
 European wild 41
catalyst 24
cats 41, 130
cattle 6, 8, 40, 61, 76
Cecidomyidae (134)
cells 5, 7, **21-28**, 38
 blood 22, 23
 chemistry 22-24, 29-30
 communication 117
 connective 22, 23
 daughter 25, 26, 30, 31
 division 25-26, 31, 131, 139
 eating—*see* phagocytosis
 energy 22-24, 25
 epithelial 22, 23
 extensions 25
 function 21
 genetic information—*see* genetic information
 germ 22, 25, 26, 131
 hair 87, 93
 haploid 134, 135
 inside of 25-27
 meiosis—*see* meiosis
 membranes 24-25, 26, 29, 42
 mitosis—*see* mitosis
 movement 27
 nerve 22, 23, 116, 117-118m (118), 119, 120, 121, 122, 123, 126, 137
 neurosecretory 126-127
 plant 38
 progeny 131
 reproductive—*see* oocyte *and* oogonia
 shape 27
 size 22
 structure 21, 27, 27
 triploid 134
 types 22, 27
 viruses—*see* viruses
cellulose 39, 40, 41, 44, 45
centipedes 9, 10
Cephalaspis 5
Cephalochordata 15
Cephalopoda 12
cephalopods 12, 44, 62, 89, 90, 107
Cetacea 19
Charadrius
 dubius 81
cheetah 81, 99, 112
Chelicerata 10
chemoreceptor 87
chewing the cud—*see* rumination
chimeras 70
chimpanzees 112
Chiroptera 19
chitons 11-12
Chlamydomonas 6
chlorine 28, 46
chlorophyll 5
Chordata 3, 13
chordates 15

D

chromatin 25
chromosome 25, 26, 27, 30, 31, 31, 32-33, 33, 131, 131, 134, 135, 136
Chrysaora
 hysoscella 9
cichlid fish 142
cilia 27, (28), 29
ciliates 6, 9
Ciliophora 6
circulation 51, **61-63**, 80, 82
clams 12, 102
 giant 39
class 3
classification **2-3**, 6-7, 15
clone 132, (134), 137
Cnidaria 7
cnidarians 8, 13, 133
coccidiosis 6
cockroaches 113
coelacanth 15, 72, 107
Coelenterata 9
coelenterates 39, 44, 132, 132
Coenagrion 65
Colaptes
 auratus 17
cold shell 81-82
Coleoptera 110
collagen 29
colonies
 coral 7, 132
 protozoan 7
 siphonophore 132, 133, 134
coloration 3
colored bodies—*see* chromosome
colored matter—*see* chromatin
Colpoda 6
communication
 and brain development 126
 and nervous system—*see* nervous system
 and smell 96
 and sound 94, 94, 96
 and vibration 96
 in birds 94, 126
 in fiddler crabs 96, 126
 in humans 126
 in primates 94, 126
community 36
competition 132
compound 28
conch shells 90
conditioned reflex 47
cone shells 40
conformity to environmental change 69
Connochaetes
 taurinus 77
contractile vacuole 70, 71
convection 53
Conus
 geographus 40
coordination and control **115-127**
 brain—*see* brain
 in multi-celled animals 116
 in single-celled animals 116, 116
 nervous system—*see* nervous system
copepods 10, 36, 37
copper 47
copulation 136
Coragyps 108
coral
 Precious 9
 Stagshorn 133
coral reefs 7, 39, 132, 132, 133, 134
Corallium
 rubrum 9
corals 7, 37, 39, 44, 99, 132, 132, 133, 134
 brain 133-134, 133
cormorants 64
countercurrent
 flow 57
crabs 9, 10, 55, 75, 101, 104, 113, 123, 124
 blue 75
 fiddler 75, 96, 124-125, 126
 hermit 118
 shore 116
 soldier 74
crawling 102, 102
crayfish 75, 119, 119, 121
Crinoidea 13
crocodile
 Johnston's 138-139
crocodiles 16, 64, 70
Crocodylus
 johnstoni 138-139
Crossater
 papperus 54
crossopterygians 15
Crustacea 10
crustaceans 10, 11, 37, 44, 63, 73, 89, 90, 101, 122, 134, 142
Cryptocheilus 142
Culex 65
curlews 60
cuttlefish 12, 44, 106, 107
 Atlantic 89
Cygnus
 cygnus 58-59
Cypselurus
 californicus 108
cytoplasm 25, 26, 33, 135
cytoskeleton 26-27

D

damselflies 65
Daphnia 134-135, 135
Dasypeltis
 scabra 34
decomposition 36, 39
decompression sickness 65
deer 19, 40, 76
dehydration 72-73, 75, 76
Delichon
 urbica 68-69
Delphinus
 delphis 107
desiccation 75, 76
development 129, 131, **136-143**, (138)
 growth—*see* growth
diffusion
 and cells 24, 25, 25, 117
 and circulation 61, 62

E

diffusion—*continued*
 and gas exchange 53-55, 56, 59
 and movements of water 70, 72, 73, 75
digestion 43-47
 and cells 44
 and enzyme action—*see* enzymes
 and fermentation—*see* fermentation
 in carnivores 46
 in cattle 6
 in cells 25, 26
 in herbivores 38, 39-41, 46
 in humans 44, 46, 47, 86
 in mammals 44
 in omnivores 46
dinoflagellate 39
dinosaurs 16, 18, 109, 112, 113
Dione
 vanillae 48
Diploria
 labyrinthiformes 133
 strigosa 133
dipnoans 16
Diptera 10, 110
disease
 and flatworms 8
 and insects 10
 and protozoans 6-7
 and viruses 33
divers 64
diversity 2, 36
diving animals (64-65)
DNA 28, 30-33, 30, 32-33, (33), 135
dogfish 100
dogs 5, 19, 41, 47, 97, 102, 112, 113
dolphin
 Common 107
dolphins 64, 74, (107)
donkeys 75
double helix 31, 33
Draco
 spilopterus 108
dragon, flying 108
dragonflies 64, 109, 111
drinking 76
ducks 64, 111
dugong 39
dysentery 7
Dytiscus 64
 marginalis 65, 107

E

ears
 amphibians 94
 bats 94
 fish 94
 frogs 85, 94, 94
 humans 94
 insects 94
 mammals 86, 93
 reptiles 94
earthworms 8, 9, 10, 11, 101, 102, 102, 116, 134
echidna
 Short-beaked 18
echidnas 18
echinoderms 12-13, 100, 136, 138, 143
Echinoidea 12
Echinodermata 12
echolocation 86-87, 87, 88
ectoparasites—*see* parasites, external
ectotherms 17, 18, 78-79
eels 15, 92, 106, 141
eelworm
 Potato root 8
egg-eater
 Common 34
eggs
 and reproduction 131-136, 141-142
 and structure 141
 and yolk 141
 in birds 17, 131, 141
 in fish 131, 141, 143
 in frogs 135, 139, 141
 in humans 131, 135
 in mammals 18, 131, 141-142, 141
 in reptiles 16, 138-139
Eimeria 6
electric organs 89, (92), 92, 93
electrical potential—*see* action potential
Eledone
 cirrhosa 123
elephant
 African 38
elephants 19, 112
emu 18
endoplasmic reticulum 26, 27
endotherms 17, 18, 79-81, 82, 83
energy 22, 24, 52
 locomotion and 102, 104, 105
 solar 5-6, 35, 36, 52
 storage 28
enteroceptor 86
environmental conditions 67, 68
 adaptability—*see* adaptation
 response to 68-69
 tolerance to—*see* tolerance
enzyme 24, 24, 26, 29, 30, 29, 40, 41, 43, 45-47
Ephemera
 danica 139
Erithacus
 rubecula 141
Escherichia coli 31
esterase 44, 45
estuarine animals 75
Euglena 29
eukaryote 25, 26
evaporation 74, 75-76, 78, 80-81, 81
evolution 2, 4-5, 67
 natural selection—*see* natural selection
 of amphibians 15-16
 of animal behavior 18
 of birds 16, 17, 18, 60
 of brain 116, 121
 of breathing mechanisms 60
 of dinosaurs 18
 of feathers 17
 of fish 15
 of flagellates 5
 of flightless birds 18
 of heterothermy 81

evolution—continued
of life 30
of locomotion 102
of mammals 18
of multi-celled animals 7, 68
of nervous system 116, 117, 118, 120, 121
of parasites 42, 76
of temperature regulation 80
of viruses (33)
of vision 89-91, 89
exafferent activity 88
excretion 41, 70 71, 73, 74, 75
in *Amphiuxus* 71
in birds 70, 75
in fish 70
in humans 71
in insects 70, 71
in multi-celled animals 73
in planarians 71
in protozoans 71
in reptiles 70, 75
in sea urchins 70
in starfish 70
Exocoetus 107
exocytosis 25, 25
exteroceptor 86
extinction
of dinosaurs 16, 18
of lions 2
of lobe-finned fish 15
of reptiles 16, 18
of thylacine 19
eyes 86, 87, 89-92, 89
Atlantic cuttlefish 89
crustaceans 89, 90, 91
fish 89, 90
humans 87, 88, 89, 90
insects 81, 89, 90, 91
mammals 88, 89
owls 88-89
Red-eyed tree frog 85
scallop 89, 90, 92
snakes 90
worms 89, 89, 92
see also vision

F

facilitation 118
family 2, 3
fanworms 11, 89, 92
farming, fish 16
Fasciola
hepatica 45
fat 80
fatty acid—see acid, fatty
feathers 17, 18, 80, 111
feces 40, 74, 75, 76
feeding behavior 34-49
in carnivores—see carnivores
in ciliates 6
in Common egg-eater 34
in filter feeders—see filter feeders
in fluid feeders—see fluid feeders
in herbivores—see herbivores
in omnivores—see omnivores
in protochordates 15
in Rock python 16-17
in sponges 7
feeding mechanisms 37-42, (48-49)
Felidae 2
Felis 2
fermentation 24, 38, 39, 40, 41, 52
ferrets 41
fertilization 26, 131, 134, 135, 136
filament 7
filariids 42
filter feeding 15, 36, 37-39, 41, 44, 48, 49
filtering of signals 87, 118
fins 15, 16
in sharks 106, 106
fish 15-16
adaptation 69
body fluids 73, 75
bony 15-16, 15, 18, 59, (82), 107
cartilaginous 70
circulation 62, 63
classification 3
feeding 5, 41
fossils 5
gills 13, 57
growth 137
lobe-finned 15
movement 105, 106
ray-finned 16
reproduction 136, 141
respiration 55, 58, 59
senses 89, 89, 90, (92), 93, 94, 96
temperature regulation 82
fish, flying 107, 108
Fissipedia 19
flagella 6, 27, (28), 29
flagellates 5-6, 6, 6-7, 39, 106
green 5, 6, 7, 10
flamecell 71
flamingo
Greater 48, 98
flatfish 16, 70, 106
flatworms 8, 13, 44, 55, 55, 61-62, 73, 75, 89, 89, 121
fleas
water 131, 134
flicker
Common 17
flies 110, 130, 138
fruit 33
mushroom 132, (134)
true 10
tsetse 10, 142
flight 107-111
fast forward 109, 110
gliding—see gliding
hovering 109, 110, 110, 111
in bats 109
in birds 17, (58-59), 60 109, 110, 111, 111
in insects 109, 110, 111
in mammals 19
powered 109-111
flightless birds 18
fluid feeders 41-42, 44, 48, 49
flukes 42, 43, 44, 133, 134

flukes—continued
blood 76
liver 8, 45
food
chain 35, 36, 37
energy from 24
requirements 17
web 36
see also feeding behavior and feeding mechanisms
fossils
birds 18
fish 5, 15
footprints 16, 112
mammals 18
record 4-5
reptiles 18
foxes 41
freshwater animals 75
fritillary
Gulf 48
frog
Common 141
Red-eyed tree 84
frogs 15, 16, 75, 94, 130, 135, 138
flying 109
leopard 69
fungi 39
fur
in mammals 18, 80
in moths 80

G

galactose 46
galactosidase 46
gamete 131, 136
ganglion 121
gas
alveolar 53, 54, 59
partial pressure of 53-55, (53), 59, 61, 64
gas exchange 51-61
in air 52, 53, 59-60, 61, 64
in body fluid 52, 53, 54-55, 56, (62)
in humans 56
in insects (60)
in water 52, 53, 56, 57, 58-59, 61, 64
surfaces 52, 54, 55
gastric juice 47
gastrin 47
Gastropoda 12
gastropods 12, 62, 90
gazelle
Thomson's 112
gazelles 16-17
gemsbok 112-113
genet
Common 49
genetics 30, 31, 33
combinations 131, 132, 134, 135
information 25, 30-33, 135
jumping genes (32)
programs 137, (138), 141, 142
test-tube 33
Genetta
genetta 49
genus 2, 4
geology 4
gerbils 76
germ cells—see cells, germ
germ plasm 135
Gerris 96
Giraffa
camelopardalis 18, 61
giraffe 18, 40, 61, 142
glands 70, 126-127
gliding 19, 107-109, (109)
glucose 24, 42, 44, 46
glycerol 43, (82)
glycogen 100
glycolysis 24, 26
gnu
Brindled 77
goats 40, 75
Golgi body 26, 27
gorilla
Mountain 76
goshawk 48
grasshoppers 10, 670, 94
long-horned 96
grazing 39, 41
grebes 64
greyhound 112, 113
growth 137-138, 142-143
guinea pigs 142
gulls 108
guppy 141
Gymnarchus 92, 92
Gymnodinium
microadriaticum 39
gymnotids (92)

H

hagfish 15, 72
hard parts 4
hare
Arctic 68, 69
hares 40
hatchet fish 107
hawkmoth
Hummingbird 110
Pine 60
heads 120-121
hearing 86, 87, 88, 93-96, 95
heart 62, 64
heat exchanges 76, 78-83
heat loss—see temperature regulation
hedgehogs 19, 80
helium 65
Hemiptera 110
hemoglobin 29
hepatitis A virus 33
herbivores 36, 37, 38, 39-41, 46
herring 10
heterotherms 81-83
regional 80, 81-83
temporal 83

heterotrophic organisms 36
hibernation 80, 83, 83
Hippocampus 16
hippopotamus 19, 40
Hirudinea 10
Holothuroidea 12
homologs 26
hookworms 8
hormones 24, 45, 47, 127, 138, 143
horsefly 91
horses 19, 40, 102, 112
hoverflies 111
humans 19
and dogs 5
and insects 10
cells 22, 25
communication 126
digestion 44, 45, 46, 47
feeding 41, 47
growth 143
movement 102, 104, 105, 112
nervous system 119, 119, 121, 122, 127, 127
reproduction 131, 135, 142
respiration 52, 56, 56, 64-65, 64
senses 86, 87, 88, 89, 90, 91, 92, 94, 96
temperature regulation 80
hummingbird
Costa's 110
hummingbirds 83, 109, 110
Hyaena
brunnea 97
hybridization 134
Hydra 130, 131
hydrogen 28
hydroids 136
hydrozoans 117, 117
hyena
Brown 97
hyenas 41
Hyloicus
pinastris 60
Hymenoptera 110, 135
Hypnos
monopterygium 93
hypophysis 127
hypothermia 83

I

iguanas 64
immune system 43
impala 104-105
Inachis
io 83
inheritance 5, 69
Insectivora 19
insects 9, 10, 17
adaptation 68
blood-sucking 76
body fluids 75
circulation 63
excretion 70
feeding 41, 44
movements 101, 104, 107, 110, 110, 111
nervous system 122, 125
number of species 2
reproduction 134, 135, 138, 141
respiration (60)
senses 89, 89, 90, 91, 92, 94, 97
skeleton 92, 101, 104
temperature regulation 78, 79, 80, 81, (82)
insulation 80, 81
insulin 33
intermediate filament 27
internal environment 67-83
regulation of body fluid—see body fluid
intestine 45
invertebrates 11, 72, 75, 91, 124
amphibious 75
marine 42, 73, 75
iodine 47
iron 47

J

Jacklin, Tony 114-115
jaguar 2
jaws
Agnathan 15
snake 36
jellyfishes 4-5, 7, 8, 9, 44, 117, 117, 118, 120, 121, 130

K

kangaroo
Eastern gray 18
kangaroos 18, 19, 40
keratin 29
kidneys 70, 71, 74-75, 76
killifishes 75
kin selection 135
kingdom 3, 5
kiwi 18
knifefish 92
koala 38
Krebs cycle 26
Krebs, Hans 26
krill 10

L

lactase 46-47
lactose 46-47
Lagomorpha 19
lampreys 15
lancelets 13, 15
lantern fishes 107
lateral line organs 92-93, 93
Latimeria 15
learning 123, 126
leeches 10, 41, 76, 106
legs
birds 18
lizards 16

lemurs 19, 107
leopard
Snow 2
Lepus
timidus 69
life, evolution of 30
Limenitis
populi 108
Linnaeus, Carolus 2
lion 2, 40-41, 41, 128, 131
lipid 26, 28, 29, 43, 44, 45
Lissman, Hans (92)
Litoria
chloris 84
live birth—see viviparity
lizards 16, 61, 70, 78, 134, 142
horned 78
llamas 40
lobsters 10, 11, 55, 57, 58m, 59m 89, 91
locomotion 99-113
and coordination—see coordination and control
and energy 102, 104, 105
and evolution 102
and muscle action—see muscles
in cells 27
in mammals 102
in sea anemones 117, 118
in single-celled animals 116
in slugs 102, 102
in snails 102, 102
in snakes 101-102, 102, 103
in starfish 118, 118
in worms 101, 102, 102
see also flight; running; swimming; walking
locusts 10, 141
Loligo
opalescens 13
Loxodonta
africana 38
lungfish 16
lungs 52, 53, 54, 54, 55, 55, 56, 59, 60, 63, 64
lysosome 26

M

mackerel 10
Macroglossum
stellatarum 110
macromolecule 28, 43
macrophage 43, 48, 49
Macropus
giganteus 19
Macrosiphum
rosae 42
magnesium 28, 46, 74
malaria 6, 7, 10
malphigian
tubule 71
Mammalia 3, 18
mammals 18-19
body fluids 73, 74
brains 18
circulation 62, 63
classification 3
digestion 45
eutherian—see placental
excretion 74
fossils 5
growth 143
marsupial 18-19, 19
monotreme 18, 18
movement 102, 104
number of species 2
placental 18, 19, 136, 141 142
reproduction 135, 142
respiration 53, 54, 56, 59, 60
senses 86, 88, 93, 96, 97
skeleton 92
temperature regulation 17, 79, 80, 81, 83
man-of-war
Portuguese 132-133
manatees 73
manganese 47
Manta
alfredi 72-73
marine animals 70-75
marsupials 18-19, 19
martin
House 68-69
mating 128, 131
mayflies 10, 138, 139, 141
measures (22)
mechanoreception 88
medusa 7
Megaptera
novaeangliae 94-95
meiosis 26, 27, 131, 134, 135
memory 123
mesogloea 7, 8, 8
message types 126
messenger RNA 25, 33, 135, 138
metabolism 17, 24, 60-61, 80
aerobic 24
anaerobic 24, 26, 52
oxidative 52, 58
metamorphosis 16, 79, 138-139, 139
mice 19, 33, 101, 130
deer 143
marsupial 19
microfilament 27
microphage 48, 49
microtubule 27, 27, 29
microvilli 47
Mictyris
longicarpus 74
migration
and adaptation 69
and soaring 108
and temperature changes 79, 80, 81
in House martins 68-69
in salmon 69
milk
birds 142
mammals 18, 46-47, 142
millipedes 10, 116, 124
mineral salts 24, 46-47, 69
Miniopterus
schreibersii 86-87

Mirounga
angustirostris 66
mites 11
mitochondria 26, 27, 100
mitosis 26, 27, 29, 30, 131, 133, 134, 136
modality 86
molecule 7, 27-30, 30, 43
moles 19
Mollienisia (Poecilia)
formosa 134
Mollusca 11
mollusks 11, 39, 63, 75, 100, 101, 106, 121, 123
bivalve 12, 13, 15, 63
cephalopod 12, 62, 90
gastropod 90
Monarch butterfly 108
Monastrea
cavernosa 132
monitor
Perentie 79
monkey
Red howler 96
monkeys 19
monoplacophorans 11
monosaccharide 43
monotreme 18, 18
moods 126
moose 48
mormyrids (92), 92
mosquitoes 10, 42, 43, 64, 65, 76
moss animals 7
moth
African moon 97
Cinnabar 80
moths 19, 80, 81, 87, 94, 96, 97, 109, 110, 138
dalcerid 80
silk 141
mouth-brooding fish 141
movement—see locomotion
mudpuppy 56
mudskippers 16
multi-celled animals 3, 7, 22, 25, 26, 30-31, 44, 68, 70, 73, 99, 100, 116, (118), 136
muscles 23, 101, (101)
action 27, 92, 100, 100-101, (101), 101-102, 110-111, 118
locomotion—see locomotion
smooth 100
striated 23, 100, (101)
mussels 12, 36, 37, 79, 101, 118, 130
mutual defense mechanism 43
myonere 27
Myotis
myotis 109
Myrtilis
edulis 130

N

names—see nomenclature
natural selection 5, 141
navigation
in bees 92
nectar feeding 41-42, 48
Necturus maculosus 56
Nematoda 8
nematodes 8, 9, 101, 101, 135
neoteny 18
nerve
cells—see cells, nerve
impulses (122)
nets 117-118, 117, 120
tracts 118, 120
nervous system 117-127
and breathing 61
and evolution 116, 117, 118, 120, 121
and senses 86m 87-88, 120-121, 123
in chordates 13
in endotherms 82-83
in heterotherms 82
in jellyfish 117-118, 117, 121
in multi-celled animals (118)
in starfish 118, 118, 119, 120
nests 10, 142, 143
neuro-endocrine system 126-127, 127
neurohemal organs 126-127
neurohormones 127
neurons—see cells, nerve
newts 16
nitrogen 28, 53, 64, 75
narcosis 64-65
nocturnal behavior 81
nomenclature 2-4, (5)
Notonecta 64, 96
nucleic acid—see acid, nucleic
nucleotide 28, 30, 31, 33
nucleus 7, 25, 31

O

Obelia 132
octopus
Lesser 123
octopuses 11, 12, 44, 55, 57, 58, 59, 90, 123, 142
Oecophylla
smaragdina 10
olfaction—see smell, sense of
Oligochaeta 10
omnivores 41, 46
Onymacris
unguicularis 76
oocyte 134, 136
oogenesis 135-136, (138)
oogonia 134
Ophiuroidea 12
opossums 18
order 3, 19
organelle 21, 22, 25, 26, 27, 27, 29, 33, 70
Oryx
gazella 112-113
oryxes 75-76
osmosis 69, 69, 70, 73, 74, 75
Osteichthyes 15
ostrich 18, 70, 112, 142
otters 41, 64, 142
ovary 135

owl
  Long-eared *88-89*
oxidation 52, 58, 100
oxygen 24, 26, 28, 39, 52-59, *53*, 60-63, 86
oysters 130

P

pandas 3
Panthera 2
  leo 2, *40-41*, *128*
  tigris 2, *3*
panting 80, *81*
Paramecium 92, 116, *116*
parapodia 9
parasites *42-43*, 137
  evolution of 42
  external 76
  fish 15
  flatworms 8
  internal 76
  intestinal *45*
  mites 11
  protozoan 6-7
  regulation of body fluids 76
  reproduction behavior 133-134
  species flocks 135
Parazoa 7
parental care *140*, 141, *141*, 142
parthenogenesis 131, **134-135**, *134*, *135*
Parus
  caeruleus 111
Pavlov, I.P. 47
Peacock butterfly *83*
Pelamis
  platurus 65
pelicans 18
penguin
  Gentoo *82*
  King 64, *140*
penguins 64, 105, *107*, 110
pepsin 45, 47
peptidase 45, 47
peptide 47
  bonds 45
Periophthalmus 16
Perissodactyla 19
Peromyscus
  maniculatus 143
pests 10, 11
Petaurus
  breviceps 108
phagocytosis 25, *25*, 26
phalangers
  flying 107, 108
Phascolarctos
  cinereus 38
pheromones 96, 97
Phoenicopterus
  ruber roseus 48, *98*
phosphate salts 74
phosphorus 28, 46
photoreceptor 87
photosynthesis 5, 7
phylum 3, 5
Physophora
  hydrostatica 132
phytoplankton 36, 37, 39
pigeons 111, 142
pigs 19, 39, 41, 46, 80
pike 68
Pinnipedia 19
placenta *141*, 142
placental mammals *18*, 19, 136, 141-142
plaice 130, 131
plankton 10, 15, 39, 41, 73, *132*, 138
plants 5, 6, 35, 36, 37, *38*, 39, 40, 52, (90)
planulae 132
Plasmodium 6
Platyhelminthes 8
platypus
  Duck-billed 18
Pleuronectiformes 16
plover
  Little ringed *81*
plovers 74
poisons
  in plants 39, *40*
polarization of light 91-92
Polychaeta 9
Polymastia
  boletiforme 8
polyp 7, *37*, *132*, 133
Polyplacophora 11
polysaccharide 28, 39, 40, 41
Pomacanthus
  paru 72
population
  stability 130
porcupines 19
Porifera 7
Porpoises 73, 81
potassium 28, 46
poultry 6
precipitated salts 74
predatory behavior 41
  snakes 16
primates 19, 41, 90, 94
privilege *138-139*, 141-142
Proboscidea 19
prokaryote 25, (27)
proprioceptor 26, 125
propulsion (28)
proteins 28, 29-30, 31, 33, 41, 43, 44, 45, 52
Protista 5
protochordates 13, (15)
protoplasm 21, 25
protozoans 3, **5-7**, *6*, *6-7*, 9, 22, 27, 39, 44, 92, 99, 104, 106, 116
Pseudoceros 55
pseudopod 25
ptarmigan 39
Pteranodon *109*, *109*
pterosaurs 16, 109, *109*
puberty 143
pumping mechanisms 58-60
Pygoscelis
  papua 82
python
  Rock *16-17*
Python
  sebae 16-17

R

rabbits 19, 40
radula 39
ragwort *40*
Rana
  catesbeiana 94
ratites 18
rats 5, 39, 41
rattlesnakes 90
ray
  Electric *93*
  Great manta *72-73*
rays 15, 70, 72, 92, 122
reafferent activity 88
receptors 88, 87, 92, 121
reflexes **123-126**, *124-125*
regeneration 118, *119*, 120, 137
regional heterotherms—*see* heterotherms
regulation
  internal change 69
  of body fluids—*see* body fluids
  of temperature—*see* temperature regulation
reindeer 80
reproduction **129-143**
  asexual *130*, 131, 132, 133
  environmental conditions and 68
  sexual 131, 132, 133, 134, **135-143**
reproductive behavior
  in aphids *134*, 135
  in coelenterates *132*, 132
  in corals 133-134
  in *Daphnia* 134-135, *135*
  in flukes 133, 134
  in mammals 18-19, 135-136
  in mushroom flies 132, (134)
  in parasites 133-134
  in siphonophores 132-133, *132*
  in social insects 135
  in tapeworms 134
  in Tarantula wasps 141, (142), *142*
reproductive cycles 130-131
reptiles 16
  anatomy 18
  body fluids 73, 74
  circulation 62, 63
  classification 3
  evolution 18
  excretion 70, 75
  fossils 16
  movement 109
  reproduction 141
  respiration 56, 60, 64
  senses 94
  temperature regulation 17
Reptilia 16
resistance to environmental change 68
respiration 26, **51-61**
  in amphibians 16, 59
  in birds 58-59, 60, 61
  in cold-blooded animals 61
  in fish 16, 58, 59
  in flatworms 55, *55*, 61-62
  in humans 52, 56
  in insects (60)
  in lobsters 58, 59
  in mammals 53, 54, 59, 60
  in octopus 58, 59
  in reptiles 60
  in snails 54, 55, 59
  in starfish 54, 55, *55*
  in warm-blooded animals 61
  in Water spiders 51
  see also breathing *and* gas exchange
respiratory quotient 52
Reynolds number 37, 39
Rhincodon
  typus 15
rhinoceroses 19, 130
rhodopsin 86
ribosome 33
RNA 25, 28, 33, 135
robin
  European *141*
Rodentia 19
rodents 81, 142
Rotifera 8
rotifers 8-9, 131, 134, 135
roundworm
  Common 42
roundworms 8, *8*, 42, 76, 101
rumination 39-41
running 80, **102-104**, (112-113)
  in arthropods 113
  in cheetahs 112
  in chipmunks 112
  in dinosaurs 112-113
  in dogs 102, 112
  in elephants 112
  in gemsbok *112-113*
  in Greater flamingos *98*
  in horses 102, 112
  in humans 102, 104, 112
  in impala *104-105*
  in mammals 102, (112-113)
  in ostriches 112
  in Thomson's gazelle 112
  in zebra 112

S

Sabella
  pavonina 11
salamanders 16
salinity 73, 75
saliva 40, 46, 47, 81
salmon 68, 69, 75, 96, 141
salt 73-75, 76
salt licking 76
salt-excreting glands 70
sap sucking 41-42, *42*, 48
Sarcomastigophora 5
scales 80
scallops 89, 90, 92
scavenging 13, 25
scent marking 96, 97
scorpions 10, 11, 41, 76
Scyphozoa 7
sea anemone
  Beadlet *117*
sea anemones 7, *8*, 13, 39, 55, 70, 118, 132, 133
sea bass 70, 73
sea cucumbers 12
sea horses 106
sea lilies 12, 13
sea snake
  Yellow-bellied *65*
sea snakes 64, 70, 73, 74
sea squirts 13, 15, *15*, 36, 37, 44, 62, 131
sea stars 118
sea urchins 12, *12*, 70, 138
seahorses 16
seal
  Northern elephant 66
  Weddell 64, 65
seals 19, 64, 74, 81
segmented animals 9
segments 9, 133
Selachii 15
Senecio
  jacobaea 40
sense organs 120, 121
  see also senses
senses **85-97**, 120
  brain and 86-87, 121, 123
  chemical **96-97**
  electrical (92)
  human 86
  mechanical **92-96**
  nervous system and 86, 87-88, 120-121, 123
  stimuli 87-89
Sepiola
  atlantica 89
shape changes 143
shark
  Great white *14*
  Whale 15
sharks 15, 70, 72, 82, 92, 104, 106, *106*, 107, 122, 130, 136
shearwaters 74
sheep 6, 8, 19, 40
  Bighorn 81
shells
  cephalopods 107
  construction of *100*, 101
  gastropods 12
  mollusks 11, 12
  tortoises 16
  turtles 16
shrews 19, 61
shrimps 89, 91
  fairy 79
Siamese fighting fish *143*
sidewinding 101-102, *103*
sight—*see* vision
signals
  and communication—*see* communication
  and filtering 87, 118
similarity 131-132, *131*
singing
  in birds 94
  in insects 94
  in whales 94-95, 96
single-celled animals 3, **5-7**, 22, 25, 68, 70, 99
siphonophores 117, 117, 132-133, *132*
size *24*, 55, 137-138, 142
  units—*see* units
skates 70, 72
skeleton *100*, 101, 111
  construction *100*, 101, (104)
  jointed (104)
skin 16
sleeping sickness 7, 10
sloths 40, 81
slugs 11, 12, 102, *102*
smell, sense of 86, 87, 88, 96-97, *97*, 122, 123
snail
  Giant land *39*
snails 12, 54, 102, *102*, 1113, 142, 143
  intertidal 75
  land 55, 56, 59, 142
  mud 75
snake
  African egg-eating *36*
snakes 16, 90, 101-102, *102*, *103*, 106, 137, 142
soaring 108-109
sodium 28, 46, 86
  chloride 69, 73-74, 76
solenocyte 71
solutes, regulation of 69-76
sonar 86-87, *87*
sound—*see* hearing
species 2, 4, 10
sperm *23*, 27
spermatheca 136
spermatozoa 131, 132, 136
spermatozoans 106
spider
  St Andrew's cross *49*
  Water *50*
spiders 9, 10, 11, 41, (82), 90, 96, 138, (142)
  jumping 90
  wolf 96
spines *118*
sponges 7, *8*, 39
sporozoans 6-7
squid 12, *13*, *49*, 62, 90, 106
  cranchid 107
  Giant 91
squirrel
  Round-tailed ground 81
squirrels 19
  flying 107
starch 44, 46, 47
starfish
  Common *119*
  Crown-of-thorns *118*
starfishes 12, 13, 54, 55, *55*, 70, 116, 118, *118*, 120, 138
starling
  European 130
starlings 131
stick insect
  Indian *134*
stomach *45*
storks 108
Strophoscheilus
  oblongus 54

sturgeons 16
subkingdom 5
subphylum 4
suckling 18, 46, 142
sugar gliders *108*
sugars 28, 41, 43, 44, 45, 46
sulfate 74
sulfur 28, 46
superfamily 4
swan
  Whooper *58-59*, 60
swans 18
sweating 81
swimbladder 107
swimming **104-107**
  in cephalopods 12
  in cuttlefish 106
  in dolphins (107), *107*
  in fish 16, 100, 105, 106, *106*
  in jellyfish *117*, 118
  in penguins 105, *107*
  in sharks 106-107, *106*
  in squid 106
  in turtles 16
  in water beetles 105, *107*
  in whales 105
swordfish 78
symbiosis 39-40, 132
  see also associations
symmetry 12, (13), 120, 121
synapses (126), 127

T

Tachyglossus
  aculeatus 18
tails
  in fish 105
  in whales 105
tapeworms 8, 42, 43, 76, 133, 134
tapirs 19
taste 86, 88, 96-97, 97
teeth
  in carnivores 41
  in Giant land snail *39*
teleosts 15
temperature
  regulation—*see* temperature regulation
  tolerance to 68-69, *68-69*
temperature regulation **76-83**
  ectotherms—*see* ectotherms
  endotherms—*see* endotherms
  evolution of 80
  in mammals 18, 80
  in terrestrial animals 76
temporal heterotherms—*see* heterotherms
tenrecs 19
terminal breeders 141
termites 135
terrapins 16
terrestrial animals
  regulation of body fluids 75-76
  regulation of temperature 76
test-tube genetics 33
Thylacine 19
Thylacinus
  cynocephalus 19
ticks 11, *42*, 44
tiger 2, 3, 41
  white *2*
tit
  Blue *111*
toads 16, 75
  green 78
tolerance 68, 75, 76, 78-79
tongue, rasping *39*
torpor 79, 80, 81, 83
tortoises 16, 59, 101
touch 86, **92**
tracheae 63
transcription 33
transduction 86-87
transposable elements (33)
trematodes 42
Trienodon
  obesus 106
Trimeresurus
  popeorum 90
tube feet 118, *118*
tuna fish 82
tunicates 44
tunnies 105, 106
turbellarians 44
turtle
  Green *39*
turtles 16, 59, 64, 70, 74

U

ungulates 19
Uniramia 10
units (22)
urea 41, 70
urine 70, 72, 74-75, 76, 81
Urochordata 13

V

Varanus
  giganteus 79
variety 131-132, *131*, 134
vasoconstriction 64
vein 62
Vema
  ewingi 39
Vertebrata 13
vertebrate animals 13
vertebrates 121, 122, 123, 127
  marine 73, 74
vibration 96, 126
viper
  Pit 90, *90*
viruses 21, (32), 33
vision 86, 87, 88, 89, **89-92**, 123
  and color (90)
  and polarization 91-92

vision—*continued*
  in bees (90), 91-92
  in humans 89, (90), 91
  in insects (90), 92
  in snakes (90)
  see also eyes
vitamins 41, (44)
viviparity 141-142
vocal sac 85
volition 125
Volvox 6-7
von Frisch, Karl R. 92
vulture
  Rüppell's griffon 108
vultures 108

W

walking **102-104**
  in humans 102, 104, *105*
  in insects 125
  in mammals 18, 102, 104
  in tortoises 16
  in turtles 16
walruses 64
wasps 110
  tarantula 141, (142), *142*
wastage of sexual products 131
water 52, 67, 68, 69
  balance *72-73*, 74
  diffusion—*see* diffusion
  evaporation loss—*see* evaporation
  gas exchange in—*see* gas exchange
  movements (70)
  osmosis—*see* osmosis
  oxygen capacity 55
  vapor 53
water beetle—*see* beetle, water
water boatman 64
water fleas—*see* fleas, water
water vascular system 12
weasels 19
weaver birds 142
weight
  of insects 10
  of sharks 15
Weis-Fogh, Prof. Torkel 111
whale
  Blue 19
  Humpback *94-95*
  Sperm 65
whales 5, 19, 64, 80, 81, 96, 104, 105
  baleen 10, 73
wheel animalcules 8
whelk 138
wildebeest 142
wings 109-111
  of birds 18, *111*
  of flying fishes 107
  of insects 10, 111
  of *Pteranodon* 109
  of Wandering albatross 109
wolf
  Tasmanian 19
wolves 41, 80
woodlice 10
worms 4, 8, 55, 68, 136
  annelid 13, 62, 89, 90
  blood 75
  earthworms—*see* earthworms
  helminth 42
  marine 9-10, 138
  nematode 8-9, 101, *101*, 135
  nemertean 138
  polychaete 9, 138
  roundworms—*see* roundworms
  segmented 9
  tapeworms—*see* tapeworms

Y

yellow fever 10
Yozia
  tigris 2

Z

zebras 112
zinc 47
zooids 117
zygote 136, 138